OPEN FOR THE SEASON

KARL P. ABBOTT

Open for the Season

DOUBLEDAY & COMPANY, INC., 1950

GARDEN CITY, NEW YORK

FIRST EDITION

A PATHFINDER BOOK REPRINT EDITION

Complete and Unabridged

Printed in the United States of America

ISBN: 979-8869055019

To my wife Esther

ACKNOWLEDGMENTS

TO EVELYN WELLS my sincere appreciation for her valuable editorial advice and co-operation.

TO MY SECRETARY, Lillian Riley, for her patience and loyalty while working with me on this book.

CONTENTS

OPEN FOR THE SEASON

Chapter One: THOSE WERE THE DAYS

ATHER ran a small hotel. He used to lean against the desk and say, "What we need is folks." He kept a pen in an Irish potato.

This hotel, The Uplands, sat on a series of terraces high above Main Street in Bethlehem, New Hampshire, in the White Mountains. Bethlehem consisted mostly of the one street, clinging to the side of the mountain halfway between Turner's Sugar Place and Cherry Valley. For nine months of the year it was a sleepy mountain village, occupying itself with farming, logging, trapping, and just being there.

But when warm weather came, it bestirred itself with vigor. Houses were scoured and aired, carpets beaten, windows washed, and every freshly hung curtain was white as snow. Women with towels pinned over their heads scrubbed front steps. The barber's pole was newly painted; in the livery stable the harness sets were polished; and down at the drugstore "Hen" Smith was shining up his showcases and the big soda fountain with all the spigots.

All over town neighbors were calling out: "Sprucin' up for the city folks?"

There were just two sorts of people when I was a boy, our kind and city folk.

The last thing Father did was paint the front porch. He never got around to it until the day before opening, and then was in a cussing frenzy for fear it wouldn't dry. Summer came on so quickly we wondered where spring had gone, and the annual rush of tourists was on us overnight.

There were thirty hotels in Bethlehem and they all opened around July 1, the day the first train of the summer season came up to Bethlehem. Opening day was the most important day of our year.

I would wake about sunup, when Fred Lewis's meat cart clattered up to the kitchen door. I'd look out and see the well-brushed horses and the clean white cart, and Fred, in his white coat and apron, climbing down from the front seat as Father came out of the kitchen door.

Father was tall and upstanding, with icy blue eyes and a high black pompadour that made him seem inches taller than he really was. He had a temper like a firecracker and a hair-trigger sense of humor, and was the most universally loved man I have ever known. I never knew him to be afraid of anything on this earth and I suspect that he was never afraid of anything beyond. He came from Puritan stock and had a Puritan conscience, with time off for a considerable amount of fun on the side.

Fred came every morning during the season, and their meeting bubbled over with merry quips. "Say, did you hear about the feller . . ." Laughing, they'd go around to the rear of the cart and pull down the hinged door, so that Fred could point out the different cuts hanging inside, and the entire cart would open up, clean and sweet-smelling. "Now there's a well-hung loin at twenty-two cents a pound," Fred would say, hauling the cut down on the tailboard that served as a counter.

Father would shake his head and wonder what things were coming to. Twenty-two cents for sirloin steak!

Father was a Yankee trader when it came to price, but he never stopped at anything short of the best. He said the basis of a good table was good produce.

Meat buying was a ceremony that started off the day and called for much leisurely conversation. Fred had the grapevine from all the other hotels inasmuch as he went to all the back doors every morning. He was a Republican and Father a

Democrat, and they would start arguing about politics until Fred would say, "Well, meat's a-spoiling!" and drive off.

A few minutes later Ed Bishop would drive his poultry wagon up to our door. I was sure to be dressed and out in the yard by this time, because Ed would always cut a slice of cheese for me, and the full cream cheese the New Hampshire farmers made in those days was something to start the morning right and help take my mind off the fact that this was the day I started wearing shoes. I was also wearing long black stockings that itched and wouldn't stay up, tight pants, a shirt with a collar, and even a necktie.

Sometimes if Ed came earlier he would meet Fred, and the talk lasted longer. Ed was a Democrat like Father, and they were always hatching plots to help defeat the Republicans. But there was no business rivalry between Ed and Fred because Ed's wagon carried only poultry, butter, eggs, and cheese.

Father would buy dozens of the big brown eggs every day. He said they were richer and fuller than the white. He considered fourteen and a half cents a dozen almighty high.

By this time the staff had arrived. The girls would start setting up the dining room, the chef would open his reign in the kitchen, and Father would take a last swing around the house to see that everything was in order. There was the last-minute worry of touching fingertips to the piazza to see if it was dry enough. It looked pretty as a strawberry bed, with the dozens of newly painted rocking chairs set out, red and green. Father would march on through the lobby to see if the floor was like a mirror—we'd polished it by hand with butcher's wax—and out along the gravel walks to see that every dandelion was dug out of the lawn—another of my jobs.

Mother would be whisking through the upstairs rooms to check the linen and see that every bureau had its fresh bouquet.

As soon as we heard the whistle of the first train, Father

would send me running down to the station to help. Lem and Dan, our driver and porter, already would be there.

Pretty nearly everyone in Bethlehem was down to see the train come in, and would be, night and evening, all summer.

Our coach stood in the long line of coaches backed into the row of stalls by the station. All the hotels had their coaches down to meet the first train and all were exactly alike, made by the Abbott-Downing Company of Concord, New Hampshire, the same company that had made all the Concord coaches that crossed the plains.

Lem made a fine figure sitting on the box. Lem was a character. He had lost the index finger of his right hand and always said he wore it off pointing out the god-damned mountains to the city folks. He was sweet on a redheaded chambermaid at the Uplands and pursued her so persistently that it annoyed my mother. Rumor had it that he did not confine his attentions to the daylight hours, and once when Father called him on the carpet and asked him if he had slept with Maggie the night before, Lem looked him right in the eye and said, "Not a damn wink, sir."

Dan was out on the platform with the other porters. Each hotel had one porter, and each porter had one uniform, and it was new and a surprise and had to last all season. There was always a lot of advance guessing as to the colors and styles the different porters would wear on opening day.

The train consisted of one engine and a couple of passenger cars, and came rushing in all out of breath with much whistle blowing and bell ringing, like a little old lady late for tea.

Dan began hollering, "Uplands" at one end of the platform, and I took up my post at the other end and yelled, "Uplands" too. Usually the first trainload to arrive would be an excursion up from Boston, run by a jolly fat man who herded his people off the train and into the coaches like a distracted shepherd dog tending his flock. The horses backed and filled, the long line of coaches wavered, porters shouted, drivers swore, and city folks climbed into the wrong coaches and out again, dropped parcels and parasols, lost their baggage, and called out greetings. Dan and I kept sharp watch for strays, and no matter where people said they wanted to go, we assured them ours was the only coach that went there. Sometimes guests were with us for days before they realized they were in the wrong hotel, and by that time they liked us so well they stayed on.

When the coaches were full, whips cracked and the horses started the race out of the station yard and up the hill to Main Street. I'd cut across lots to tell Father the first coach was coming.

Lem brought the coach in on the gallop, and there, alighting at the side piazza of the Uplands, were the summer people—the wonderful foreign "city" folks from far away.

Later I would find words to fit these people—assurance, authority, *savoir-faire*. Then I could only wonder, helping Dan carry their luggage in to the desk. "Help Dan with those bags, Karl," Father found time to say in a low voice. "Don't let him sweat out his uniform!"

Father and Mother were always out in front to welcome their guests, Father at the foot of the stairs and Mother at the top, and young as I was, I knew that in dignity and good looks none of the city folks had anything on them. Mother was beautiful, tall and willowy, with black eyes that laughed, and she wore her lovely black hair in a huge pompadour and always had a bunch of fresh flowers at her waist. Her complexion was peaches and cream and she never used a cosmetic in her life. Everyone loved her, and she was the intimate and friend of every woman guest who came to our hotels. She had a temper to match Father's, and when I erred she had a way of thumping me on the head with her thimble that would leave a bump aching for hours. But when the going got rough, she had pioneer New England courage that never faltered.

Father and Mother were a team. They were New Hampshire to the bone, and the land there is so rocky they have to sharpen the sheep's noses so they can reach the grass between the stones. Three or four generations born in the White Mountains insure hardy stock.

Father had left home at fourteen and found work in a potato starch factory, shoveling potatoes from twelve noon to twelve midnight. Another fourteen-year-old boy worked the other twelve-hour shift.

My parents married with no insurance against the future except courage and good health, and they made their way up with hard work, frugality, and good will.

They started in the hotel business the way it started in early America. First the farmhouse, with maybe a room or two for guests, then a larger kitchen, a croquet ground, perhaps eventually a tennis court. This was the evolution of the country inn and its keeper, "the friend by the side of the road." Father opened his first hotel in 1884. Multiply each year since by two seasons, summer and winter, and I have just completed without a break our one hundred and thirtieth season as hotel men, father and son.

The arrival of the "regular" guests was most sedate, with murmurs of polite greetings and the quiet renewal of old acquaintances. They were mostly from New York, Boston, Hartford, New Haven, and Stamford, and another large contingent from Jacksonville and Tampa. Among these families I remember the Wilkies, Taliaferros, Corchmans, Davidsons, and Stocktons. Some would arrive with their own teams and coachmen.

There were quiet flutters of greeting. "How well you look! How the children have grown!" They were delighted to see Father and Mother and one another again. Father and Mother, welcoming them, offered these sophisticates the comfort and savor of a home in a pastoral setting of great beauty and a gracious mingling with old friends. This was the charm of the resort hotel that brought the city folks back to us, year after year.

Our little lobby swarmed with men in single-breasted coats, pants with creases, stickpins in their Ascot ties, derbies, and gold watches with heavy chains. Later they would appear with straw hats and white flannels and blazers of a brightness we never saw at any other time in Bethlehem. The younger men carried mandolins. All a practicing Lothario needed in those days was a mandolin and a pound of Huyler's chocolates.

The women were decked out with bustles and leg-o'-mutton sleeves and big hats piled with feathers, birds, flowers, and veils worn over high pompadours. Voluminous as their dresses were, women brought no more luggage than they do now. Today it is not unusual to see a woman guest with ten pieces of luggage—one for nothing but shoes.

My furtive attention was focused on the children. Resort hotels frown on children now, but large families then were taken for granted. The little girls didn't interest me much, with their buttoned shoes, ankle-length skirts, and high collars like those their mothers wore.

But the little boys were eyed with plans in mind. How we country kids loved enticing the city kids onto a hidden wasp nest or into eating a Jack-in-the-pulpit root with results excruciatingly funny—to us!

We put most of the excursion people in "Angel Alley." This was a series of small rooms up under the roof, with bowl and pitcher and slop jar, which we sold for two dollars, American plan, the standard excursion rate. Not a hotel in Bethlehem had rooms with private bath. Uplands had one public bath on each floor and charged twenty-five cents for the use of it.

Behind Angel Alley was a big room with about twenty beds which was a dormitory for the young men guests. Father called it "the Ram Pasture."

The "regulars" occupied the front and side rooms. Year after year they had the same rooms and the same seats in the dining room, and woe unto the casual guest who sat in one of their favored chairs!

The dining-room windows overlooked the garden, where Father made a great last-minute show of selecting the juiciest ears of corn just as the guests sat down and rushing them into the kitchen where hot milk and butter waited on the stove.

Each table seated eight, and we took pride in having centerpieces of fresh, fragrant sweetpeas all summer.

In the little kitchen the staff worked in concert to produce the perfectly cooked, perfectly served meal. I started my apprenticeship there at an early age, standing on a box to serve vegetables from the steam table for one hour during dinner. On the other end of the table were the roasts and sauces which no one could touch but the chef. Father always came in to supervise the cutting, and stood by, tall and frowning with concentration, while our white-coated and -hatted chef, a red-faced man with a handlebar mustache, majestically carved the first slice. The meals that came out of that New Hampshire kitchen were something to dream about. (I just came across this old menu. It is an average Sunday dinner which was just one of the three tremendous meals that were part of the "room and board" at two dollars and fifty cents a day.)

SOUP

Chicken Broth   Julian

FISH

Fresh Salmon, Worcestershire Sauce   Fried Trout

BOILED

Cold Neat's Tongue   Fowl and Pork
Cold Pressed Corned Beef   Lamb, Caper Sauce   Cold Ham

ENTREES

Chicken Pie   Lamb's Cutletts Breaded   Macaroni Plain
Alamode Beef Chicken Salad   Beef's Liver Broiled with Salt Pork
Baked Beans and Pork   Rice Croquettes

ROAST

Sirloin Beef   Ham, Champagne Sauce   Lamb, Mint Sauce
Turkey, Cranberry Sauce

VEGETABLES

Tomatoes   Green Peas   New Beets   String Beans   Onions
Boiled Rice   Hominy   Potatoes Plain, Mashed, and Browned

RELISHES

Olives   Pickled Beets   Cucumbers   Pickles

PASTRY AND PUDDINGS

Apple Pie
Damson Pie   Currant Pie   Blueberry Pie
Sponge Pudding, Wine Sauce   Cocoanut Pudding

DESSERT

Wine Jelly   Charlotte Russe   Blueberries   Italian Cream
Boiled Custard   Vanilla Ice Cream   Roman Punch   Pine Apple
Layer Raisins   Pecans   Almonds   Filberts   English Walnuts

COFFEE

The girls hurrying in and out with their heavy trays were
fresh-cheeked and capable. Each girl cared for two tables of
eight people, memorized sixteen lengthy orders and kept them
all straight! Between meals they made the beds and cleaned
the rooms of their sixteen charges, picked flowers for the
rooms, laundered their own uniforms, stayed sweet-tempered
and cheerful, and, if they weren't caught, climbed out of the
dormitory windows after dark to dance at some country
grange until dawn.

Our pastry cook was a New Hampshire farm woman who cooked for us through the summer, and in the fall, winter, and spring cooked three big meals a day for thirty-two farmhands —including griddlecakes and johnnycakes and pie for breakfast, and played the piano in the grange halls half the night three nights a week.

Between the kitchen and the dining room was the storeroom. Father kept the key on a long chain buttoned onto his suspenders. Every time I passed I gave the doorknob a shake, just in case. Once it turned—he had forgotten to lock it! I tiptoed in and stood in the cool semi-darkness afforded by the one small window that faced the girls' dormitory.

Standing there, I drank in the sights and smells of well-filled shelves stocked with large boxes of raisins, crystallized ginger, fruits, and cookies of every shape and kind. A ten-pound box of fig newtons, my favorite delicacy, was on the top shelf. By wriggling the cracker barrel under the shelf I was able to lift the box to the floor. It had a glass front, and as I sat gloating over my treasure and cramming my mouth full of fig newtons, I chanced to look up. Through the window in the adjoining building I saw a big blond waitress, naked as the day she was born, standing in a washbowl, taking a sponge bath. This was the end of the world. All I could do was tear out of there, and when I came to a stop, I was in the middle of the lobby, my eyes bulging and my mouth and hands crammed with cookies. At that time I didn't know which I liked better, the girl or the fig newtons.

The last thing Father did at night was to walk up the front stairs, down the halls, and through the dining room and kitchen—turning out lights and shutting windows. He inspected the kitchen carefully to see whether anyone had left any dirty dishes or food about, and if anyone had, he'd hear about it in the morning.

He looked to see whether the storeroom and cooler (a walk-in icebox) doors were locked, and even peeked into the swill house to see whether the cans had been washed. Then he would come in our apartment and sigh: "Well, Emma, another day, another dollar." His had been a busy day—up at five-thirty and to bed at midnight. He had to see to everything himself and to his own satisfaction. He couldn't trust to heads of departments. There were none. Uplands, like hundreds of other resort hotels in America in the nineties, was a family affair.

Everyone was busy. The summer days were never long enough. One of my many jobs was in the lamp closet, about six feet square and filled with lamps and oil cans. I kept the lamps filled and polished and their wicks trimmed and went through the house before dark "lighting up."

One summer a pitch man introduced "unbreakable lamp shades" in Bethlehem. He'd pitch one on the sidewalk and catch it on the bounce and it didn't break because it was made of celluloid. A lot of people bought them. Can you imagine the furore in town when lamps were lighted under those inflammable shades?

Once a week I sold the weekly *White Mountain Echo*, on Main Street for ten cents a copy. Its star reporter was a young fellow named Channing Cox who later became governor of Massachusetts.

Nights I ushered in the Opera House for free seats to Lorin Ellwin's Stock Company productions and the Tallahassee Minstrels.

There was always something around a hotel for a boy to do. I don't know where I found time for so much mischief. Once I found an empty candy box and went around catching crickets. I had about a hundred when Mother called, and I got scared and dumped them in an umbrella in her bedroom. When darkness came, they started chirping, and Father and Mother were up all night catching crickets.

Dan, our porter, didn't have much to do—just mow the

lawns, help weed the garden, turn the ice-cream freezer handle, meet the trains twice a day, serve as watchman every third night, and do all the portering. Dan liked the night watchman part best because he loved a fight. There were always a lot of young fellows hanging around the hotel watching for a chance to get into the girls' dormitory. Dan threw one "city slicker" into the swill barrel.

Father was busier than anyone else, but some time during the season he found time to go visiting. He'd hitch Dennis, our chestnut Morgan, to the Concord buggy, and we'd go over to Whitefield and up the long hill to the Mountain View House to see the Dodge family, or down through the Notch to visit Joe Elliott at Deer Park. Once we went to the Fabyan House to see Hal Barron. Going up, Father mentioned that most of Hal's guests were Jewish. I don't know what I expected, but I was terribly disappointed—they looked and acted exactly like everyone else.

That was the day we decided to do some trout fishing on the way home. When we reached Twin Mountain, Father dropped into the hotel to visit while I went back of the barn and dug worms. When we reached Little River, we crossed a corduroy bridge, unhitched and tied Dennis, and began casting upriver under the thick trees. Watching Father, I knew I'd rather be with him than with any boy I knew. He was a lot of fun, and he knew more.

I waded upstream after Father, pulling in a trout now and then and wondering if there was any country on earth as beautiful as the White Mountains in July. Finally the black flies took to biting along with the trout, so we started back to where we had left Dennis tied to the tree. Father carried the legal trout in the basket and I stuffed the little ones in my pockets.

We found Dennis raring to go, but a terrific thunder shower was coming up. Father said, "Let's get the wagon across the bridge before we hitch up. It'll save trouble."

Father got between the shafts and I pushed, and we started over the bridge. Dennis looked around the tree and his ears pointed together in sheer astonishment. I never saw a wilder horse; he thought we were taking the buggy and going home without him! He squealed, reared, snapped his halter, and passed us, tail in air, sailing down the logging road like a bat out of hell. I leaned against the wagon, weak from laughing, and Father glared at me. "What do you think is so damn funny?"

It didn't seem so funny to me either after we had pushed the buggy four miles to a farm where we borrowed another horse. Dennis was waiting for us when we got home.

On one of these trips we drove to the Profile House to see Charlie Greenleaf. There was a spot near the lake where one stopped and stood awe-struck, staring up at that tremendous stone profile against the sky. The "Old Man of the Mountain" was on our New Hampshire calendars, post cards, and stereoscopic views, and of course Nathaniel Hawthorne had helped immortalize it in his story the "Great Stone Face." But familiar as this natural wonder was to me, it was always inspiring, and I often wondered what its discoverer thought, looking up and seeing that tremendous profile, so human in outline it seemed forever readying to speak.

Charlie Greenleaf who ran the Profile House also ran the Vendome in Boston. He was a cheerful short man who catered to Ward McAllister's Four Hundred. I remember him saying that day that he lived by the adage: "There's a good deal to everything."

He asked me if I intended going into the hotel business. I nodded. "Well," he said, "it's the easiest business in the world to learn. Just get a hotel, stand behind the desk, and the first guest who comes into the lobby will tell you how to run it."

Then he quoted Kim Hubbard: "I've just been over to the poorhouse to see an old friend who used to run a hotel to please everybody."

Who would have believed that I, the small boy taking in every word, would someday run the Boston Vendome and operate a newer, larger Profile House and own all this magnificent property, including the Franconia Notch and the Old Man of the Mountain, to my mind the greatest natural wonder of the world!

Whenever I got too big for my britches Father would say, "There are two kinds of people in a hotel, help and guests. Everyone who puts money in is a guest. Everyone who takes it out is an employee. That goes for my family."

So I had great respect for guests.

Those we favored dined with us at the host's table, which was equivalent to being asked to the captain's table on an ocean liner.

In turn many of our guests invited us to their homes in Boston and New York. Crossing a parquet floor under a crystal chandelier, I'd be impressed most of all by the culture and ease of manners that made us welcome. These visits to some of our greatest American families showed me the way they were accustomed to live and how to care for them when they were away from home.

Our guests had no planned sports or amusements but filled their days with simple enjoyments. Breakfast was one. Every morning they faced a choice of steaks, chops, eggs, bacon, ham, sausages, griddlecakes, coffee, and fruit. Today, given the same list, guests order orange juice, toast, and coffee, but in those days people ate their way through the menu.

Then they went out and sat in the red and green chairs. They had to; after that breakfast. The men sat in one group and the women in another. The men read the Boston *Globe* or the New York *Tribune* and the women sewed and talked.

After an hour or so they played croquet, or walked up the hill to the Indian camp, or down into town to look around the stores. Midday dinner was twice as impressive as breakfast. In the afternoon they climbed into the long mountain wagons and drove to Sugar Hill or to see the Old Man of the Mountain.

After supper most of them just sat around. Mother kept two stereoscopic sets and stacks of "views" on the marble-topped table in the parlor. These pictures were made at the Kilburne View Factory at Littleton, only five miles away, and many of our townspeople modeled for them. "Where's George?" someone would ask, and the answer, "He's over at Littleton working in the views."

Some of the guests made up charades or parties for whist, euchre, or hearts. They did not play for money but for inexpensive prizes. Every Wednesday evening there was a progressive card party, with a lot of moving around between tables. Each player had a tasseled card, and I had to go from table to table with a conductor's punch and punch the points.

Tuesday nights the tables were removed from the dining room. A three-piece orchestra came from Whitefield, and our city folks and guests from other hotels appeared in all their finery and took their places in the chairs that went all around the room for the "hop."

It opened with a grand march and circle, usually led by Father and Mother. Dancing followed—the lancers, two-step, waltz, in rotation, with an occasional polka or caprice. There was no stag line, as the ladies' programs were filled out days in advance. Everyone was very gay.

At twelve light refreshments were served, and then the ball continued into the small hours. After it was over the staff had to reset the dining room, and frequently the waitresses had time only for quick baths before serving breakfast. Queer as it may seem, the help looked forward to the weekly "hops" because there was no curfew.

The "hops" did not always go according to plan. One summer a dashing young grass widow arrived from New York with her two boys, about six and seven years old respectively and the most resourceful pair of hell-raisers it was ever my misfortune to meet. We called them the "Heavenly Twins."

The other women looked askance at the widow. She had a better figure and was prettier than most of them. All summer they tried to get something on her, but her behavior was beyond reproach.

Then, during a hop, and right in an intermission when everybody was seated, a hush fell on the assembly. Through the wide doors marched the cherubs, pajama flaps down showing bare bottoms, and trailing after them on the polished floor came a long line of their mother's lingerie tied together with every stocking she owned, and this, mind you, in an era when a lady getting into a coach inadvertently showed the calf of her leg caused strong men to faint and horses to run away.

Some of the underwear was silk. That really did it!

She took a boy by each hand and they left the ballroom, trailing the lingerie. A buzz of satisfaction went around the walls. Then I saw Mother leave her chair and quietly go out after the widow. They came back a few minutes later, Mother's arm was around her waist, and they were chatting away as if nothing had happened.

How can I expect a generation of sun bathers in G strings to appreciate the almost fatal implications of this incident? But Mother understood her guests, and she also knew that her showing preference for anyone carried a lot of weight. I've heard her often bring a guest up short for criticizing another, but she could do it in the nicest way.

Major disaster could threaten even in those easy-going times. Once a doctor staying with us left the crowded dining room in the middle of breakfast and came out quietly to Father. "Frank," he said, "someone in that dining room has smallpox. I can smell it. I think it is the waitress who is serving me."

Father drove the girl to the county physician, and, she did have smallpox. He left her to be cared for at his expense but came back sick with worry. Quarantine in the middle of the season would ruin our business. That doctor proved a friend. He did not mention the subject again. Father kept his mouth shut, and the Uplands survived another of those unexpected crises that take years from a hotel man's life.

We were not entirely without worldly entertainment. In July the Dorothea Dix girls came up from Boston to "play" the hotels. To me this was the soul-shaking event of the year. Ten little girls were chosen from the Dorothea Dix home for actors' children, and they were dressed exactly alike in blue skirts, blue sweaters, and blue tams, and carried identical gray suitcases. They were chaperoned by a motherly woman with a beaming smile and a gimlet eye. No matter which hotel they performed in, I was on the porch that night looking through the window. One of the little girls was Millicent Orme. She was my first love! Millicent had a twinkle in her eye and a lilt in her voice, and when she sang, "Shine, Little Glow Worm, Glimmer," I wanted to run up and down the screen. She grew more beautiful every year, and by the time she was a dazzling ingénue with Anna Held, she had me practically in a state of apoplexy.

There were also the visiting elocutionists. One, who was Mother's favorite, was a tall, thin woman with eyeglasses and a tremolo voice, who recited a sad poem about a little boy sinking in quicksand, inch by inch. Just as the sand was about to reach his chin she would pause, give a stately nod to the waiting pianist, and interrupt her recital with a quavering "Nearer, My God, to Thee." Father and I suffered, but the ladies thought it perfectly beautiful, and wept all the way through.

Every year I had to help out an actor by sitting in a chair dressed like a girl while he knelt before me singing "Oh, Promise Me." The ladies listened and became all unglued. We went through that once a season, and I never stopped dreading it. Years later I saw George Arliss in the *Green Goddess* and with a poignant rush of memory recognized on the program the name of the actor I used to assist.

Best of all the summer events was the "Coaching Parade." This was apparently purely New Hampshire in origin and for some reason was always held on August 22. Coaches were brought from all over the White Mountains weeks in advance and hidden in barns to be decorated; meanwhile, the wagons met the trains.

Sometimes as much as thirty-five hundred dollars was spent trimming a coach. Decorators and costumers came up from New York, and the guests of each hotel donated and even helped with the decorating.

The parade was on a par with the Fourth of July. Every coach that rolled along was a picture, drawn by teams of six, eight, and even twelve horses, and strung out along Main Street for more than a mile. I knew all the famous drivers— Hod Wilder, Charley Wilson, Free Bede, Sime Connery, George Fiske, and Jerry Johnson. They were men who could bring any sort of vehicle over dangerous mountains, in sleet or snow, but on this day they were pictures of elegance.

Lem, our driver, hated dressing up for the parade. One year we took the prize with a coach decorated entirely in white. Mother and the women guests sewed for weeks, making white rosettes, and the half-dozen beautiful girls who sat on top were all in white. So was Lem, even to a white silk hat. Just before the parade started he heaved a mighty sigh: "White coach, white horses, white women, white parasols, and white doves. I never felt so g'damned pure in m'life!"

But the high light of summer was the Grand Ball and Cotillion at the Maplewood Casino off Main Street.

Weeks before the event the coveted invitations were received, and young belles lived in a dream of anticipation and their mothers in a dither of anxiety.

On the night of the ball the cream of the White Mountain summer cotillion set drove into the circular driveway of the Maplewood in coach-and-four, tandem, surrey, and six-wheel brakes. Bugles blew, grooms rushed to horses' heads, and footmen helped down bedecked and bejeweled guests.

Up the splendid stairway and into the mammoth high-ceilinged ballroom swept people whose names made the society columns in New York, Boston, and the southern and European spas. Men in full evening dress squired beautiful women in décolleté gowns of every hue who handled their long trains with grace and bore their heads proudly under bird-of-paradise plumes. Pretty faces flirted over ostrich fans, saucy beauty marks added fairness to young cheeks.

Against the walls and in the spectators' gallery the full-bosomed dowagers sat with the dignity of pouter pigeons, gasping in their lacings, with diamond tiaras on their heads.

The twenty-piece orchestra was composed of musicians from the Boston Symphony. Master of ceremonies was plumpish, jolly Mr. Clifford, the cotillion leader who knew all the McAllister set by their first names and whose badge of authority was a little golden whistle. Often, as I grew older, I served as his assistant, finding lost partners or stacking the slippers for the Cinderella dance. I'd wear white gloves and be dressed to kill, and the next morning be out in my oldest clothes, fishing. Continual sharp contrasts have whetted my appetite for life and perhaps my ability to get along in all sorts of situations.

The Cinderella dance was staged long after midnight. Ladies and gentlemen sat at opposite ends of the ballroom and the ladies tossed their left slippers in a pile on the floor. Mr. Clifford blew his golden whistle, the men caught up slippers, and hurried to find the girls who owned them, who would be their partners for the set. Many summer romances began with a slipper and many a hapless swain was stuck with his aunt Minnie.

It was almost dawn when the guests departed, the lights dimmed, and I remember standing on an empty floor littered with programs, confetti, and wisps of ostrich plume in a vast hall returned to gloom and solitude.

I would rather have lived in that era, between 1895 and 1910, than any other. Then a uniform was a costume an officer wore to a ball in Vienna, then a lady was a lady (or she wasn't), and a boy grew up knowing all was for the best in the best of all worlds. Radio, television, airplanes, and motion pictures have speeded up our metabolism and our daily lives, but they have not made one contribution to the pure happiness of living.

If only we could have thirty years of peace! It would all come back.

I remember one summer Father fulfilled an ambition of many years by adding a ballroom to Uplands like the one his friend Bill McAuliffe had in the Sinclair House. We sent invitations to two hundred people, and twenty minutes before the ball was to start we learned that the orchestra could not come. Bill heard of our trouble and sent over his entire orchestra to play for our opening.

If a resort kitchen ran short of anything during a meal, the owner could always send over to the nearest resort to borrow.

Honesty and good neighborliness weren't talked about. They were taken for granted.

Life moved on in this tranquil way all summer, with picnics, hayrides, coaching parties, and, three times a day, the sumptuous meals.

Labor Day came and went. The September crowd took on a new energy, as if in protest against summer's ending. Our guests huffed and puffed over mountain trails, chewed spruce gum, cut long mountain sticks. They took longer rides, and mailed bushels of post cards. They seemed to be crowding in the last of the joys that would not be theirs for another year.

Then the harvest moon rose over the White Mountains. Trunks were hauled down from the attic. There were farewells and promises to write, to return, to exchange visits during the winter.

The hotels were closing. The city folks were going home.

Chapter Two: INDIAN SUMMER

*T*OWARD the last of September we'd hear the little train going down over the hill with its whistle wailing farewell to the season.

Glad as we had been to see the city folks come, we were as glad to see them go. We were like farmers whose harvest was in. They were our bread and butter; they left us with money in the bank, the interest on the mortgage paid, and the future assured—for another season.

Oh, the relief of not having to be polite to everyone and worry over someone else's creature comforts every minute of the day! We were plain folks again, content with the church social, the Sears-Roebuck catalogue, and the monthly meeting at the grange. Over us closed the golden refulgence of Indian summer, and we had it all to ourselves.

I had a little cocker spaniel named Sport and a single-barreled twenty-gauge shotgun bought from Sears-Roebuck for twelve dollars. Every day after school Sport and I went hunting, through Turner's Sugar Place, or the woods on Strawberry Hill. The warm autumn sun shone down through leaves of crimson and gold, and when I got tired I'd sit against some giant maple and daydream until I heard Sport's excited bark over the next ridge. He usually had some partridges up a tree. Saturdays we went into the dark reaches of Waumbek Swamp rabbit hunting.

Sometimes I went hunting with the little boys of the Abnaki tribe who lived back of our house on Strawberry Hill, who made and sold sweet-grass baskets and bows and arrows to the summer visitors. Often, coming home late, I'd have supper with some of my Indian friends in their wigwam.

No matter how late I stayed, Mother and Father never seemed to worry about me. New Hampshire boys are brought up to be self-reliant, and they seemed to think I could take care of myself.

Sundays in the fall I had to go to church, morning and night, because I hadn't gone much during the summer. Father and Mother were Methodists, which was a handicap because most of my friends went to the Congo Church—old New England for Congregational—and I didn't have anyone to throw spitballs at. We had a Deacon Smithers who used to get down on one knee in the aisle at prayer meeting to pray. He was a tall, gaunt man in a long black coat who invoked the Lord in a voice loud enough to be heard by St. Peter. One Sunday before church I came around Smithers's barn and the old deacon in his Sunday clothes was teaching a calf to drink. He was shoving the calf's nose into the milk and singing at the top of his lungs, "Jesus, lover of my soul, I'll push your damn head through this pail" without a break in the rhythm.

Every Tuesday night there was band practice under Cruft's Hall. Father couldn't play any instrument, so they made him drum major. He had a wonderful red-and-blue uniform, and someone put this poem in the local paper:

> When I was young and in my prime,
> And that was back, oh, yes, some time,
> There wasn't anything so grand
> As our own Silver Cornet Band.
> The uniforms had much gold braid
> And all the horses were afraid.
> The gay drum major wore a hat
> That weighed ten pounds, yes, all of that.
>
> Of generous design 'twas built,
> And loaded down with sparkling gilt.

> His uniform was showered with gold
> And cost a fortune, we were told;
> He wore nice patent-leather boots,
> And kept step with the umpah toots,
> And whirled a stick high in the air,
> Which made the townfolks gape and stare. . . .
>
> The music wasn't very grand;
> The clothes were what made up the band.

I don't know who wrote the poem. Maybe Will Carleton, our town poet, who was famous even outside of Bethlehem because he had written the popular poem "Over the Hill to the Poor House."

Some of us boys trailed along to the band practice. During intermission we tootled on the horns, and I got so I could play an alto pretty well.

A family on a farm near by belonged to some obscure religious cult that believed the world was coming to an end on a certain day. That day, along toward milking time, a boy named Eddie and I stole a couple of alto horns, climbed to the top of the hill above their house, and began a mournful blasting that sounded like the last trump. The old farmer came out of the barn on a dead run, threw the bucket of milk over the fence, and hollered to his wife, "Mira, praise the Lord! The day has come!" The family rushed out of the house all dressed up in long white robes they had prepared to meet their Maker.

Evenings after supper Father would say, "Emma, I'm going down to the store," and I'd go with him. Nearly all the men in town would be down on Main Street and most of them would gather in "Hen" Smith's drugstore. Father said Henry Smith was one of the finest men he had ever known, and a great philosopher. He always had a handful of chocolates for every kid that came in and a cheaper kind for dogs—he called them "dog chocolates" and kept a big pail of them on the shelf next to the sink.

The chairs around the potbellied stove filled up with leading citizens and it was like a club. The men talked politics, told stories, and discussed hunting and fishing. "Hen" had one of the new Edison phonographs with a purple bell and cylinder records. Ada Jones and Sousa's Band were the favorites. Every once in a while someone would say, "Hen, give us a little piece of Ada," and they would all laugh.

Hen was more cosmopolitan than most of our townfolk. He had lived in Boston while attending pharmacy college and had "advantages." He held the fellows spellbound with accounts of the way people lived in cities. Up our way folks found it hard to believe that city men not only bathed, but shaved, every day. A bath was strictly for Saturday, and twice a week did for a shave.

A story never lost flavor in the drugstore. One of the favorites was about the time Hy Dillsmore, who ran one of the inns, got up at four o'clock one morning to cook breakfast for a guest who had asked to be called for the early train. It was a freezing morning, and when Hy went upstairs to rouse the guest the man went down farther under the covers and said he guessed he'd wait over and catch the later train.

"You kin if you like," said Hy, reaching right down after him, "but I got up and cooked breakfast for you, and right now, by gum, you're going to get up and eat it!"

George Turner, Father's closest friend, ran a farm and small hotel near ours called Turner's Tavern. He liked telling about the time a slick salesman came along during spring planting and sold him a half-dozen packages "guaranteed to kill all potato bugs." Mr. Turner was warned not to open the packages until he was ready to use them and by that time, six weeks later, the salesman was long gone. When the potato field flowered and the pests came, Mr. Turner opened his packages. Each contained two little blocks of wood painted green. On one was printed, "Lay the bug here," and on the other, "Hit it with this."

When the men stopped telling stories and started arguing politics I'd wander out of the drugstore and along Main Street. Another crowd was loafing around Burt Parker's grocery. He began missing change out of his cash drawer under the counter one winter, so he set a mink trap in it. That night a man sitting on the counter let out a surprised yell and was caught dead to rights with three fingers in the trap.

I'd drift on past Hugh Carr's livery stable. This was a wonderful place, where horses tossed their heads and stamped in the stalls and all sorts of shiny rigs stood in rows. The big office had a box stove and its walls were hung around with harness sets and long six-horse whips. The place smelled of saddle oil and smoke and was inhabited evenings by a number of weather-beaten characters in boots and denim overalls, faded shirts, and big hats. In my eyes these drivers were heroes. They logged in winter, drove tourists in summer, and tolerated small boys with the lofty detachment peculiar to champions in any field. I stood in awe before the whips that were the badges of their calling, and my greatest ambition was to handle one. Once I took a coveted whip into the yard where I became entangled in the long lash. A red-hot iron seared my little bottom and I turned around to see Hugh Carr grinning from the office door and coiling a whip back around its handle.

My last visit was usually to Clint Mason's harness shop. There was always a crowd, mostly teamsters, farmers, and lumberjacks, sitting around there in an aura of strong leather and stronger tobacco. The stories were racy and the swearing so beautiful it made my blood congeal.

There was a lot to be seen and learned along Main Street.

In November we had elections. Father was a Democrat but most of his friends were Republican. The Republicians were led by Father's friend, George Turner, and when our side got licked, Father used to say, "George, the damn Democrats always do the right thing at the wrong time." Before election there were caucuses in Cruft's Hall. I went to both the Republican and the Democratic caucuses because both gave out free popcorn, apples, and cider. The same men made the same speeches every year, and everyone got excited and stamped and pounded one another on the back.

Before every election Father went to Boston. He'd hitch Dennis to the Concord wagon and I'd go with him to Littleton, then he'd turn Dennis around, warn me, "Now don't you stop before you get home," and turn him loose. He knew the horse wouldn't stop until we reached the barn.

Two or three days later Father would be back. All the talk would be about the "railroad interests," "lumbering interests," and "wet or dry." On election day Father and I went to the polls early. Elections were held in a large hall off Main Street. As the men arrived, some of them would be steered over into the church horse shed. I'd hear some hot political arguing going on inside, and then the men would come out smelling of strong whisky and cigars and go right in to the polls and vote.

This quaint custom was known as "horse-shedding the voters."

One year Father ran for representative against Colonel Ringerford, one of the "big bugs" of Grafton County. He stood at the polls in a black Prince Albert coat and made a great to-do over the voters as they filed in. Father waited quietly on the other side of the gate.

About noon it was apparent that the election was going Republican. The colonel turned majestically to Father. "Things aren't going just as you expected, are they, Frank?" Just then seven or eight hayracks loaded with men drove up from the junction and piled out into the street before the polls. They stomped in single file, led by a big Irishman in a red-flannel undershirt named Jim Flannagan. The colonel bowed and beamed. "How are you today, Mr. Flannagan?"

There was a glint in Jim's eye as he scowled back, "Ah, t'hell wit yez!" Here were sixty or seventy solid Democratic votes delivered on schedule and insuring victory for Father.

Father spoke up from the other side of the gate. "Things aren't going just as you expected, are they, Colonel?" And the colonel replied, "This is dirty business, Frank, dirty business."

I never understood how they could be such good friends as soon as the election was over.

Elections were followed by a big dinner in Cruft's Hall, which was almost like a second Thanksgiving—good New England home cooking, than which there is none better: roast spareribs, chicken pie, big bronze-skinned turkeys, venison steak, bowls of creamy mashed potatoes, cranberries jellied and in sauce, and the desserts! And what desserts our New England women can produce! They would put Hubbard-squash pie and cranberry cobbler on the table and flush with pleasure at the praise of the menfolks.

The hunters were out in November, and the music of the deerhounds echoed and re-echoed across the hills. The ringing chorus summoned me through the windows of the musty schoolroom and almost drove me mad with longing. What did geography mean to me when I knew from the sound of her voice that old Bess was in the lead!

Eventually the practice of dogging deer was made illegal. The next year, when we went deer hunting, we took with us a town character named Ollie. Ollie was "teched in the haid." He'd locate a deer track in the snow and follow it all day, howling like a dog. Come noon we all had our lunch down in an old logging camp. Some of the boys put some hard dog biscuits in Ollie's lunch. He carried his lunch in a two-quart lard pail and when he opened it we winked and nudged, but he ate the biscuits with relish. The next day he looked in his lunch pail and grumbled, "What, no cookies?"

Years before this logging camp had been bossed by a man named Bannion Fonne, who, we were told, killed his wife. The lumberjacks cut a grave marker from a slab of pine and carved this inscription:

> Here lies the body
> Of Bannion Fonne,
> The meanest man
> The sun shone on.
> He murdered his wife
> On a winter's night
> When the stars shone down
> Their eerie light.
> Where she has gone
> No one can tell
> But we're damn sure
> That Ban's IN HELL.

What vivid memories to treasure! A little half-frozen mountain boy slogging home through the woods after dark—hungry, wet, and dogged tired; aching in every muscle after the day's hunt. The damp snow clinging to his mackinaw falls down the back of his neck as he plods along, head down, slipping on the smooth-soled moccasins, tripping over a fallen log.

The wind sighs through the naked branches and light scuds of cloud skip by, their phantom fingers clutching at the treetops. Weighted down with his rifle that in the morning seemed so light, he follows the unerring homeward course of a woodwise lad, proud of his self-reliance, yet conscious of the ever-haunting fear of getting lost. He thrills to the warm joy of reaching home, to a wonderful supper of fried salt pork and baked potatoes with a big piece of hot mince pie, and so to bed, and to the dreamless sleep of youth.

Soon the snow got too deep for hunting. We kids skated on Bishop Pond or slid two miles down the long hill on Travis sleds. On sunny mornings Father pulled on his coon coat, hitched Dennis to the pung sleigh, and we would start for Grandfather's with Duty racing behind. Duty was big even for a Saint Bernard and had been brought from Switzerland as a puppy and given to Father by Dick Croker, the well-known sportsman.

Just as December seemed the best part of the year, and I was enjoying it most, it was time to leave for Florida.

Like the birds, we made ready for our annual flight and the adventure that was always new.

The night before we left for Florida I didn't sleep much. I had been busy all day helping Father put up the shutters and turn off the water. We were out early in the snow before Uplands with all our grips and trunks, waiting for the "stage" to take us to Littleton.

The stage was a three-seated mountain wagon drawn by a pair of horses, driven by a red-faced, cheery fellow named Fred Gardner. For years Fred made two trips daily between Bethlehem and Littleton, and he knew everyone in the county and all the local gossip.

"So you're going 'way off to Florida," he always said, and we knew the whole region was marveling because "those crazy Abbotts" were traipsing off to Florida again.

There isn't a trip you could take in the world today as far-away seeming as our annual trek from Bethlehem, New Hampshire, to Orlando, Florida, in the nineties. We were going to travel for days, by mountain stage and jerkwater train, by boat and special car, changing at Boston, again at Washington, and last at Jacksonville. We were exchanging one remote American frontier for another that was its antithesis in every way, the little-known Floridian frontier.

Mother and I sat in back, tucked under robes that smelled strongly of the horse barn, and we started off down the long hill.

The dark green spruces and hemlocks, silhouetted against the towering far-flung Presidential Range, framed a Currier and Ives scene of a long road struggling over the snowy hills, past little white houses and large red barns. I looked over my shoulder to get a last look at the Uplands, covered with snow.

I was anxious to get on the train and torn between two emotions—anticipation of the exciting trip and the sadness of leaving home.

The Boston and Maine local steamed into Littleton at nine o'clock. The car was overheated and filled with shrilling women and crying babies, and I divided my time between pressing my nose on the window, gazing on the countryside, and deviling Father every time the news butcher came by for those wonderful glass pistols full of candy beans.

At noon the train stopped thirty minutes in Plymouth. Everybody rushed into the lunchroom in the basement of the Pemigewasset House adjoining the station. The long counter was served by pretty girls in spotless white, who dispensed food fit for the gods. Our old friend who owned the hotel sat behind a roll-top desk in a corner where he could survey the entire room. Joe was known all over the White Mountains. He was a big man with a loud voice and a merry twinkle and one of my extra-special friends. About halfway through the meal he would look up and bellow, "Maggie, that's Frank Abbott's boy from Bethlehem; give him some mince pie with ice cream on it and don't charge him a cent."

All during the long afternoon the train trundled its way past the wide reaches of the Winnepesaukee, through Concord, Manchester, and Lowell. It was dark by this time, and as I looked out the misted window at suburban lights rushing by I was awed by the thought that we were getting into the big city of Boston.

We alighted into the din and glare of old North Station, carried our grips up the platform and through the station and out into the street, where we waited for a streetcar. The lights, the teams, and the crowds were exhilarating, as was the ride up Washington Street to Adams Square. Here we left the streetcar and walked up to the old Quincy House.

The average small-town New Englander swore by the Quincy House. One reason Father stayed there was because it was frequented by his friend Charlie Sinclair, son of the Honorable John G. Sinclair of Bethlehem, New Hampshire, and Orlando, Florida, a power in the Democratic party for many years, who had been responsible for Father's first going to Florida.

Once, in the Quincy House, Father pointed out a tall, well-dressed man to me. "He carries the Boston and Maine Railroad in his vest pocket."

While Father registered, Mother and I waited in the lobby. Through the open door at the left I saw a long bar and a room for billiards and pool. Opposite was the dining room with its white napery, gleaming silver, and smiling colored waiters.

Father had thrift in his bones but no penury. We had come from the station by streetcar because it cost only five cents apiece and a costly hack would add nothing to our enjoyment. After we were in the dining room, Father had a little speech for Mother and me.

"Now we've had a good summer," he'd say, "and we're going to have a good dinner."

Then Father ordered the steak and everything that went with it, and the dinner was wonderful. He didn't even wince when he picked up the check, although it was $3.50, and for only three people. Father would say firmly, "It was worth it."

Meals were relished in those days. People entered a restaurant with a sense of expectancy, ordered with care, selected the wines that went with each course, then settled down to a leisurely meal with enjoyment. In Delmonico's in New York—and there was no more famous restaurant in the world —you could get a filet mignon of beef that would melt in your mouth, plus trimmings, for a dollar and a half. Now people go into restaurants, order highballs, and start table-hopping and screaming, "Hi!"

A few nights ago in New York three of us had a steak dinner at a famous restaurant, and the bill came to eighty-five dollars. The steaks were no better than those at the Quincy House when I was a boy.

Each year we spent two weeks in Boston, buying supplies and getting a crew together for the Florida hotel.

The next morning I heard Mother say she was going to Jordan Marsh and R. H. White's. I knew what that meant. If there was anything humiliating to me it was dragging up miles of store aisles and revolving on countless stools while Mother talked about yard goods, trimmin's, and whether or not sheeting would shrink in the wash.

Once a clerk trying to persuade her to buy a more expensive brand of sheets used the wrong argument. "These are the kind Mrs. Austin buys," he said, naming a woman who ran a larger summer resort than ours in Bethlehem. Mother pushed them right back. "Yes, but I intend to pay for mine," she said.

But I loved to go buying with Father!

We'd start for the market district at South Market and Blackstone streets. This was a busy section where big horses pulled large wagons of produce and men staggered about carrying great chunks of meat. First we went to Batchelder and Snyder's, the meat company, and climbed a long flight of stairs to pay our respects to Fred Snyder, the president, an old friend of Father. They had gone to Florida together in the eighties. Then we went down the hall to Mr. Bolton's office.

Of all the people I have ever known, L. R. Bolton was the most unusual. He was six feet four, fair, and stout, with a peaches-and-cream complexion, very masculine, always fault-lessly dressed. He was the Diamond Jim Brady of the resort hotel industry. As head salesman for Batchelder and Snyder and afterward president of Bolton-Smart Company, he traveled the resorts, North and South, winter and summer, for about fifty years, and the power he wielded in the industry was amazing, particularly when one stops to consider that in the last analysis he was merely a purveyor of meats.

The big hotel operators who were on their way South collecting their crews and ordering supplies for the winter, made Bolton's office their Boston headquarters.

Bill McAuliffe, on his way to run the Alcazar in Saint Augustine; and Harry Priest, who was going to the Carolina in Pinehurst, North Carolina; Andy Creamer, Fred Adams, and all the other headliners of the industry were there. Bolton presided over the talk as if his only care was making them feel at home. They gossiped, talked "grapevine," and smoked big cigars, and I sat in a corner and wondered if I would ever be a big hotel man.

Batchelder and Snyder maintained an employment service which Bolton directed in addition to his other duties. Outside his private office was a large room with benches that seated about one hundred and a number of small consultation rooms. Stewards, chefs, headwaiters, cooks, and various other applicants were in regular attendance and were sent to various hotels throughout New England, New York State, through the Carolinas, Florida, and even as far as California. There was no charge for this service, and it was a great source of Bolton's power.

Sometime during the morning Father and I went over to the Faneuil Hall Market, where I was fascinated by the countless stalls displaying such game as moose, bear, deer, and festooned strings of rabbits and ducks. Under the market place was Allen-Hurd and Company, dealers in fresh fruits. Fred Allen always had a big red Northern Spy or a bunch of grapes for me.

Father did his ordering and we got back to Batchelder and Snyder's before noon.

Sometimes Mr. Snyder took us up to Marston's Restaurant, where he had a regular table. A restaurant serving such food as Marston's would be famed around the world if it could exist today. Other days we went with Mr. Bolton.

It was his custom to take some of the hotel men, stewards, and chefs who were with him at noontime over to Durgin and and Park's, the famous old eating place above the produce houses "where your grandfather dined," and Mr. Bolton and his guests were treated like royalty. The patrons were nearly all market men. Ten or a dozen ate at each of the tables, which were covered with red-checked cloths, with a pound of butter set at each end, and were served by big, motherly-looking women who bustled around and knew nearly all the customers. It was the custom for the market men to wear their white butcher coats and straw hats into the restaurant all year round, even in winter. Many were wealthy, several were millionaires, but they wore these coats and hats with a sense of tradition.

We were offered our choice of the many generous items— heavy, thick-cut steaks, broiled live lobsters, huge servings of broiled fish, every kind of game, and great slabs of johnny cake. For dessert we had to choose between an entire plate of fresh strawberry ice cream, a mountain of strawberry short- cake, pies of every variety, or tremendous bowls of Indian pudding topped with vanilla ice cream.

After lunch Father set out to buy groceries. This was the part I liked best. It meant going to Cobb Bates and Yurkzies and S. S. Pierce. Of course we had to try all the cookies, raisins, olives, and crystallized fruits. We sat in Bill Harding's private office while boys brought cans of peaches, plums, and pears, which they opened for us to sample, and by the time the vegetables came, all we could do was sniff. Last, a large box of candy was given me at Pierce's which really topped off the ceremonies, glazed my eyes, and put me in a stupor.

This was the one time of the year when the hotel man was treated like a king. Father, buying supplies wholesale later, was brought into the president's office, given the best chair, the finest cigar. Today the hotel steward is mailed an itemized list and checks off what is wanted. But in the nineties buying was a ceremony with polite conversation and consultation that resembled the leisurely Chinese fashion of doing business, with wonderful samplings of food and being taken to lunch.

It was Father's day and he reveled in it. So did I.

Once when Father dragged out his buying in Pierce's I wandered out of the store and onto Tremont Street. I discovered I was lost when a voice said, "What's the matter, little boy?" and a friendly, helmeted policeman took me to the station house where a burly Irish sergeant lifted me onto his desk and asked my name. I told him my father ran the Uplands in Bethlehem and there was no mistaking which hotel it was, because, I explained, "Father says it has the biggest damn mortgage in the state of New Hampshire." I was disappointed when Father rushed in, very much excited, and led me away with the caution, "For heaven's sake, don't tell your mother!"

That evening we went to see Joseph Jefferson in *Rip Van Winkle*. We were in a box with Mr. and Mrs. Harry Priest and some other friends, and I sat in front where I could see. When the gnomes came up from behind the stumps they scared the living daylights out of me, and I let out such a wildcat yell that Father had me out in the back corridor before my feet touched the floor. I never have seen the rest of that play.

The next day Father learned that he would have to stay in Boston longer and decided to look for rooms. After supper we walked up Columbus Avenue, hunting for a nice genteel boardinghouse, and Father selected a neat-looking brownstone with a friendly light shining through lace-curtained doors. I liked the vestibule because there were so many pleasant-looking people in it. Father started chatting with the "host-ess," then his face turned gray and he muttered, "Holy cat-fish, Emma, let's get out of here!" He grabbed my hand and I landed on the sidewalk. When I asked what the trouble was, Mother bit her lip and Father told me to keep my mouth shut. How was I to know we innocents from Bethlehem had stumbled into one of Boston's "nicer" houses?

Our gypsy caravan left Boston from the old Park Square Station on the Federal Express, which was the only through night train to Washington. In those days hotel help was not allowed to ride in the Pullmans, where Father and Mother had a section, so the crew of men and women were in two day coaches hooked onto the end of the train, and I preferred being with them. The day coaches each had a barrel of apples, a barrel of beer, and several crates of cookies at either end, and in these cars our boys and girls were to eat, sleep, and sing through the six or seven days by train, from bitter cold to southern heat, and the trip was like a picnic all the way.

Someone had left about a half-inch of whisky in a bottle in the men's room. I wandered through the cars with this, won-dering what use I could put it to, when I saw Dan, our porter from Uplands, had fallen asleep in his seat. I poured the whisky over the front of Dan's coat, then told the brakeman there was a drunken man in our car. Before Dan was fully awake the brakeman had him hustled out into the vestibule, and Dan had a hard time getting back.

After a few more activities on my part Father and Mother ordered me into bed in their section. But they promised to wake me when we reached New York, where I sat up, staring sleepy-eyed out of the window, as our cars were put on lighters and towed seventeen miles down the river to the Jersey side.

In the morning we arrived in Washington, crossed the city by trolley, and after breakfast caught the Richmond, Fredericksburg, and Potomac train. Father wired ahead so that breakfast was ready for our troupe at the station. There was an old colored man at the entrance of the dining room who took the men's hats and never gave out checks. Father tried to fool him, and when he handed Father his hat, Father said, "That's not my hat." The old colored man smiled and bowed. "Sir, I do not know whether or not that is your hat, but I know it is the hat you gave me."

All day we trundled through Virginia and North Carolina, stopping at every little town. It was very dusty and tiresome, and along in the afternoon I went to sleep. Dan was still brooding over the whisky episode; he found a cork, burned it, and blacked my face. When I woke up, I walked up and down between the cars and was pleased because everybody seemed so happy. I didn't know until I washed for suppertime why they were laughing.

That night on the train has always been one of the most poignant memories of my childhood. I lay propped up on pillows in the lower berth, looking out of the window, watching the silhouettes of the stately long-leaved pines in the moonlight and the sand, white as the snow we had left in New Hampshire. This, to me, was fairyland.

There never was a musician who played as beautifully on any instrument as the old-time colored firemen played the whistle of those locomotives. The pathos and tragedy of an exiled race ran through the whistle cord. Sometimes they were merry and used to play a little tune—"Beatin'est thing since I been born, people still a-comin' and the train done gone."

In Savannah, where we stayed a couple of hours, the warm air filled with song. The colored porter, who swung his lantern as our train backed into the station, sang, "Railroad, railroad, hot line from the No'th! God's chillen's train!" But everyone else in Savannah in those days called it the "Damn-yankee Train."

In the restaurant where we had breakfast the colored waiter came up to the table and sang:

> "Beefsteak, lamb chops,
> How yuh ha' yu' eggs cooked?"

Across the room, at a table facing us, was a big Georgia "cracker" filled to the ears with corn liquor. He was a "backlander" from the turpentine camps. He was resentful and fighting mean, and he was just finishing off his second dish of bacon and eggs when a great big Savannah cockroach peeked up over the table. The "cracker" hiccoughed, swiped at it, and missed, and the insect raced across the table and down the other side.

The cracker swung around to his waiter. "Nigger," he yelled, "how come this restaurant is all cluttered up with cockroaches?"

"We don't have no cockroaches in here," the startled waiter replied. "This is a strictly first-class place."

The cracker reached into his hip pocket, pulled out a pistol, and laid it on the table.

"Nigger," he breathed, "what did you distinctly see run across this table?"

The waiter stiffened and turned a light ochre.

"Boss," he whispered, "I distinctly saw a cockroach run across that table!"

He was just one heartbeat from death.

Memories flooded in. I had been making this trip since I was nine months old. The South was a different world from Hampshire. The people were different.

The Yankee was temperate and suspicious of change. He chose to avoid trouble. The endless rigors of winter had taught him patience.

The cracker we saw that morning was an exception, but, even so, the cracker temperament can be as hot as Florida's sun. The term "cracker" originated when the early cowboys drove their cattle through the southern woods, cracking their long whips with the sound of revolver shots. "Here come the crackers," folks would say. The whips were made with oak handles about eighteen inches long, and a lash of plaited rawhide from eight to twelve feet long with a thin leather thong or "cracker" at the end. I used to watch the crackers toss a silver dollar in the dust and with a crack of the whip snap the dollar up into the air and catch it. This was their method of gambling.

Even time was different in the South. They used three kinds in Savannah: northern, southern, and city time, and some member of our crew usually miscalculated and missed the train.

When our train pulled out of Savannah, Father and I were on the back platform watching the Negroes working in their little garden patches and catching snatches of song, "Swing Low, Sweet Chariot."

Now I was wild with excitement. I went through the cars telling the help we were getting into Florida.

Father knew where the Florida line was and he sang a little song he had learned from the darkies:

> "Florida, that beautiful land,
> The home of the black snake and chigger,
> Where the rattlesnake roams
> O'er the red-hot sand
> And bites both white man and nigger."

Wild, unspoiled, and beautiful, Florida was a wondrous virgin land, stretching from Georgia to the Keys. It was a land of sunny skies and great tempest, beautiful flowers and stinging insects, unbounded hospitality and short tempers. A kindly land, where one could regain health and solace. A cruel land, where one could lose his life just off the highway. A land of tiny lakes and mighty rivers, reflecting in their depths gorgeous sunsets and countless thousands of snowy heron, egret, and ibis. An arid land, sun-baked and dusty, whose sole inhabitants were the buzzard, the rattlesnake, and the scorpion. A land of everglades and giant cypress, where the Seminole glides at his hunting.

And to this land I had returned, a little New Hampshire boy, bubbling over with life and eagerness, inquisitive of the high adventure which lay beyond. Every year of my life we had been shuttling between this country and New England. For this reason I was to think of myself as a Yankee cracker, having two homelands, loyal to both.

To FATHER Florida was truly the land of perpetual youth, and he loved it with a passion that has permeated every Abbott down to the present day.

He went there in the eighties as a contractor for the Honorable John G. Sinclair, who, among other interests, owned the Sinclair Real Estate Agency in Orlando.

There was no railroad below Jacksonville then and Father and Mother went by boat down the St. Johns River and drove over the sand roads to Orlando. They were in a small hotel there when yellow fever swept Florida. Father came down to breakfast one morning to find the crew had deserted. A panful of eggs was still frying on the stove. Father and Mother cared for the guests as well as they could. When the owner showed up, he took a look around and said, "I think you can run this."

This started the Abbott family in the hotel business. Father went back to New Hampshire and bought Uplands.

My first memory of Florida is of Father running the San Juan Hotel in Orlando in the winter of 1894, the year of the "big freeze."

The season started well. In December the hotel was filled with commission merchants and citrus buyers from New York and Boston markets who were offering the local growers fifty, seventy-five, and one hundred thousand dollars for the oranges on their trees. Grapefruit was not yet popular.

One day about noon a chill wind blew in under a leaden sky and big raindrops scattered the red-clay dust in the street.

Growers began to drift into the lobby to state nonchalantly that they had decided to accept the prices quoted an hour or so before. The buyers hurriedly left the lunch tables and went out of doors to view the weather. The big thermometer in front of the hotel indicated unusual cold.

By two o'clock the San Juan was in an uproar. Prices had dropped to "No Sale." Commission merchants were frantically trying to get out of options and heated debates and fist fights flared up in the lobby. The temperature continued to drop and the wind increased. By nightfall the thermometer registered sub-freezing and was still going down.

About nine o'clock in the evening a fine-looking gray-haired man in a black frock coat and Stetson hat walked up the street in front of the hotel and looked at the thermometer, groaned, "Oh, my God!" and shot himself through the head.

The hotel had no heating plant and Mother and Father made me sleep in their room where they had an oilstove.

Father had the damnedest habit of getting out of bed in the morning in his long white linen nightshirt, clapping his black derby hat on his head, and marching bare-shanked to the window to survey the sunrise.

As he peered out of the window that morning he looked black despair in the face. The "big freeze" had killed all the citrus groves in the state. As far as the eye could see the orange trees were withered and dead.

For three days the icy winds blew over a dead world. The gloom in the San Juan Hotel was something you could feel and touch, and for probably the first time in my life I behaved myself.

Then, one morning, we awoke to find the land bathed in sunshine. People stirred out of gloom and began to take a count of stock. This was the time to pick out the men from the boys; the fit from the unfit; the fighters from the weaklings. Many pulled up stakes and left. Others plowed up their dead trees and started anew. The wise sawed off the frozen trees at the ground and in another year new shoots ten feet high had grown from the old roots. These were seedlings, so many groves were bearing within two or three years.

Severe as the blow was, it wasn't fatal to our community inasmuch as the citrus industry shared only an equal place with the cattle industry. Orlando and Kissimmee, twenty miles to the south, were big cattle towns, and together with Arcadia, Punta Gorda, and Fort Myers were as wild and woolly as anything the West had to offer.

Visitors to modern Florida cannot imagine what the country was like in the nineties. We Northerners seemed as strange to the Floridians as the city folks had seemed to us in Bethlehem. The Floridians were the most hospitable, easy-going people in the world, but under the soft-spoken gentleness of the men lurked pure dynamite for anyone who stepped out of line.

Nor is it easy to convey the difficulties a northern man encountered doing business in South Florida. The entire state was unreconstructed, particularly in the rural sections, and Damnyankee was just one word. Somehow Father got through those early years without getting into trouble, in spite of being in the hotel business where all sorts of factions met and matters were argued out.

Orlando lay in hilly country surrounded by lakes. Many of our guests were sportsmen from New England, who brought their families to stay for the winter. They could venture out of the pretty little town in any direction and get all the fish and game they desired. People were beginning to settle there and many real estate men hung around the hotel.

The cattlemen resented the influx of Northerners, and the citrus growers and native Floridians resented the Johnny-come-lately real estate operators. There were times when feeling ran high. Father had a loud-mouthed carpenter from up North working at the bench with a Florida boy. The Southerner happened to say, "There's a lot of Yankees coming down here now, ain't they?" Big-mouth replied, "There was a lot of them came down here once when you didn't want to see them." The touch on the unforgotten tragedy of war whitened the face of the southern boy. He pulled out his gun and stuck it into the other's ribs. "Brother," he said softly, "there's a lot of them never went back."

Father got between them and it was only because of the love and trust the natives had for him that he was able to rush the carpenter out of the hotel and out of town "before night-fall."

A movement was started to pass a law to make the cattle-men fence their ranges, and a big rally was planned for Orlando at which the Honorable John G. Sinclair was to speak in favor of the new law.

The morning of the rally a rangy, haggard-looking cow-boy on a spotted pony rode up in front of the San Juan Hotel, dismounted, and lounged into the lobby. A gun hung low on each lean thigh and his belt was stuffed with car-tridges. He demanded something to eat and added as an after-thought that he had been sent over from the west coast "to shoot Mr. Sinclair if he makes that speech."

After breakfast the gunman went out, sat down in a chair tipped back against the wall, pulled his Stetson over his eyes, and went to sleep.

Charlie Young, who later ran the Boston Tavern in Boston, was tending bar for Father, and he adored Mr. Sinclair. He was back of the bar in his white coat when he heard about the gunman. He reached for a bung starter, jumped over the bar, went out to the killer, and tapped him on the shoulder. The man started awake. Charlie said, "I hear you've come over here to kill Sinclair." Then he knocked the killer sprawling with the bung starter.

When the gunman got up, he was so embarrassed that he climbed on his horse and left town.

There were a number of remittance men from England

living in Orlando. One, who lived in our hotel, used to take me riding all over the country with a mule and buckboard. There were no bridges, and I had to hold my feet up crossing the fords.

Once we drove by a twenty-acre tract being cleared of underbrush. We couldn't see the back half because so many brush fires were going and the smoke was thick. The owners, three "Johnny-come-latelies," extolled the fertility of the soil and the beauty of the location and my friend bought the place. The next day he drove Father and me back to view his purchase.

The fires were out and we could see that most of the back acres were useless swamp.

The Englishman didn't say a word. He just turned the mule around and drove home.

A few days later he bought a lot at the entrance to the cemetery and set up a large tombstone which read:

"There was a man who came down from Jericho and fell among thieves; their names were . . ." followed the names of the real estate sharks who had sold him the land.

The gale of merriment that swept Orlando forced the three to give the Englishman back his money, buy his cemetery lot, and take down the tombstone, without a shot being fired—an unusual proceeding in those days.

There was a great deal to keep me occupied. I'd hitch Nicodemus to his little red wagon and go visiting. Nicodemus was a goat of great dignity and great smell and my constant companion. I drove him down the one sidewalk when the city marshal wasn't looking and hung around the firehouse because young Johnny Weeks, a friend of Father, was the chief. His full name was John W. Weeks and he was later Secretary of War under Harding and Coolidge.

One hot morning I drove Nicodemus around back of the hotel and found a couple of Negroes digging. A lone drifter who had "cashed in" one night in the barroom had hastily been put away in the nearest convenient place. Father had permission to remove the body to the cemetery, but it had taken a great deal of persuasion, a bottle of whisky, and twenty dollars, to get two men to undertake the job.

Nicodemus and I watched, fascinated. The darkies were in the hole up to their waists, pausing to pull on the bottle and mutter piously, "This po' lost soul!" Suddenly one of the shovels hit something with a crunching sound. I gave out with a prolonged groan and the two erupted out of the ground and down the road. I was sagging in hysterics with my arms around Nicodemus's neck when Father plunged through the back door yelling, "Emma, get this kid into the house! Now where in hell can I get any more men to dig up this body?"

The county jail was about a block away from our hotel. Once, when they were going to hang a man, Mother sent me and Nicodemus out to Formosa, about three miles away, to stay with "Auntie Sinclair." The Sinclairs had a lovely big house in an orange grove by a millpond, and "Auntie" Sinclair always gave me the most wonderful things to eat, which Nicodemus and I enjoyed out on the dam. I could also catch pollywogs and take them home in a jar to put in the hotel bathtubs.

The next morning I looked out of my hotel room window and the man was hanging on the gallows. Mother had miscalculated the event by a day. At the luncheon table, which we shared with about ten guests, she noticed I was dangling a peanut on a string. Mother asked what I was doing, and, to her horror, I answered it was the man on the gallows.

Our New England guests went on wonderful Sunday picnics. Even the children were invited. We camped at the edge of one of the lakes and spent the day feasting, lounging, and playing games. At nightfall the teams wound their way back through the piny forests, and I can still hear the singing as the great Florida moon came over the treetops.

In the main these were simple, gentle, peaceful days.

The next fall found us even deeper South. The small sun-baked town of Punta Gorda, sprawling along the banks of the Peace River, was then the last outpost of Florida's west coast and a rip-roaring, hell-raising cattle town. The Plant System had pushed the railroad south to this point, and F. Q. Brown built the large new Punta Gorda Hotel that towered over the one-story wooden shacks of the frontier terminus.

This was the largest hotel Father had operated, and it proved to be very popular. Since Punta Gorda was railroad's end, everyone going down the coast had to spend the night with us before taking the morning boat to Fort Myers. The regular winter guests who filled the hotel were sportsmen and their families from the North. These men devoted practically their entire days to hunting and fishing, and when they came in at night everybody rushed down to the wagons or boats to see their game and fish. On a day's trip up the Peace River one party of hunters sighted one hundred and nine deer and thirty-eight wild turkeys.

Our guests were true sportsmen and formed lasting friendships with the local hunters and guides, who forgathered evenings on the wide piazza of the Punta Gorda to spin tall tales of the western coast. There were stories of big fish and mighty hunts, pirates, cowboys, and of the bad men who were not legends but realities in our region. I remember so well these evenings—the men slouched in their chairs, weary after the day in the open, the low murmur of their voices, the lazy cloud of tobacco smoke, the Florida night winds soughing in the palms, and the hum of insects. Below the steps, in the soft dust, the sleeping dogs whimpered their dreams of game pursued.

In the middle of the season Father received word that an English nobleman was coming. W. K. Vanderbilt brought his yacht to Punta Gorda to take the celebrity on a hunting and fishing expedition and Father prepared to "roll out the red carpet." We were all on hand the next day when Lord

Warwick arrived in his private car. He stepped down leading a pair of beautiful English pointers. A couple of hound-dogs belonging to a cracker in the crowd started for the English dogs.

"Call off your dogs, won't you?" the lord asked civilly, whereupon the cracker took umbrage. "Don't you put a hand on my dogs, you ol' soft Lord of Creation!" And he made a pass at the lord, who countered with a stiff uppercut that floored the cracker. Warwick collared his dogs and led them off, and the cracker, regaining his feet, stared after him in admiration. "Doggone!" he exclaimed. "That's a real man!"

Nothing was too good for Lord Warwick in Punta Gorda from then on.

In this sportsman's paradise Father was hard pressed to supply his table. There were no markets in Florida catering to fine hotels. He could buy ten plump quail for fifteen cents and all the wild turkey and venison he needed for a song, but in a land teeming with cattle there was not a quart of milk for sale. Our milk and cream were shipped by boat from Vermont to Boston and the rest of the way by boat and slow train. A little benzoate of soda kept it fresh. When we went farther South, to Fort Myers, another boat trip was added.

Imagine the cost of every drop we put on our tables!

The hundreds of cowhands around Punta Gorda considered our sending all the way to Vermont for milk a curious business, but of greater interest to them were the pretty New England girls we brought down as waitresses. Southern girls did not go out to work, and any girl who did was likely to be suspected of being "fast." This fallacy spread a lot of hope around the local ranges.

The Punta Gorda had been open only a month when a big cattle drive came through. Several thousand head traveled down from Kissimmee and were shipped from Punta Rassa to Cuba. After the cattle were loaded, the range boss paid off, and the "cow pokes" proceeded to take Punta Gorda. Whooping like Indians, they rode their cow ponies up and down the street and into barrooms, shooting up the town. One contingent got roaring drunk on brandied peaches and decided it would be great sport to have dinner at the "damnyankee hotel." They marched in headed by a six-foot-four range boss named Bill Post. I was standing by the door, and he swung me up onto his shoulder and we led a deafening grand march around the lobby and into the dining room. Dinner was in full swing for our dignified guests, and the cowboys let out a concerted whoop and each grabbed a waitress.

I'll never forget Father sauntering up to Bill Post with his broadest smile. "Now, how in hell do you figure I'm going to serve you supper if your boys don't turn my girls loose?"

They left peacefully enough after dinner, but later on several came back, liquored to the boiling point and looking for girls. There was no reasoning with them, and the last I saw of Father that evening he was settled for the night on a chair in our lobby, with his Winchester rifle across his knees.

There was plenty of excitement and wild characters around Punta Gorda. Only a few months before the city marshal had prevailed on the city council to build a jail that would "stand the strain."

Presently the town filled with gunrunners engaged in running arms and ammunition to Cuba, which was at war with Spain. The Cuban leaders of the outfit stayed at our hotel. So did the secret-service men sent down from Washington to watch them.

The famous gunrunning ships *Dauntless* and *The Three Brothers* stealthily slipped up and down the coast, keeping rendezvous with their conspirators ashore.

The United States authorities captured a small fleet of Cuban fishing smacks and took away their sails so they could not leave, and a large side-wheel United States gunboat lay off our dock. Officially, the United States was neutral, but sympathy ran strongly with the Cubans, and an air of hushed excitement permeated Punta Gorda.

Yellow fever broke out in Cuba and the Windward Islands, and a strong cordon of boats guarded the Florida coast from Key West to the Anclote Keys with the orders "shoot to kill." Thus the coast was doubly guarded and gunrunning became even more dangerous.

At 9:40 P.M., February 15, 1898, Father rushed upstairs from the cable office to tell us that the battleship *Maine* had been blown up in Havana Harbor! We knew it before President McKinley did, for the news had been flashed from the cable station at Punta Rassa and thence through the Punta Gorda Hotel to the White House in Washington.

The slogan, "Remember the *Maine*, to hell with Spain," was on everyone's lips.

For weeks nothing happened, and the papers were calling the President an old maid for not declaring war. Public and press did not realize that the two little Plant System steamers, the *Olivette* and the *Mascotte*, were busily transferring American citizens from Havana to Port Tampa. Not until two months later, when the *Olivette* cleared Morro Castle with the last American citizen, was war declared.

Then there was real excitement along our coast! We expected the Spanish Fleet to shell us at any moment. A battalion of volunteers formed and marched and countermarched. Port Tampa and Punta Gorda were the main shipping points for troops and supplies going to Cuba, and there was great confusion as contingent after contingent sailed. Schooners set out with army supplies, half of which was sold along the Florida coast.

Our hotel filled to overflowing with army officers, contractors, and camp followers. The lobby was a shambles of newspapers, stray letters, and telegrams, and reeked of sweat and stale tobacco smoke. Men crowded there, pushing up to the desk to ask for mail, send telegrams, argue, and spread rumors. The hotel help was exhausted, and Father hardly slept for weeks.

America had not been at war since the sixties and it was a new and exciting experience for all of us.

In my eyes the most important people on the Florida west coast were the reporters and war correspondents—Richard Harding Davis, Caspar Whitney, John Fox, Jr., and Frederick Remington. Clara Barton came with her Red Cross units. Cowboys flocked into town on the chance of joining up with Colonel Teddy Roosevelt's Rough Riders.

I made my customary contribution to the general confusion. Our only water supply was rain water, and there were a number of huge wooden cisterns beneath the hotel. It was cool down there in the semi-darkness and just the sort of place I liked.

By chance I opened the big valve of one of the cisterns. The amount of water that gushed out led to my building a system of miniature canals, ponds, and lakes under the hotel. At the end of the day Father came looking for me. He took one look, shut off the valves, and pounded on the cisterns. They were almost empty.

This was a serious situation, which he impressed upon me with the aid of a paddle. What were we to do without fresh water for the balance of the winter? Father was worried and I was frightened to death!

That night one of the worst storms blew up that I have ever seen in Florida. It rained four nights and days without stopping, and a forgiving providence filled the tanks to over-flowing.

To me there is always a thrill and a challenge in going to new places—new sights to see, new problems to meet, new friends to make, and so it was that day in December of the following year when we left Punta Gorda for Fort Myers on the beautiful stern-wheel steamer *St. Lucie*. We were exhausted after the trip down from winter-bound New Hampshire by the side-wheel steamer *Pilgrim* of the Fall River line, from Boston and New York, and the three grueling days and nights by train.

This winter Father was to operate an even more splendid caravansary, the new Royal Palm at Fort Myers, built, furnished, and outfitted by Hugh O'Neill of O'Neill's famous department store in New York.

I climbed to the upper deck of the *St. Lucie*, curled up on a life raft in the shade of the wheelhouse, and went to sleep listening to the rhythmic chug, chug, chug of the great paddle wheel. I was awakened by the welcome sound of the big brass luncheon bell in the hands of a smiling Negro.

Off across the bright green water lay the jungled mangrove mass of Lacosta Island, and in the distance the shimmering sands of Sanibel. We crossed San Calos Bay in the late afternoon and neared Punta Rassa at the mouth of the Caloosahatchee River where it enters the Gulf of Mexico.

The only building there was the Punta Rassa Hotel, an old white clapboard building of about thirty rooms, jokingly known to some of its exclusive clientele as "Murderer's Row." It was run by George Schultz, a respected and popular hotel man. Guests dined at one long table, where, rumor had it, a barrel of whisky always stood at the head, and spent their holidays fishing, loafing, and playing cards. They had a peculiar custom of pulling long white nightshirts over their clothes after they dressed in the morning, donning wide-brimmed straw hats, and wearing this costume all day.

When our boat whistle blew about twenty big fat men in nightshirts and straw hats strolled down to the dock. They looked exactly like a flock of dignified penguins. Their dignity was not unwarranted, for in their ranks were some of the top executive, business, and political figures of the United States.

We steamed on up the broad and beautiful Caloosahatchee.

Along the river cattle grazed neck deep in floating hyacinths. Snowy egrets frosted the dark green of the jungled mangrove. I saw a great bald eagle atop a giant pine, and laughed as flocks of coots skittered across our bow, or ran across the water, holding up their feathered skirts like frightened girls. Countless thousands of blue-billed ducks whirled and circled in long festoons against the sunset sky.

Captain Warner pointed out a large house set well back from the river and surrounded by bamboo and orange trees.

"That's the home of the inventor, Mr. Thomas A. Edison," he said impressively. Fort Myers came into view and I fell in love with the town at first sight—the clusters of little houses set in the lush green of the giant banyans; the dock running out into the river; Harvey Heitman's grocery and his big white house across the street; the Silver King Bar and Billiard Hall with a dozen cowponies hitched to the tierack in front (Finest Bar and Ball Tables in South Florida, Whisky from two and a half to five dollars a gallon); a dozen other saloons near by; Frank Carson's Livery Stable; the courthouse; the fish house and jail down by the river; a couple of churches and, rising over all, the unfinished Royal Palm Hotel.

Father couldn't wait to have supper before he had us all over the new building from top to bottom. He had never before operated a place so big and fine, and he was so proud he could hardly contain himself.

There was a merry-go-round in a vacant lot back of Frank Carson's Livery Stable. It was the first one that had ever come to Fort Myers, and the cowboys were deserting the saloons to ride it. It was comical to see the big hard-bitten fellows in their ten-gallon hats, chaps, and spurs, riding the little painted wooden horses round and round to the loud music. When the tired owner wanted to close up, the cowhands started shooting at the organ, so around they went again, and round and round, far into the night.

The Royal Palm opened after much fussing and fuming,

arranging of furniture, and arguing with decorators. Dozens of guests appeared on the first day, and Father planned a great dinner for opening night. That afternoon I was out catching minnows in a little creek near the hotel, and when I came in to dress for dinner, I was carrying them in a Mason jar.

The dining room was decorated with tropical flowers. The tables gleamed with silver and spotless linen, and in the center of each a large glass carafe sparkled to the brim with clear water. A wonderful idea struck me. Why not put a litt minnow in each water bottle? In a few minutes it was done. They looked wonderfully silly swimming around in that festive setting and magnified by the bottles to three or four times their actual size.

Paul, our dignified headwaiter, came through the door. One look, and all was consternation. He rushed out, marshaled the waitresses, and rushed them in to empty the bottles. As the water gurgled through the narrow necks, the little fish stuck to the sides, and when the bottles were refilled, they again swam around merrily. It was only a few minutes until the dining-room doors must open, and into this bedlam came Father with the suggestion that they use water pitchers from the bedrooms and leave the damn fish in the carafes. Then he warmed my pants to a fare-thee-well and sent me upstairs to change.

A formal dinner in those days was majestic with pomp and ceremony tempered with charm. The dining room filled with townfolk of local prominence and hotel guests. Now and then the conversation was broken by an expectant hush as a noted personage entered—Thomas A. Edison and Mrs. Edison; Colonel Henry Watterson (Old Marse Henry himself), the fire-eating editor of the Louisville *Courier Journal*; Joseph Jefferson, the famous actor, in his seventies and fresh from playing *The Rivals* on Broadway; Harry Payne Whitney, the socialite; Chauncey M. Depew of the rapier wit; A. M. McGregor, president of Standard Oil of Ohio, and "Tooty" McGregor, his beautiful wife, who was to play such a large part in our lives, and a party of guests from their yacht, *Whim;* H. P. Plant, president of the Plant system; Richard Crocker, known to society pages as "the eligible bachelor"; and a host of others.

I realize now why Father was called the "dean of the art of hospitality," and I envy him the privilege of having been host to the great and near-great of that golden era.

Dinner was served with a flourish. Paul attended the guests with a grave courtesy, and the staff rendered adequate yet unobtrusive service. Course followed course in stately procession—appetizers, soups, roasts, entrees, game with stuffing and sauces, a frozen punch, desserts, sweets, each course attended by its proper wines, down to the last liqueur. Repartee was then a fine art, and light laughter rippled across the room. Finally the ladies retired and the men settled over the tables to their cigars, their brandy, and their stories.

I wandered out on the back stoop. On the wall was a giant Florida house spider. He was so large he could have run up a two-by-four with his legs on the outside, only he was dead.

I looked at that spider and saw a clear picture of the stairwell running down through the four stories of the hotel, and, at the bottom of the grand staircase, the bench where the bellboys sat.

In no time I was up on the fourth floor with a spool of black thread and the spider attached. Peering over the banister and down into the lobby, I was surprised to see, instead of the bellboys, Father and a gray-thatched gentleman sitting on the bench in deep conversation. I recognized the gray-headed man as Thomas Edison.

Mr. Edison was in evening dress and his dress shirt bulged in front as he bent over, his hand cupped to his ear, listening to Father. Oh, well, since no bellboys were available, they would have to do! I lowered the spider slowly until it reached the level of their heads. I saw Father make a pass at it, and I yanked it up a few feet, then let it down again. I heard

Father cussing as he rolled up a newspaper and went after the monster in earnest. They both looked up and saw me. Mr. Edison's mild features wore a broad grin, but the look on Father's face sent me skittering down the back stairs.

Father met me at the bottom. The opening of the Royal Palm was a black day for me.

We came to know the Edisons intimately during the years we spent at Fort Myers. They had two children, Charlie, about my age, and his younger sister Madeline. Charlie later became governor of New Jersey.

I have always been fascinated by stories of Edison, some true, some folklore, and have sat through many a quiet afternoon listening to him and Father reminiscing. He once told us that when he first started to sell his inventions he sold them outright instead of arranging for royalties.

He said he was plodding along on one of his early inventions, meeting with repeated discouragements and sorely pressed for money. Eventually he succeeded and was able to sell the invention for a considerable sum. The buyers gave him a check, which he took to the bank. The teller was a fussily important young man in a great hurry, who told the inventor he would have to be identified. Edison, being deaf, did not understand. Thinking the check was worthless, he sat on the steps of the bank in deep despair.

A friend entering the bank asked what was wrong and Edison confided in him. The friend explained that he needed only to be identified, and took him to the teller. When asked how he wanted his money, Edison replied, "In big bills—tens and twenties." Edison stuffed the bills into all his pockets, buttoned his overcoat tightly, and went to his boardinghouse room.

He put the money in his trunk and sat on the trunk all night worrying. Next morning he went back to his friend and told him of his dilemma. The friend explained that Edison should deposit the money in the bank and stop worrying.

And, Mr. Edison told us, smiling, after he deposited the money life went along like a song for six months. He bought machinery and supplies for his laboratory and anything else he wanted, and all he had to do was write out checks. As his friend had promised, he had no worries at all.

One day he was shocked to learn that he was broke. He hadn't thought to keep a balance.

Mr. Edison said that when he was a telegraph operator for a railroad he had orders to flag down a freight train with his red lantern. But while waiting at his desk he became preoccupied with an idea. The freight train rushed by and before he realized it he was staring at the lights of its caboose vanishing up the line.

"I resigned then and there," the great man told us. "I just picked up my coat and hat and walked out."

He was a gentle, kindly man with a wonderful smile, and usually wore a somewhat rumpled linen suit and a standup collar which was frequently awry, as was his unruly gray hair. He had a way of making young folks adore him. When I was a youngster, he foretold to me radio, television, and atomic energy years before their discovery.

Thomas Edison told me many things. Some of them I remember. He said I would probably live to see the day a large ocean liner going to Europe would be run by a small box of energy "about the size of a wastebasket located in the center of the ship." "There will be no more machinery," he told me, "or power plants, or bunkers for coal." That clear, kind look of his pierced far ahead of our horse-and-buggy turn of the century.

One of the great privileges of my life as a hotel man and a hotel man's son has been meeting many of the great personages of this country. People away from home are apt to let down the barriers of natural defense they usually assume owing to business or social pressure. Many we knew as friends would be unapproachable at any other place or time.

North or South, no matter where we were, Mother started a garden the day after we arrived. She was always puttering around flower beds. The vegetables were in Father's department. At the Royal Palm she had a big Negro named Pink Green to help her with the flowers. He was powerfully built and black as coal, with a sunny disposition. Pink was on the chain gang, but the authorities let him off when we came down in the fall and put him back again when we left in the spring. I never knew what he had done to make his sentence so long.

Pink was a great crony of mine.

Father used to send us down-river to get curved-bill curlews for the table. Pink would row eight or ten miles down the Caloosahatchee to a rookery island. We would get there when the sun was still high, hide the boat, and lie in the sand in the center of the island waiting for sunset. Beside us were our guns and a big tin dishpan and iron spoon.

About sundown the beautiful white birds would start converging on the island from all directions—in small flights of eight or ten to large flocks of hundreds. They would come in "V" formations or long, undulating lines from near and far, until the trees were white. They would flutter through the trees gossiping and squawking until their cries merged in a roar.

When they had quieted and the sun started to dip over the horizon, we would have to work fast, since there is no twilight on the Gulf. Pink would start to beat on the pan with the spoon and the curlews would rise in one great cloud and slowly circle the island just at treetop height. We were awed by the glory of this solid white formation of birds, so thick one couldn't see the sky, moving slowly around the island in a snowy feathered cloud with the crimson rays of sunset tinting their breasts.

We would shoot until our gun barrels got hot, and would cool them in the water, and shoot again. A half barrel of birds was the work of half an hour. By the time the last curlew was in the boat it was dark.

On Sunday evenings our guests often gathered in the ballroom of the Royal Palm for an impromptu forum. I recall one evening when the topic under discussion was "The Three Greatest Men in History," and the debaters were A. M. McGregor of Standard Oil, Thomas A. Edison, Colonel Henry Watterson, and the famous Dr. Curtis R. Teed, who founded the Koresham Unity down the coast below Fort Myers. Colonel Watterson held forth wittily on the thesis, "As a navigator Noah was no slouch." In retrospect, I realize what a rare treat it was to have witnessed the lightning flashes of these brilliant minds.

William Jennings Bryan, the "Great Commoner," stayed with us the latter part of the winter and entered into the Sunday-night forums with great enjoyment. He had the ability, when speaking to a crowd, of making you think he was speaking directly to you. Bryan was a large man, given to informal dress, and he always carried an old-fashioned palm-leaf fan around the hotel. He was a great favorite among the other guests, even those who disagreed with him politically.

Laughing, he explained to a group one day, "Karl comes from New Hampshire, where they have pie for breakfast." I demanded, "Did you ever eat any better pie anywhere?" to which he replied seriously, "Come to think of it, young man, I don't believe I ever did."

The placid atmosphere our guests enjoyed was in direct contrast to the wildness of the country. Cowboys, 'gator hunters, and fugitive renegades lived dangerously in pioneer southwest Florida.

Frank B. Tippens, later federal marshal of Miami, was sheriff of Lee County and brought his men to justice without fuss or feathers—in fact, his reputation among the lawless element was so great that many times he just sent word for them to come in.

Famous guides worked for the Royal Palm—Tillit Henderson, Captain C. B. Able, George West, Bill Bartley and his son young Bill, Captain Hugh Cooper, Philip Bylaski, and the Mickle brothers. They brought me presents of young wild life found on their trips afield. Soon I had a menagerie—an American eagle named Baldy, who roosted on the water tank over the hotel and soared down to select his share of fish when the fishermen came in at evenings and laid their catch on the dock; a pair of otter who spent most of their time in the drip pan under the big refrigerator in the kitchen; a covey of quail which lived in Mother's geranium bed; and a pair of sandhill cranes, Jack and Sandy, who amused the guests with their stately dances. But the prize was my pet pelican, Noah.

I'd keep a fish on ice until it was stone cold. Noah would run after me on his short legs with much wing-flapping and his big mouth open. The regular guests smiled—they knew what was coming. Noah took his fish whole, closed his eyes contentedly, and waited for the comforting processes of digestion. Instead, his tail would twitch, his belly oscillate, and his eyes fly wide. The most surprised look would come over his dignified countenance. That fish was damn cold, and Noah brought it up in a hurry.

I had two wonderful friends about my own age, Stanley Hansen and Dan Floweree. Stanley was the son of Dr. William Hansen, and later the white medicine man of the Seminoles, who brought the Seminole Indians to the New York World's Fair. Dan was the son of D. A. G. Floweree of Helena, Montana, who wintered in Fort Myers. We boys fished and hunted, rode cow ponies, matched fighting cocks, and hunted for birds' eggs in the bayous.

One morning I woke to find the old stern-wheel river steamer *Gray Eagle* tied up to the head of the dock. Mr. O'Neill, the owner of our hotel, had chartered the quaint steamer for a trip up the Caloosahatchee to Fort Thompson, and I was to go along.

As I remember her, the *Gray Eagle* was about seventy feet long and flat-bottomed, painted gray, with a large deckhouse over all and a wheelhouse on the hurricane deck. Year in and year out this comfortable old craft had plodded up the river against a four-mile current to Fort Thompson and back. She had wood-burning boilers and a single stack that belched great clouds of smoke, and, as the country was flat, you could see her coming for miles.

We pulled away from the dock about ten that morning with Captain J. F. Menge on the bridge and headed up the Caloosahatchee through high banks overgrown with live oaks and palmetto. Our party consisted of Mr. and Mrs. Edison, "Tooty" McGregor, Mr. and Mrs. A. D. Hermance, Father and Mother, Mr. O'Neill, and myself. I sat in the bow, exhilarated beyond measure as each turn of the tortuous river gave new and haunting vistas. Birds by countless thousands hovered over a small island—Indian curlew, lady of the lake, blue crane, egret, white ibis, and others of marvelous plumage.

We passed a picturesque old sugar mill, vast fields of sugar cane, and gleaming orange groves where the dark branches were heavy with gold. Huge alligators, lazily sunning themselves on the banks, slithered into the water and sank without a sound. We passed historic Fort Denaud, where immense cypresses towered, their great branches extended as if in perpetual prayer, with long strands of Spanish moss hanging from them like vestments.

Fort Thompson was simply a location. As soon as we tied up at the riverbank the men took their guns and disappeared over the side into the eerie twilight of the jungle, while the ladies took up their fishing tackle—they had no intention of being idle spectators!

As the great red sun dropped over the palms, our sportsmen came trooping aboard with their spoils. A long table stood amidships on the cargo deck and the colored cooks and waiters set out a dinner to warm the heart—venison, wild turkey, ducks, pigeons, quail, snipe, and fish, and a variety of other good things.

That evening we lounged on deck listening to an impromptu concert provided by our genial Captain Menge and his crew. After the concert his men set fire to the Spanish moss hanging from the oak and cypress trees along the shore. The sheets of flame racing from tree to tree were reflected in the dark mirror of the river. The silence was broken only by our gasps of admiration and the cries of jungle birds startled from their resting places.

Next morning we left for the homeward journey.

On the deck of the *Gray Eagle* were laid out the fish and game caught within a small radius and the space of a few hours—sixty black bass averaging in weight from six to eight pounds, several dozen terrapin, fourteen pigeons, fifteen ducks, seven wild turkeys, seventy-five quail, and many jacksnipes, curlews, flintheads, and ibis.

Caloosahatchee—crooked river of the Seminoles—is to me an enchanted river.

The old *Gray Eagle* is now in Henry Ford's museum at Dearborn, Michigan, and the last I knew Captain Menge was still its custodian.

The railroad came to Fort Myers in 1904, just a short time after the first long-distance telephone lines linked it to the outside world. Florida was growing up and I was growing with it.

WE USUALLY arrived home about the middle of April. Father and Mother would get off at Littleton, where the stage was waiting, but I'd stay on the train and go on up the line to Wing Road.

From there I had a three-mile walk over the hills to Grandfather's farm in Cherry Valley to get Dennis and Duty and bring them home to Uplands in the morning.

The New Hampshire hills are wonderful in April: brooks running bank full and chill winds blowing off the snow-capped mountains scenting the pine and balsam. As I trudged up the narrow country road, jumping over the puddles, memories of palms and sleepy lagoons slipped away.

At the summit of the first long hill I would perch on a rail fence under a giant pine and drink in the sweet dark breath of spring. A saucy red squirrel might sit on a limb above my head and cuss me out for disturbing his solitude, and in the surrounding trees his uncles and cousins take up the chant.

From here I would take a short cut along a cowpath through a thicket and my heart would skip a beat as a ruffed grouse whirred from under my feet and sailed off over the alders. I'd cross the stream on a fallen log and Duty, our beautiful big Saint Bernard would run up on a knoll in the pasture and bark. He was nearsighted and did not recognize me. Then he would hear my voice, and rush forward in an ecstasy of canine greeting, knocking me down to lick my face with his long, rough tongue.

My grandparents were always so glad to see me. Grand-mother would take me in by the kitchen stove, remove my coat and rubbers, and bring caraway cookies and a pitcher of milk. Every minute since leaving Florida I had been think-ing about new maple sugar. There would be a large tub of it out in the buttery, and Grandmother always gave me a big spoon and let me dig for myself.

As I sat up to the kitchen table to gorge myself, I'd look out of the window and see Grandfather coming through the dusk of the far woods with an ax over his shoulder; this time of year he would be fixing fences. He would stamp up onto the piazza and come through the door with a merry shout: "Hello, young feller, I spied you a-comin' over the hill. How's my leetle Florida cracker?"

Grandfather was a short man, about as wide as he was tall, and he smelled of the barn and good pipe tobacco. He was a lumberman and farmer and ran a string of horses up Mount Washington before the cog railroad was built. He had torn his section of land out of the New Hampshire rocks in pioneer times and was always quoting Daniel Webster's remark about the Old Man of the Mountain: "God Almighty has hung out a sign to show that there He makes men," and then he'd say, "And that goes for the Abbotts, by God!"

After supper I would climb the narrow stairs to the small bedroom under the eaves with its little multi-paned window, hand-hooked rugs, and big feather bed. When I had the patch-work quilt tucked up under my chin, Grandmother would blow out the light and leave the door open so I could hear the hum of the voices of Grandfather, Uncle Fred, and the hired man talking politics.

Grandfather was the sort of old-fashioned, red-hot Demo-crat they called a "Copperhead," and he liked telling about the time he went down to Concord with his friend the Honorable John Sinclair to hear him make a speech. He sat in the bal-cony, and when the crowd started to heckle Sinclair, Grandfather put his hand on the balcony rail, jumped down into the aisle, walked up beside Sinclair, rolled up his sleeves, and said, "John, I ain't much at speechmakin', but I'm damn good at this business."

After this fracas Grandfather and Sinclair went over to the little hotel across the street from the State House, where they were rooming together. Sinclair was very deaf. Grandfather came into their room and said, "John, as I was comin' up the hall there was a door open. I looked in and there was a dern pretty girl in the room combing her hair before the mirror. She looked at me and smiled, and I wanted to say somethin' to her, but I heard the voice of my wife saying, 'Daniel, you mustn't do that!' And John, I didn't! This morning I got up and went to the water closet, and her door was open agin. She was combing her hair with hardly no clothes on, and she smiled, and gosh, John, I wanted to say something to her but I heard the voice of my wife saying, 'Daniel, don't you do that!' And I didn't. John, what would you 'a' done?" John laughed and said, "Oh, Daniel, I'm so deaf I shouldn't 'a' even heard her." Their laughter ran up the stairs.

As my sleepy eyelids dropped I'd catch snatches of conversation—"shot a bear over on Ladderpole Hill"—"came up through Hell's Half Acre with ten pounds of trout"—"the snub rope broke and slued the team right off the damn mountain!" Soon they tramped off to bed, and I lay drowsily listening to the sounds of the night—the mournful moo of the cow in the barn, the sharp bark of a fox on the hill, and the call of the wild geese. Hi! Hi! Geese in the sky! I shared with them the passionate freedom of their migrating urge. Like the wild birds, the Yankee had come home.

In 1904 I was fifteen years old but because of my background, experience, and environment, was very old for my age. Like most youngsters then, Jack London was my idol, and I lived by the adage: "I'll try anything once." It was a carefree world, and my education was a sketchy affair gleaned from any school that I happened to be near—North or South.

By this time I had thrown off the parental restraint usual for boys of my age and as soon as the season was over in Florida I would start North alone—sometimes not showing up for two or three months. Why my mother and father didn't worry themselves to death I don't understand, but I suppose Father felt that I was gaining self-reliance and a lot of worldly wisdom that would stand by me later on. He had left home to earn his living at the age of fourteen, which gave him a sympathetic understanding of a boy with an itching foot.

I had an old suitcase that would almost pack and unpack itself, and if stranded in a strange town, I could always go to the nearest hotel and get a job. Or I could lean against the desk and talk to the clerk, or sit on the bell row and talk to the bellboys, and the hotel grapevine would tell me where I could get a job. Father's name was good in any hotel for a free meal and a night's lodging, and I am glad to say that the quaint custom of professional courtesy among reputable hotel men has continued until the present time.

I never took a drink until I was forty years old, not that I had anything against it, but because it seemed a sucker's game to me. There had always been plenty of free liquor around, but I didn't need any to keep my motor running.

I could smoke anything that burned—cornsilk, grapevine leaves, "rabbit tobacco," or a half-burned cigar that Father left on his desk. Given a package of Sweet Caporal cigarettes and a Nick Carter dime novel, I was set for an afternoon.

Down South they used to tell the story about two little colored boys. The older said to the younger:

"Boy, how old is yo'?"

"I don' know."

"Is yo' eight?"

"I don' know."

"Is yo' twelve?"

"I don' know."

"Boy, does yo' like girls?"

"No!"

"Boy, yo' is eight."

I was *fifteen!*

That winter I worked a "hitch" on the desk at the Royal Palm from after school until ten at night and had about one hundred and thirty-five dollars saved by spring. So I went to New York and hung around until my money gave out. I heard Bert Williams sing "I May Be Crazy, but I Ain't No Fool," saw Rose Stahl in *The Chorus Girl*—and stayed in love with her all summer.

I was crazy stage-struck, particularly when it came to minstrel shows. I was a great fan of Bert Williams, McIntyre and Heath, and Lew Dockstader. I'll never forget Bert in his big, high-topped shoes, wrinkled dress suit, and battered tall silk hat, shuffling onto the stage with an ingratiating smile and speaking his songs, nor the utter dejection of McIntyre and Heath as they moped on carrying a big bass drum and sat under the imaginary ham tree.

I left New York to the tune of "Give My Regards to Broadway" which George M. Cohan was singing in *Little Johnny Jones*, and headed for home.

When I reached home this spring of 1904 Father was building a large addition to the Uplands. It had thirty rooms and thirty baths, a really spacious and beautiful white-and-gold ballroom, and a wide veranda going all around. It cost fourteen thousand dollars and about eighteen thousand when furnished. It would cost more than a hundred thousand today provided you could get the materials and workmanship. The summer inn had grown into a fine resort hotel, and since it was on a series of terraces, I got Father to rename it Upland Terrace.

Our old guests were there for the opening, and a steady stream of tourists poured through all summer. We made enough that season to pay for all our improvements.

It was always "ours" with Father and Mother and me. I'd been deeply interested in the hotel ever since I could remember. I was doubly interested and proud of the new Upland Terrace, the only hotel so far that was Abbott-owned. I helped out all over the place, in the kitchen, dining room, behind the desk, and on the bell row. It was wonderful schooling which put me far ahead of my years in the profession and was to enable me to operate my first hotel at the age of twenty-four.

At odd times during the next ten years I sold papers, drove cattle, worked on a stone crusher, operated a moving-picture machine, went to sea on a tramp steamer, ran a bowling alley, drove a streetcar, played semi-pro baseball, went on the road with small-time minstrel troupes and medicine shows, played in a band, rode freights, and worked on a farm. I taught in a dance studio, took sport pictures, rode quarter horses, trained bird dogs, took out hunting parties, cakewalked on the Circuit, went into the Everglades with the plume hunters, and other things I can't or won't remember.

But I always came back to hotel business.

It was show business. It held all the elements of chance. To make a success of it you had to have ingenuity and the gambling instinct and a genuine liking for almost everybody.

The hotel was full one afternoon when I happened to glance at the board in the lobby and noticed that a room had registered. There were no room telephones but push-button bells with a big annunciator in the lobby over the bell row. When a room rang in, a white spot showed under its number on the board.

Little signs above the buttons in the rooms read as follows:

> 1 ring for bellboy
> 2 rings for ice water
> 3 rings for hot water
> 4 rings for chambermaid
> 5 rings for porter

The bellboy was busy so I took the front stairs two at a time and knocked on the indicated door. A feminine voice said, "Come in," and in I walked. Before the mirror a stately dowager in her drawers and corset looked at me in utter amazement. She said, "Young man, I rang for a chambermaid, but as long as you are in here you'll have to do. Help me lace up my corset." With fumbling fingers and my knee in the middle of her back, I went to work. The perspiration rolled down my face and I was covered with confusion, but finally the damn strings were tied and I got out of there with a shiny new dime.

We had a hotel band of our own this year, a lady orchestra composed of violin, piano, cornet, and drums. The lady pianist was a little pint-sized brunette named Dinah. She was pretty in a saucy way, with long, dark eyelashes.

There were a few automobiles scattered through the mountains, but we didn't own one. Father had a small black mare named Southern Queen that could trot like blazes and in her early days had done 2.19 on the track. Dennis had grown too old for my present purposes, so I persuaded Father to lend me Southern Queen for Saturday night. There was a dance over at Littleton.

Dinah got another girl to fill in for her in the band and we left after dinner. She came downstairs wearing high heels, a black silk accordion-pleated dress, and a big black picture hat. I had Southern Queen hitched to a buggy with pneumatic tires and a three-quarter seat, a blue plush robe, and a red ribbon around the whip. It was a gay turnout.

The dance was held in the Opera House. There were a number of couples from Bethlehem there and after the dance, when we started the five-mile drive home, we young bloods raced to show our girls which had the fastest horse. Southern Queen won, but when I got her into the barn she was white with lather.

I didn't have time to thank Dinah for the lovely evening

or anything else. Southern Queen was the apple of Father's eye. I washed her off with warm water and walked her up and down the stable yard to cool her off, then I curried her, brushed her down, polished her with a rag until she shone, and led her into the barn and started to make her a bed of clean straw. I heard the funniest snort, and turned around. Southern Queen was gone—she had fallen through the scuttle hole onto the manure pile under the barn. I raced around back and under, frightened almost to death, but Southern Queen was standing up, hale and hearty, and coated with manure from forelock to tail.

I led the mare around in front of the barn, washed her off with warm water, walked her up and down the stable yard to cool her off, curried her, brushed her down, polished her with a rag, and put her in the stall and raced for my room. By this time it was six o'clock in the morning.

My room had a side window. I slid through, pulled my nightshirt over my clothes, and jumped into bed. Just as I hit the pillow Father opened the door.

"Well, young fellow," he boomed, "have a good time at the dance last night? I want you to get out of that bed and paint the dining-room roof."

I got up, grabbed breakfast, a brush, and five gallons of green paint, and went at it. Don't try to imagine how long that day lasted or how hot the sun beating down on that tin roof. But I finished it before night.

Along toward the last of the summer Father received a telegram that almost broke our hearts. The O'Neill estate had sold the Royal Palm! That left the winter gaping ahead without a hotel, but the hotel grapevine started to work, as it always did for us, and within a few weeks Father was called to operate the Berkshire and Harvard hotels in Pinehurst, North Carolina.

When we went South that fall of 1904 we stayed at Young's Hotel in Boston. Father collected a party of about sixty help for the Pinehurst hotels. They were to sail one morning on a Merchant and Miners steamer for Norfolk, and I went down to see them off. I was always fascinated by the Boston water front. It was a busy place, teeming with activity. I loved the roar and the rumble of the great wagons over the cobblestones; the sloshing of the dirty water through the piling; the tooting whistles of the little puffing tugs, churning the water like frustrated ducks, and the great freighters leaving for unknown ports. From the semi-darkness of the long sheds came the cries of the stevedores and the smells of a thousand cargoes.

I waded through the general confusion incident to the last few moments before sailing. The first call of "Al-l-l ashore, gooooin' ashore," had been sounded, and as I reached our party it was hard to make myself heard above the shrill good-bys and general hubbub. Off to one side was a tearful group of a dozen New Hampshire girls who had signed to go South as waitresses, and a more terrified and homesick lot you never saw. They had decided not to sail. But I knew Father had to have them. So I said easily, "Now you girls just forget your troubles; you don't have to go unless you want to. You've never seen a big ship, so why don't you let me take you over the boat before it sails?" I winked at Charlie Jones, the steamship agent, and I knew he would get their luggage on board and tell Father I'd left.

The girls had a gay time as I showed them over the boat, and just at the right moment I was leading them down through the engine room, the galley, and the dining salon. When we came up on deck we were passing Fort Warren in Boston Harbor, and you never saw a more frantic group of women. They wanted the boat stopped, but they were on their way South.

The next morning, when they came up on deck, it was bright and sunny, and they were glad they had been shanghaied.

When we arrived at Norfolk we found that we had to stay overnight and take the train in the morning, so I took the party to a small hotel. The girls and the boys sat around the lobby on their suitcases while I undertook the arduous job of registering. The manager came along and asked me what kind of group we were. I told him we were an "Uncle Tom's Cabin Troupe." Of all the dumb things to say in Norfolk, Virginia, in those days! He hit the ceiling and told me to get them out. He wasn't going to let us stay in his hotel. I had to argue about a half-hour before I convinced him that they were really hotel help. Then he smiled and extended some real southern hospitality.

While all this was going on two of our best cooks got disgusted, walked off, and joined the Navy.

We spent two winters in Pinehurst. It was much smaller then than it is now. There were four hotels and the rudiments of a town, a clubhouse, two golf courses, kennels, and riding stables. The largest hotel was the Carolina, run by Harry Priest from New Hampshire, a lifelong friend of Father.

Mornings I went to school, but afternoons and evenings I worked in the bowling alley, the golf club, the trapshooting field outside of town, or down at the kennels. I liked the kennels best. They had a fine bunch of pointers and setters and I helped feed and train them and learned their pedigrees—all the way back.

The trapshooting was taught the guests by the world-renowned Annie Oakley of Wild West show fame, one of the greatest shots in history and a very great lady. She was a sprightly little woman with graying hair and searching eyes, and usually dressed in tweeds, laced boots, and a felt hat with a gay feather. But Annie Oakley was just another job to me. I'd do anything to earn a dime, and I carried her ammunition and did other odd tasks to help her.

There were the usual round of resort social activities—the

gymkhanas, trapshoots, and dances at the Carolina and Holly Inns. I had never before been in a resort that featured golf and it was very interesting. The golf "pro" at Pinehurst was Donald Ross, probably the most famous golf architect in the world. He was to golf what Babe Ruth was to baseball. I met the usual crowd—bankers, brokers, socialites, sportsmen and their wives—who forgather in a resort community imbued with a festive vacation spirit.

Sometimes I rode the little trolley car out to the golf links. How different this land was from New England and Florida! Here sandhills rolled as far as eye could reach, and the dark green of pines intermingled with the lighter gray of scrub oak and the golden fields of sedge grass.

Only one man operated the trolley, so some mornings I collected fares for him. On the nine-o'clock trip a small, slightly stooped elderly man was always first to enter the car. He was memorable for his inquisitive eyes and the almost shy smile with which he always greeted me. "Have you change for a half dollar?" he'd ask, and bring out a silver dollar neatly cut in half. It was our usual morning joke. He was John D. Rockefeller, Sr. Another gentleman who often came from his home in nearby Aberdeen to dine at our hotel was Walter Hines Page, editor of *World's Work*, and afterward Ambassador to Great Britain.

The big springtime event was the Pinehurst Minstrels organized by Charlie Baxter. Charlie was station agent, telegraph operator, and, I sometimes suspected, practically ran the diminutive Aberdeen and Asheville Railroad.

I started hanging around the railroad station with the idea of learning something about telegraphy, but we were soon talking show business, and that is how the Pinehurst Minstrels were born. We gathered talent among guests and employees, rehearsed for weeks, and put on a really creditable show. Charlie taught me a lot about dancing, make-up, timing, and how to sell a song, and we had one skit called "The Ragtime

Oyster Man" that never failed to bring down the house. We had an idea of hitting the road with our skit, but I was beginning to give serious thoughts to my education, and nothing came of the idea. It was the last of my life at Pinehurst, as the next fall I went away to school.

When I attended Goddard Seminary in the little town of Barre, Vermont, Father was willing to give me what money I needed. But I was accustomed by this time to going along on my own, so we agreed that he send me a dollar a week. Every Monday I got a letter containing a brand-new dollar bill. With one hundred and fifty girls in the school—and they raise beautiful girls in Vermont—my social obligations soon required considerably more cash.

Victor Olsen, my roommate, and I had an old bell rope which we would throw out of our window and so scramble down or up the side of the brick building like squirrels. This was our protest against the ridiculous rule that said we had to be in bed by ten o'clock! With the rope as stock in trade I organized myself into a "late-snack" delivery service. Orders slipped under my door for hot dogs, pork sandwiches, apple pie, et cetera, were delivered after hours.

But how to deliver into the girls' section! Our room was next to the girls' side, which was divided from the boys' by a brick partition. Vic and I went into our clothes closet with a ball bat and chisel and knocked a hole about a foot square through the bricks. It opened into the clothes closet of the girls' room next to ours. By sweeping up the debris, hanging a raincoat over the hole on our side, and persuading the girls to keep a dress hung over their side, we had a convenient means of communication.

It served us well for months. One evening we heard the customary knock on the wall and, taking down the raincoat, looked through the hole into the smiling countenance of

Headmaster "OK" Hollister, who informed us that we were both "on the hill" for the balance of the semester.

I liked everything about Goddard except my studies. I hated to study, and was content with marks that just scraped me by. But in the spring of 1908, owing to the "grace of God and the Continental Congress"—also a weak moment on the part of a lady language teacher who gave me a passing grade —I graduated from Goddard.

That summer I wrote all the correspondence, kept all the books, and "sold" rooms in Uplands Terrace, a hotel with one hundred rooms. The first time Father had put me on the desk I was seventeen and an excursion run of sixty people came up from Boston. The coach made three trips. I had the list of names that had been sent on ahead and was writing down room numbers opposite names and giving out keys and Father got so nervous watching me that he went out into the garden and hoed six potato rows.

It was grand experience for a budding hotel man.

George Hodson, president of the Winchester Arms, and Mrs. Hodson I put up at five dollars a day apiece, American plan, rooms and meals. The average in 1908 was twenty-one dollars a week per person. The other hotel men in Bethlehem went around shaking their heads. "That boy is going to ruin Frank Abbott," they prophesied, "charging guests five dollars a day."

I took particular interest in reservations from parties that included sons and daughters. Upland Terrace was famous for its young element, and we had gay times, with dances, picnics, parties, and summer flirtations—some of which turned into terrific cases of young love and furnished never-ending topics of conversation on the piazza.

Touring was now in vogue. People in linen dusters and goggles raced over the dusty mountain roads in bright red Pope-Hartfords, Ford Sixes, Stanley Steamers, and the other cars of the day, and pulled up, tired and dusty, at our hotel.

The head of the family usually got out and started for the desk to inquire whether accommodations were available and at what price while the ladies sat in the car in anxious anticipation of a hot bath, a good dinner, and a night's rest.

While the man was inquiring about the rates, our alert bellboys whipped the luggage off the car to the piazza. If the rates were too high and the tourist came out determined to drive on, one look at his grips and the thought of the hard work of repacking them would change his mind and keep him with us for the night.

Some of the cars had chauffeurs. We made it our business to be friendly with these drivers because, whether the owners knew it or not, they "ran the works." If there was but one room with bath available, the chauffeur got it, along with a couple of bottles of cold beer. The next time the party was in our vicinity, though they might be fifty miles away by nightfall, the chauffeur brought their car to Upland Terrace because "something" had gone wrong with it that only the mechanic at our garage could fix. If the chauffeur knew one of our waitresses, sometimes the car wasn't fixed for days!

Orville Wright went aloft that summer of 1908 and stayed up for more than an hour. "Ain't it awful, Mabel?" was the phrase of the hour. Young people gathered around the piano to sing "Take Me Out to the Ball Game" and "Cuddle Up a Little Closer, Baby Mine" and the songs Elsie Janis was singing. Evening entertainment by young ladies included welsh rabbit or fudge made on a chafing dish.

Into our pastoral setting that summer came a handsome serpent named—so he said—Roy Spencer. He intimated that he was a "prominent contractor from Boston," and he arrived, by a strange coincidence, several days in advance of the wealthy Donley mother and daughters whom he had "chanced" to meet in Atlantic City. We learned later that he had found out from the family chauffeur that the Donleys were to spend the summer at Upland Terrace.

The girls were delighted to see him again. He was a solicitous courtier and offered to be of any service possible, particularly after a cocktail party the Donleys gave in their suite, when a large amount of their jewelry was missing.

Father, without a word to anyone, wired to Boston for a detective.

The detective brought along a complete file on Spencer's prior activities. Spencer, confronted by evidence, never turned a hair. Another detective was sent for who was an expert in third-degree methods. He grilled Spencer for six straight hours with no results. Father telephoned Mr. Donley, who drove all night and arrived early in the morning. I remember his chauffeur was driving a big Model Y Stevens-Duryea and it was blanketed in dust and the steam was popping out of the radiator.

Donley came right up to Father. "Frank, where is this Spencer? I know how to handle punks."

Spencer was in his room, and I took Mr. Donley there and stayed outside the door.

Donley walked in, announced, "I'm Donley," locked the door, tossed the key out of the window, and began taking off his coat. "Spencer," he said, "I know your kind and I know you've put a fast one over on my girls. You've pawned those jewels and I want the tickets or I'll spatter you all over this room."

While he was talking, he grabbed Spencer by the throat and bent him over the foot of the bed. I heard Spencer crying, "All right, all right!" The pawn tickets were in his shoe. Donley didn't want any publicity, so he gave Spencer thirty minutes to clear out.

Fifteen years later I bumped into Spencer in a store in New York.

"How's everything?" I asked.

"Fine! I've just finished four years up the river." He seemed glad to see me, and apparently felt on top of the world.

Father had every intention of going back to Pinehurst in the fall. We missed Florida. We missed the Royal Palm at Fort Myers. We had felt it a personal loss when its owners sold it several years before.

Now a wire came from "Tooty" McGregor. She was staying at the Royal Palm. "I'll buy the hotel, Frank," she wired, "if you'll come down and run it."

They don't make women like "Tooty" McGregor any more. The world knew her as the wife and later the widow of the president of Standard Oil of Ohio, a multi-millionairess, member of the Rockefeller and Flagler set, and the owner of fabulous jewels. But to the Abbott family she was stout, good-natured "Tooty," with a grand sense of fun and a warm heart.

She had met A. M. McGregor when he was working in the Pennsylvania oil fields. Later they went to India, where he was head of Standard Oil, and she acquired a collection of jewels, one a pigeon-blood ruby, so fabulous that I was told McGregor had to get permission from the King of England to take them out. One night I was working in the private office of the Royal Palm, and she came in, took a chamois bag from under her belt and, leaning over my shoulder, poured onto the desk jewels set and unset, emeralds, diamonds, and rubies. And she laughed, seeing how startled I was.

When McGregor died, she was left with millions. They say "Tooty" had their schooner yacht, the *Whim*, on which they had entertained the great of the world, soaked in gasoline and with all sails set put to sea on the Gulf of Mexico. All ablaze, it sailed into the sunset.

She built another, a three-masted schooner, for Dr. M. O. Terry, the doctor she married later on. Dr. Terry had no liking for the sea, and the Gulf was rough the first day they went out in the new ship. Among other suggestions, he asked the sailors to "tie the boat with the anchor string." "Tooty" was so incensed that she went ashore and turned the boat over to a boat broker to be sold that very day.

"Tooty" and Mother were fast friends. Once she asked Mother to ride down to Fort Myers railroad station with her to "look at her car." They went aboard, and before Mother realized it they were off on a trip to the Canadian Rockies and down the Pacific coast and back again to Florida. Mother had a wonderful time.

This was the heyday of the big American plan resort hotels.

Henry Flagler had developed the east coast of Florida, pushing the rails of the Florida East Coast Railroad as far south as Miami; Henry Plant, with his Plant system railroad, had marched down the west coast to Fort Myers. In the earlier days there was a rivalry between Plant and Flagler, the two great pioneer financial giants of Florida.

Flagler, backed by his millions from Standard Oil, and Plant, the owner of the Southern Express Company, were racing for supremacy in a tropical wilderness.

Coming down the east coast, Flagler built the Ponce De Leon Hotel in Saint Augustine. It was a marvel of Moorish architecture, a great pile of two hundred and fifty rooms, adorned with towers and hanging balconies, amid beautifully landscaped grounds. The architects, contractors, decorators, and landscape gardeners were given carte blanche to produce the finest resort hotel in the world, which they did.

The Ponce was authentic, even to the roofing tile which was brought from Morocco and laid in place with loving care to be forever bathed in Florida sunshine. It took a little more than three years to build, and the hotel opened for guests in January 1888. It is still in operation.

I do not believe that Henry Flagler ever thought that he would make any money out of the lavishly run Ponce De Leon Hotel. It was built primarily as an adjunct to his railroad, and, in a way, a monument to his pride.

The architects had chosen its style to reflect Saint Augustine and the old Spanish town with its narrow streets, slave market,

Fountain of Youth, the City Gate, and Old Fort Marion. Guests alighted from the carriage that brought them from the train before massive entrance gates of filigree handwrought iron, and they were met by giant Moorish doormen in native costume.

It mattered not from whence they came or from what station in life, they stood in awe at the beauty and grandeur of their surroundings. The staff had been selected with infinite care and produced a cuisine and service calculated to anticipate every wish of the most exacting traveler.

The Ponce De Leon was an instant success and it became necessary to build the fine Hotel Alcazar across the street and the beautiful Cordova a block away. The latter two hotels were built to accommodate those whose pocketbook precluded the exceedingly high tariffs of the Ponce, but they were fine hostelries. The Alcazar opened in 1889; it is now used by the Lightner Museum of Hobbies.

To show you how the hotel grapevine works, when Flagler walked from his residence to the hotel, the doorman, the instant he came in sight, told the bellboys, the boys told the clerk, the clerk phoned the housekeeper. Three hundred people passed the word, "The old man's coming" before he was in the door.

Henry Plant met his challenge by building the Tampa Bay Hotel at Tampa. This also was a great Moorish building, even larger than the Ponce De Leon. It sprawled throughout Plant Park, its many towers and minarets—some adorned with mystic crescents—towering above the treetops.

Botanists had searched the tropical world for rare and exotic plants to make its setting. It was a hotel of magnificent distances—a full hundred yards from the lobby down the long corridor to the main dining room. The tea service cost sixty thousand dollars, the parlor floor was covered with a Parisian carpet at twenty-five dollars a yard in those days, and the paintings and *objets d'art* ran to a cool million.

Flagler wired Plant: "I hear there has been a small hotel built on the west coast. How do I find it?"

Plant telegraphed back: "Follow the crowd!"

Each train that arrived at the Tampa Bay Hotel was met by a group of porters and a snappy brass band in red uniforms. At the beginning of the first season business was a little slow and the managing director wired Plant that he thought to save expense they should do without the band. Plant wired back: "If business is slow, hire another band."

It is alleged that when Plant first projected the idea of building the Tampa Bay Hotel to his board of directors they were all against it. So Plant built it himself.

Along in February Plant wired his manager that he and his board were coming South in his private car and if it took all the manager's relatives and friends to fill the place be sure not to have an available room.

One sunny morning in February, so the story continues, the train backed slowly into the hotel grounds with the private car coupled on the rear. The band was playing as Plant and the dignitaries alighted. The moment the music stopped, the managing director rushed up to greet them. He was apparently greatly embarrassed.

He said, "Mr. Plant, I am happy to welcome you and your directors to the Tampa Bay Hotel, but I'm in a terrible dilemma."

"How's that?" asked Plant.

"I hardly know how to tell you," the manager said, "but I haven't a vacant room in the hotel."

"You mean to say you have no accommodations for myself and party?"

"Mr. Plant, I'm desolate, but we are full to the roof with season guests. In fact, I'm at my wit's end to know just where to put people."

Plant beamed as he turned to his directors. "Well, boys, it looks as though we will have to live in the car."

The directors admitted that Plant had been vindicated and he magnanimously allowed each one to purchase an interest in this glowing venture so that when they went to bed that night —in the car—Plant personally did not own any of it. As a matter of fact, the hotel did a wonderful business for years.

Flagler's next move was to build the great Hotel Ormond, at Ormond Beach, Florida, followed by the Royal Poinciana at Palm Beach.

The Royal Poinciana opened in January 1894. Additions followed swiftly, until the hotel had a thousand guest rooms. It was the largest frame strictly resort hotel in the world, and so far as I know there has never been another so large. The hotel accommodated seventeen hundred and fifty guests and required a staff of about twelve hundred employees, all of whom were housed and fed in a dormitory which was a great hotel in itself. There were approximately three hundred colored waiters, and as they left their dormitory on a sunny day, dressed in their uniforms with snowy white shirt bosoms, they looked like a miniature army advancing upon the hotel. The dining room accommodated two thousand guests at a single sitting, and to quote Ring Lardner: "From one end of the room to the other was a toll call."

Business tycoons, the Newport set, theatrical stars, politicians of the day made the Poinciana a mecca for their winter vacations, and the winter colony round about grew apace; Colonel Bradley built his wonderful gambling Casino; Flagler, his beautiful residence, White Hall, and the magnificent hotel Breakers on the beach.

In Miami the Hotel Royal Palm was constructed in 1897 and Flagler began to contemplate his railroad across the Keys. All up and down the eastern seaboard great resort hotels were flourishing: the Greenbrier, at White Sulphur Springs; the Homestead at Hot Springs. Spring Lake and Atlantic City were popular. At Saratoga Springs, New York, the United States Hotel and the Grand Union, great caravansaries held over from the Victorian era, were still going strong. New England, the pioneer of the resort hotel business, boasted many fine hotels—the Griswold at New London, Connecticut; the Ocean Side at Magnolia, Massachusetts; the Wentworth by the Sea, at Portsmouth, New Hampshire; and Mount Washington at Bretton Woods, built as a hobby by Joe Stickney, the coal baron. In Maine the Ricker Brothers had built the Poland Springs House; the Samoset and the Kineo on Moosehead Lake—and so it went. Wealthy Americans had become foot-loose and fancy free and these wonderful summer and winter American resort hotels catered to their whims.

When the gay "Tooty" McGregor Terry purchased the Royal Palm at Fort Myers and she had Father's promise to operate it, she wired her friend Flagler on the east coast:

"I have bought a small hotel on the west coast of Florida."

Flagler flashed back: "Another one in the family gone wrong."

In the spring she was able to send another message: "My hotel has made money."

The hotel czar wired Tooty: "You are hereby appointed manager of all the Flagler east coast hotels."

When the time came for me to branch out on my own, the resort hotels were a vast industry that offered splendid opportunities to a young and ambitious hotel man.

Chapter Five: FRONT!

At this point there was a slight interruption.

I attended Tufts College on the outskirts of Boston, where I learned that a college boy possessed of evening clothes, a few social graces, and a love for dancing can find himself in a surprising number of places.

Delta Tau Delta put me in with a great crowd of fellows. I already knew many of the Boston families who spent their summers in the White Mountains.

I found my way around Commonwealth Avenue, Brookline, and Wellesley.

Boston was wonderful—deb parties at the staid Somerset on Commonwealth Avenue, where we did "that awful turkey trot" in the corner of the ballroom out of sight of the chaperon's reproachful eye; walking through the Fenway on Sunday afternoons with the Conservatory girls in their new hobble skirts; drinking beer at the Pops Symphony Concerts, or watching the boat races on the Charles.

Anyone who thinks of Boston as staid may find it difficult to imagine the gaiety, life, and laughter of its night life before World War I. I could listen to the subdued, exciting roar of the city and recall how rich this section was in literature, culture, and history, and of stories Father used to tell of the big Boston fire when, as a volunteer fireman, he was stationed for three days on the roof of the old State House. It seemed to me that we had always been more or less mixed up with Boston, 'way back to the original Daniel Abbott who lived there when the town was new.

In later years, when I operated the Vendome and Somerset hotels in Boston, the thought that this big friendly city was family homesite came to me many times.

Within three weeks I knew every headwaiter in Boston by his first name. That was easy for me, being, one might say, in the business.

The Touraine was in its prime. The Adams House, Youngs Hotel, Old Boston Tavern, United States Hotel, Revere House, and the Crawford House down in Scollay Square, which "specialized in sea foods," were nationally famous. Memories of the broiled live lobsters and musty ale at Billy Parks bring tears to my eyes, and so do the thick, juicy steaks dripping with butter at Locke-Obers, called the Winter Palace in Pie Alley, and the dinners at the Bell in Hand.

At Ye Olde Oyster House on Union Street, built before the Revolution, oysters were opened before your eyes.

In the hushed respectability of the Crystal Room in the old Parker House meals were served with gracious dignity. And for the aristocracy there was the red-plush Vendome 'way out on Commonwealth Avenue.

Evenings after the theater depended on the mood—perhaps the noisy Rathskeller of the American House on Hanover Street, patronized by prize fighters, wrestlers, and their followers. Mieusettes, Charlie and Jacob Wirth on Kneeland Street—the beer was the best in Boston—or the Woodcock at upper Washington Street for a hot bird and a cold bottle. At The Thorndike the savory roasts were carved in reverence at the tableside. And that bon vivant par excellence, "Papa Coulon," father confessor of the Harvard boys, officiated at the Westminster Grill which served a French cuisine with many a truffle and piquant sauce.

Later one might look in at the Dreyfus and Brigham's Café on Washington Street, or the Hayward, on Hayward Place, the gayest spot in town. The popping corks, shrill laughter, and hurrying waiters gave a gay student the feeling of a devil-may-care man about town.

Sometimes we journeyed out to the Wayside Inn at South Sudbury, now owned by Henry Ford, where chickens roasted on a spit over the open fire and ghosts of a glorious past seemed to hover.

Boston was a great theater town and drew a galaxy of glittering stars, and over a period of years I was to see these—Blanche Bates in *The Girl of the Golden West* at the old Boston Opera House, and next door, at the Tremont, Mabel Taliaferro in *Polly of the Circus*, or Donald Brian in *The Merry Widow*. Across the way at the Colonial Anna Held starred in *Miss Innocence*, to be followed by Eddie Foy in *The Orchid*. Down Tremont Street, at the Majestic, William Hodge played *The Man from Home*. Thomas A. Wise and Douglas Fairbanks, Sr., were opening in *A Gentleman from Mississippi*. Down at the Hollis Maude Adams starred in *Quality Street*, or possibly it was George Arliss in *The Devil*.

I may have my names and dates mixed, but all the great stars were there at one time or another.

Imagine the thrill of hearing a Victor Herbert tune for the first time, gazing at the splendor of an early Ziegfeld production, or sitting enthralled at the realism of a David Belasco stage setting, to witness a master craftsman such as John Drew or David Warfield sway an audience from laughter to tears.

What wouldn't I give to be carried away again into the realm of fantasy by one of those opening nights! The musicians tuning their instruments . . . the dimming lights . . . the curtain going up . . . and the lilting voice of elf-like Fritzie Scheff singing "Kiss Me Again!"

The old Castle Square Theatre was beloved by the middle-class family trade and the white-collar people, many of whom purchased season tickets. The John Craig Stock Company, which included John Craig, Mary Young, his wife, Donald Meek, and a number of others who later became famous, played a different show each week, from farce to tragedy, with six evening performances and five matinees, using mornings for rehearsals.

B. F. Keith's, at which Boston aristocracy had first raised a supercilious eyebrow, was packing them in with Gus Edwards's *School Days*. At various times I saw there Eddie Cantor, Al Jolson, Fannie Brice and George Jessel. . . . Julian Eltinge, the great female impersonator, leaving the stage smoking a big black cigar. . . . The dancing Pat Rooney. . . . Lovely Annette Kellerman in a black bathing suit, and Harry Houdini with his mystifying wizardry.

Mr. Clark, from Bethlehem, was the manager of Keith's, and Hugh Carr, who used to run the livery stable near the Uplands, was on the stage door, so I made myself at home.

Sometimes we went down to the Orpheum to hear Harry Lauder sing his wonderful Scottish songs as he pranced up and down the stage with his crooked cane, or to the Gaiety on Washington Street to see some hot burlesque, or to the Columbia Theatre.

Fortunately I could do with very little sleep, and by getting up early in the mornings I got in enough study to make passing grades. The upperclassmen in my fraternity worried, and many times I received a long lecture beginning: "Kid, how do you ever expect to amount to anything?"

For a future hotel man these extracurricular activities were the finest training one could have. But the seniors didn't know that, and neither did I, at the time.

So it was no surprise to the majority of my fellow students, though it did surprise me a little, when I interrupted my higher education to go on tour with the Tallahassee Minstrels. When I was a little boy in Bethlehem I had worked as an usher to see this troupe.

We started west through Vermont and upper New York State, playing one-night stands in the smaller towns. I was third end man in the "bones" section, had a skit with a couple of other fellows in the oleo, sang "I Wonder Who's Kissing Her Now?" to a soft-shoe dance, and joined in the chorus of the "afterpiece."

We'd get into a new town about noon, go to the opera house to change into our uniforms, and line up wearily for the parade. Some of the fellows had played poker all night, or been out chasing the girls in the last town, and the morning sunshine didn't go far toward lifting the general melancholy. When all was in readiness the band leader called out, "Come on, boys! 'S.I.B.A. March,' and sock it!"

The way the little band hit that tune rattled all the windows on Main Street, and down the street we swung, with springy steps and smiling countenances, led by our "interlocutor," in white satin-trimmed suit with long coat, doffing his white silk hat, swinging his cane. After him strutted two local boys in ill-fitting red coats, carrying large red banners emblazoned in gold: "Tallahassee Minstrels." Small boys yelled, crowds gathered on the wooden walks, and town girls giggled and gaped.

I never tired of the minstrel parades. I started with the minstrels on an alto horn and before long could pinch hit almost anywhere in the band. We would parade up the main street to the leading hotel, form a circle, play a gallop and quickstep with much blaring of the slide trombone, and troop in to lunch.

Small towns were not so sophisticated as they are now, and we minstrel men were city-slicker heroes to the locals.

Being small town myself, I got a great kick out of it. In all my life I have never felt so important.

I remember the smell of those cold old dressing rooms, the burnt cork, the walls covered with old posters, and messages scrawled by hundreds of small-time troupers before us. From out front would come whistling, catcalls, and stamping of impatient feet; then the callboy crying, "All up for the first part," and we would march on the opera-house stage for the "walk around," stopping at our appointed chairs. The interlocutor would drone, "Gentlemen, be seated," the audience burst into friendly applause, and the show was on. "Mr. Bones, who was dat lady I seen you wif las' night?"

Perhaps the minstrel tour was a crazy project for an ambitious youth, and time wasted, but somehow I cannot think of it in that way. I learned a lot about human nature and doing things the hard way.

The sometimes latent Yankee conscience won in the end, and after a flying visit home to Bethlehem to smooth things over with my folks for having taken the "flier" with the minstrels, I entered business college—Bryant Stratton in Boston—with high resolve. But it was soon the same old story. I sat in the classroom day after day watching the earnest faces of my fellow students as they concentrated on their work and speculated on their future. Some turned out work that was copperplate, and I could visualize them, lean and fiftyish, bending over worn desks, their green eyeshades high lighting the lines of defeat and disillusionment on their faces, while others with foresight and that certain spark, or by sheer will power, would get the breaks.

I transferred to the Wharton School at the University of Pennsylvania to take special courses and lived at the Delta Tau Delta House.

Through the local Delts I was soon involved in the life of Philadelphia as I had been in the life of Boston.

There are wonderful memories—riots after the Cornell game and parties out on the "Main Line"; the late-afternoon sun shining down on Franklin Field with the crowd roaring in the stands; or standing with uncovered heads to the majestic strains of "Hail, Pennsylvania."

But the things that appealed to me weren't found in books.

One gloomy December day in my second year at Penn I was lying on my bed in the Delt House reading commercial law when it started to snow. Overcome by an intense longing for Florida, I threw the book across the room and said, "To hell with it!"

My roommate looked up. "What's the matter, kid?"

"I just can't take it any longer." I lit a cigarette and started pacing the floor. "I'll never belong to the intelligentsia. I've got to get to work, and in the hotel business at that. It's in my blood."

"You're crazy as hell," he said. "The courses you are taking now will be valuable to you later on."

"Valuable or not," I replied, "I'm off to Florida."

I borrowed a wheelbarrow from the janitor, packed my trunk and wheeled it down to the Broad Street Station. The folks were back at the Royal Palm but I didn't want to ride on Father's coattails any longer. I was going South to find a job in some big resort and start out on my own in the hotel business.

On the train I fell in with some boys who were going to work in the Royal Poinciana at Palm Beach. One said:

"It doesn't make any difference to me which hotel I work at as long as it isn't the Alcazar at Saint Augustine."

"How's that?" I asked.

"Why, that's the damnedest workhouse in the South. Does a whale of a lot of business, but it's run by Bill McAuliffe and he's a slave driver."

Right away I was interested. Bill McAuliffe was Father's portly Irish friend who ran the Sinclair at Bethlehem. He had come up the hard way, starting as a bellhop, working as room clerk at the Poinciana and the old Saint James in Jacksonville. Knowing him as I had all my life, I knew he was genial and lovable on the outside, but when operating a hotel he was a strict disciplinarian and a hard taskmaster.

I went on down to Saint Augustine. The Alcazar occupied an entire city block. I went into Mr. McAuliffe's office and told him, "I've quit college and want a job."

He wasn't smiling now. "Why come to me?"

I had my answer prepared. "Because I know you are the toughest man in the business to work for."

A slow twinkle grew in his eyes. "Karl, if you have half the stuff your old man's got, perhaps you'll do." He hired me as front clerk at sixty dollars a month, room and board, and told me to go downstairs and report to Harry Loud, his assistant manager. Mr. Loud turned me over to Dugan, the room clerk, who was the head of my department.

Dugan seemed highly amused. He looked me over from head to toe and commented, "So this is what Loud has sent me for a front clerk!"

Then he walked all around me. "Abbott, how much do you weigh?"

"A hundred and twenty pounds."

He chuckled. "By the first of March there won't be anything left of you but a grease spot."

I walked around him and asked, "Dugan, how much do you weigh?"

"A hundred and sixty-eight."

"Well, I figure you'll be just forty pounds more of a grease spot than I will be by that time. I'm here to do my work, and I know my job, so pile it on, and I'll be on my feet when the season closes."

A front clerk in those days "fronted up" at the main desk— answered questions, sorted the mail, supervised the service in the lobby, and gave incoming guests their rooms when the room clerk was off duty. My hours were from seven in the morning until eleven at night, with one hour off duty from 11 A.M. until twelve noon. I say that my hours were from 7 A.M. until 11 P.M. with qualifications, because there was a train due at eleven in the evening and if the damn thing was late, which it usually was, I had to stay on duty until the bus came and the incoming guests were registered and in their rooms.

I didn't mind the hours too much, but there was no place to sit down! My legs and feet ached along the latter part of the afternoon and in the evening. Then my smile was somewhat forced as I stood listening to the long, drawn-out complaint of a pampered guest. And how I longed for a smoke! Sometimes during the dull part of the afternoon I'd slip behind the key rack and catch one, but getting caught meant being fired, as front clerks were a dime a dozen. I wonder what some of the boys in the business today with their easy hours, time off, and their "short and long day" would think of a stint like that. Sometimes I woke up in the morning fully clothed, face down across my bed, having fallen asleep before I could get undressed.

One of the first things I noticed at the Alcazar was the caste system among the employees. I had always been around small hotels where the employees worked as a team and there was camaraderie and good fellowship.

At the Alcazar everything ran like a military regime, as all good resort hotels do today, and orders came through channels. Mr. McAuliffe, as the managing director, headed up the organization and had his private suite and his choice table in the dining room. Then came the heads of departments, who were known as the "first officers": the assistant manager, room clerk, auditor, headwaiter, housekeeper, porter, steward, chief engineer, and Mr. McAuliffe's secretary. They all rated unobtrusive seats in the rear of the main dining room.

Mr. McAuliffe entered the dining room through the main entrance, but the "first officers" entered and left through a side door. This rule also held going in and coming out of the hotel.

The "second officers," of which I was one, comprised the cashiers, front clerk, assistant housekeeper, head bartender, dining-room captains, assistant steward, superintendent of service, and the like. We had our own private dining room with the main hall menu, although the choice and expensive items were crossed off.

The balance of the "help" ate in a cafeteria which adjoined the kitchen and which they called the "Zoo." They roomed in the help's dormitory as did the "second officers"—although in a separate wing. The "first officers" roomed in the top of the hotel proper.

The present-day holders of these jobs have high-sounding titles, until it almost seems a matter of providing them with big titles in lieu of wages. The night clerk is the night manager; the room clerk the executive assistant manager in charge of sales; the porter is assistant manager in charge of transportation; the headwaiter is the maître d'hôtel; the housekeeper is always the executive housekeeper; the chef steward is now the catering manager—some even go so far as to call the clerk of the cigar stand the assistant manager in charge of cigars. These titles sometimes prevail in hotels of less than a hundred rooms, particularly when they are written up in the trade papers!

While our relations with the "first officers" were cordial, there was a sharp line of demarkation between us. Evenings they held their social gatherings and we held ours. The line of social prestige was drawn fine, but it made for the respect and prestige of the "first officers" and for the betterment of the service throughout the hotel.

Mr. McAuliffe, having been one of the best room clerks in the business, was a crank on that angle of the operation. We used the old-fashioned register, and when thirty or forty guests arrived on the late train at night I had to register all and send them up to their rooms, then write their room numbers down opposite their signatures from memory! The Alcazar and the Hotel Cordova were connected by an enclosed bridge over the side street and functioned as one operation. It was nearly a quarter of a mile across the lobby, up the elevator, over the bridge, and down through the long corridors of the Cordova. If people were coming in fast and we happened to get a particularly cantankerous or finicky person who wanted to hold a long conversation about accommodations and rates while other incoming guests waited wearily in line, I'd say:

"Sir, I think I have the very room for you," and hand a key to the bellboy and "send him to Siberia," as we called it. This meant that he was taken to look at a room at the far end of the Cordova, which I knew he wouldn't accept, but by the time he got back I would have everyone else registered. After trudging wearily back from his long trek to "Siberia," he was apt to be a trifle easier to please.

We also had a number of poor rooms in the top of the hotel that we called the "North Pole." We were trying to keep a high "house count"—the number of guests registered in the hotel—so as to show as much profit as we could from our department, therefore it was necessary to fill these poor rooms each night. After many unsuccessful attempts to rent them I evolved a strategy.

In the late afternoon, when guests would arrive weary from their long train trip and ask for accommodations, I would reply:

"I believe we have some guests going out in a short while. You just rest easy in the lobby or go in and have your dinner and I will try to have something for you." Of course I had ten or twelve vacant rooms at the North Pole. After dinner they would come up to the desk and I would shake my head.

"Nothing yet, but I'm working on it." By this time they were getting apprehensive. About nine-thirty I would call them up to the desk and say:

"I've some rooms for you; you're not going to like them, but they are perfectly comfortable and have their own baths. Take them for a day or two and I'll change you into something more desirable."

They were always delighted, and the rooms were sold out every night.

And here's a tip I'll pass along with the hope that it will do some good: Don't ever try to beat a room clerk's ears down. He knows that you have had a hard trip and that you are tired and hungry and anxious to get settled and he makes due allowances, but if you stalk up to the desk and try to show how important you are, brother, you'll be sent to the "North Pole" whether you know it or not. After all, the room clerk has handled thousands of people who are more important than you are, he's had a hard day, his feet hurt, and, frankly, he is bored.

He isn't easy to fool on any terms.

The oldest hotel tradition in the world is the one about the new shoes. If a couple comes up to the desk and both are wearing new shoes, the clerk knows he has a bride and groom. If hers are new and his old, they have been married some time.

One day, in the middle of the winter, when the house was full to the roof, Mr. McAuliffe stopped by the desk and said, "Next week we have a convention of four hundred people coming in—the Traveling Passenger Agents of America. They are arriving in two Pullman trains and will sleep aboard, but we will have to feed them. This means setting up the dining room twice each meal for four days and it will be all cash business, so you boys will have to sell the meal tickets and collect for all food and wine charges at the desk."

Here was an emergency. The entire staff would have to double up and work almost round the clock, but they were a good crew and jumped to it with a great deal of enthusiasm.

The convention group arrived in the holiday spirit. We had an immense wastebasket back of the desk and when Mc-Cracken, the chief cashier, and his assistant started to collect money from the delegates, the cash drawers overflowed and they started throwing folding money into this wastebasket. When it got too full, McCracken put his foot on it and shoved it down.

One evening I heard a commotion in the dining room. A tall young man raced through the lobby as if the devil were after him, and I guess he was, because he kept screaming, "Don't let 'em catch me!" The headwaiter and a couple of other men appeared at the dining-room door shouting: "Stop that man!" I didn't know what it was all about, but I vaulted over the front desk and gave chase, followed by a couple of the bellboys.

As we turned the corner by the front entrance we took a cop in tow. The young fellow was making great speed until all at once he stopped, threw his arms across a fence, and laid his head down on the top rail. When we reached him he was stone dead. The poor fellow had had his last drink and his last race with the d.t.'s.

Walking back to the hotel, I remembered a story McCracken used to tell about a man who rushed into the house physician's office in a highly nervous state.

"Doctor," he said, "I want you to come up to my room just as soon as you can. My roommate is going blind."

"What happened?" asked the doctor.

"Well, you see," said the man, "he and I were having a party and we have killed three quarts of liquor."

"Oh," said the doctor, "you're being bothered by pink elephants."

"They're there all right," replied the man, "but the damn fool can't see 'em."

Father used to say that the only reason he remained in the resort hotel business was that he was curious to see what would happen next.

One evening a busload of guests filed up to the desk at the Alcazar and I looked into the face of "Smiling Diamond Joe" Connor. Most of the hotel boys knew of Diamond Joe, and I recognized him at once. He was one of the top jewel thieves in the country—a suave, well-set-up man about forty years old. He had a lovely old lady about seventy-five years old with him that he registered as his mother.

As there were a number of guests in line and more about the lobby, I didn't want to cause a scene, therefore I gave him a cordial greeting. After I had all the guests registered and in their rooms I turned the desk over to the night clerk and hot-footed it up to Mr. McAuliffe's apartment. "I hate to disturb you at this hour," I told him, "but Diamond Joe Connor just checked in. I didn't want to cause any commotion at the front desk, so I gave him a suite and he has just gone up."

"That's using your head. Now go to Connor and tell him Mr. McAuliffe sent you, and that Mac wants to know whether he is working or on vacation. Connor is the slickest jewel thief in the business but his word is as good as a government bond, and if he says he is on vacation don't worry about it any more."

I went down to Connor's suite. Connor came to the door in his shirt sleeves. He was having a drink and offered me one, which I declined.

I said, "Mr. McAuliffe sent me to ask whether you are working or on vacation?"

Connor laughed and called to the old lady: "Hear that, Ella?" He walked about the room for two or three minutes, then turned around and looked me straight in the eye.

"You go back and tell Mac that I'm on vacation."

I couldn't help wondering why a man so gifted and likable should choose to make a living in such a precarious manner.

Diamond Joe and his "mother" stayed out the month as dignified and retiring guests. They left the Alcazar about the middle of February and went to another Florida hotel.

The big event of the Palm Beach season was the Washington's Birthday Ball. It is alleged that Connor attended the ball disguised as a woman and during the festivities picked a priceless diamond necklace from a lady's neck in the powder room and disappeared.

Speaking of Washington's Birthday balls, we had one at the Alcazar. I had been on duty all day as usual and about ten o'clock McAuliffe walked up to the desk and said, "Karl, have you a tuxedo with you?"

"Yes, sir."

"Well, I want you to go up and run the Washington's Birthday Ball. Find the wine steward and make up a punch and keep that band on their toes. Let the music run until two o'clock with a three-quarter intermission. Now jump to it!"

This was sheer murder! I was tired enough as it was. I felt no particular thrill at the prospect, but I was proud that McAuliffe had picked me for the job. Any opportunity to make me stand out from the rest of the help was welcome.

I found the band leader and picked out some of the newer popular numbers, such as: "After You're Gone," "Waiting for the *Robert E. Lee*," "Everybody's Doing It," and a few older ones that would go over well with our type of guests. They were on the sedate side and it had to be ragtime with a fast tempo and a lilt instead of the slow numbers that took more balance.

Gone was the decorum of the lancers, the two-step, and the old-fashioned waltz, the program filled out days in advance. Instead, middle-aged couples huffed and puffed around the floor doing the Gaby glide, the turkey trot, the bunny hug, and the grizzly bear. The more sophisticated danced the fox-trot, one-step, and hesitation waltz. Some executed the intricate steps of the maxixe and tango with remarkable grace and dexterity, acquired, no doubt, from the dancing establishment of Irene and Vernon Castle or some lesser studio. The women seemed to be more expert than the men, possibly having had more opportunity for instruction or from frequenting the dansants where they danced with gigolos.

When the dancing was well under way, the wine steward arrived and we concocted a champagne punch.

The weather was warm and the music lively. One blond

debutante practically wore a path through the dance floor to and from the punch bowl. I tried to warn her, but she was a headstrong miss. By intermission her baby-blue eyes had taken on a bewildered stare.

So I said, "Honey, you and I are going to have some black coffee and a fast walk around the block; this champagne is beginning to catch up with you."

She stared at me haughtily.

"Give me no trouble," I said. "Do you want to get into a jam with your folks?" I hustled her down the back stairs to the kitchen and made her drink a couple of cups of strong coffee, took her by the arm, and walked her at a good fast pace, making her breathe deeply.

There was a patio in the center of the Alcazar, beautifully landscaped, and a little pond with a Japanese bridge. After we had walked around the block two or three times we started through the patio to the ballroom. She was pretty well sobered up, and we stood chatting a moment on the moonlit path.

I looked up and saw the portly form of McAuliffe coming across the bridge. Not by any amount of explaining could I make him believe the truth—that I was a Boy Scout doing my good deed. As McAuliffe neared I placed my right hand on the girl's chest and shoved. The low privet hedge caught her under the knees and she landed on her fanny in the shrubbery. "Don't speak!" I whispered. "Here comes Mac, and if he sees you I'll be fired."

I was lighting a cigarette as he passed. He said, "How's everything at the dance?"

"Fine! I just came out for some air."

"I knew you wouldn't let me down." And he went in.

When Jerry, the night watchman, rapped on my door at six o'clock to wake me, it seemed to me I had just closed my eyes.

Old Jerry was fat and bald and had flat feet, as he had been tramping up and down hotel corridors, lo, these thirty years.

One evening I spied Jerry on a stair landing leaning over the banister to look through the transom of the room below. The room was occupied by a movie actress who was one of the great sirens of the silent screen and Jerry was watching her undress. Just as I came along he leaned over too far, lost his balance, and crashed over the banister onto the floor below. I rushed down to help him but I was shaking with laughter. When he got to his feet he looked at me with a dazed expression and said, "I might have been killed, but by God it was worth it!"

The star opened her door and asked, "What happened?"

"Oh," I said, "one of your fans got too enthusiastic."

"Well!" she began. Then she chuckled. "As long as I can keep 'em falling out of balconies, I know I'm giving a good performance." She was a grand sport.

But I couldn't get along with Dugan, the room clerk. He was a know-it-all and out to "get me," and I tried desperately never to be remiss in any detail.

When you walk up to a hotel front desk and engage the room clerk in conversation relative to accommodations and he turns his head from time to time to glance in back of the desk, he is not inattentive, but looking over his room rack. This is a large rack divided into columns and these are divided into slots. Each slot has a number corresponding to a room in the hotel—thus, if the hotel has four hundred rooms there are four hundred slots.

Into these slots the room clerk slides multi-colored slips of cardboard, each coded to a particular significance; the room is single or double; it has a tub or shower; it is part of a suite; its exposure; its price; et cetera.

The rack is like a chessboard with four or five hundred chessmen constantly moving on or off. Some of the slips show departure dates and under these are other slips showing later arrivals. Between these dates the room is available. In describing this room rack I'm concerned only with resort hotels and not the large city hotels where the room clerks come and go in shifts and each has his own section to handle.

The public knows little of the bewildering complexity and the infinite amount of attention to detail that the room clerk has to cope with in order to keep every room occupied. Not only is it necessary that he fill the rooms each night, but also that he get as many people into a given number of rooms as possible. This procedure is called the "average rack" and means the average number of persons per room—say 1.5 or 1.66—the difference means a great deal of money to the hotel. The third element he has to cope with is the "price per person," which is known as the "per capita," and which is contingent upon a great many factors.

An expert room clerk, glancing at a given number on his room rack, should be able to tell instantly where the room is, its approximate size, its exposure, whether it is for single or double occupancy, how it is furnished, and what the rate is. So be a little patient with him, for nine times out of ten he is doing his best to secure accommodations that he feels will please you.

We trained ourselves in the early days by walking around the hotel in the evening and, seeing a light in the window, recite the number of the room and all its qualifications. To check his room rack, the room clerk received a list of check-outs several times a day from the housekeeper, testifying that the room had been vacated and was now in order.

After the height of the season there came an afternoon when Dugan was late in reporting for duty. A train due at five was usually late, so sometimes we took a chance. On this particular day the train arrived on time and we had a large number of new guests. Mr. McAuliffe was standing in the lobby and noticed that Dugan was not on duty. I suppose he felt I was not experienced enough to handle the situation so he came around back of the front desk to help me run the room rack. When he glanced at the rack it did not show a vacant room available, and he turned to me, demanding, "What in the world are we going to do?"

I said, "Mr. McAuliffe, if you will just step back from the room rack, I'll show you." I knew there were about fifteen "sleepers" in the rack. A "sleeper" is a room that is vacant and in order, but through some accident or negligence the slip has not been pulled from its designated slot. If Dugan had checked thoroughly with the housekeeper this could not have happened; but, as I said before, he was such a cocksure individual that I suppose the other departments were not too anxious to help him.

I had been carrying the sleepers in my mind and knew the number of each, but I had strict orders from Dugan never to touch the room rack or make any suggestions as to how it should be handled; when he went off duty he left me an "availability list" to work from.

I stepped up to the room rack, took a pencil, and knocked out all the sleepers and started to room the people. It happened that there were just enough rooms to take care of them all. In the middle of the work Dugan rushed across the lobby and started behind the desk. He was a little out of breath and looked as if he just had had two or three rapid cocktails. Mr. McAuliffe had strolled out into the lobby and as Dugan passed him Mr. McAuliffe inquired: "Where are you going, Dugan?"

"Why, in back of the desk to room these people."

"Seems to me you are a little late. You may notice that we have a new room clerk on duty and he seems to be doing rather well."

So that is how I got my first promotion!

Chapter Six: FIRST COMMAND

WHEN the season closed at the Alcazar and the crew started North, we boys on the desk went up together. We chipped in and bought a drawing room and upper berths on the same car and started a poker game at Jacksonville that wound up at Manhattan Transfer. Some of the boys arrived in New York without much to show for their winter's work and had to think about getting another hotel job immediately.

A peculiar psychology governs the actions of the typical resort employees. They are a gypsy lot who live more like circus people than any other I know—here today, gone tomorrow. New England in the summertime—Florida or California in the winter. Following the sun and tourist trade.

It is a world of its own that the uninitiated never enters and where its denizens know where everyone else is. I have not walked into a large resort hotel in thirty years that I haven't known many of the employees, and can always find where Joe is by asking Bill or Jack. Unconsciously, they keep track. They love the uncertainty and the gamble, and no other life seems to interest them for very long.

I had worked so hard all winter that all I could think about was a vacation. New York, for once, held no attractions. I went straight to Bethlehem, and it was exactly as it always had been.

Father had about forty French-Canadians doing some excavating outside Upland Terrace and the sand had caved in and buried one. The men were shouting and tearing at the sand with their shovels and Mother ran for her camphor bottle—in any emergency she always ran for the camphor—and to quiet her Father leaned over the piazza rail and drawled: "Don't waste time diggin' him out, boys, we can get a new man cheaper." Mother was so mad she didn't speak to Father for a week.

With several other Bethlehem fellows I planned a camp back of the mountains. We hired an old French-Canadian guide named Myat to do our hauling, and after our supplies were together started for the woods. It was the sort of May morning that can't be so beautiful anywhere as in the White Mountains. First came an old Democrat wagon drawn by a big bay mare owned by Walter Clark, who, with his brother Millard, Henry Smith, and a couple of other fellows, made up our party. The wagon was loaded with foodstuffs, bedding, horse feed, old clothes, mosquito netting, and fishing tackle. Next came Myat driving a pair of large draft horses hitched to a hayrack piled high with everything we had been able to think of that might be needed for a home in the woods.

Lastly I came trundling along on our old horse Dennis, riding a western saddle, with bags of feed and other gear tied on behind.

We went down by Maplewood and headed for Gale River. Off across the great valley to the east the snow-capped Presidential Range glistened in the sun and the green slopes of the Franconias shone like emeralds. The pungent smell of damp earth assailed our nostrils, and great beds of pink trailing arbutus, like carelessly flung counterpanes, adorned the banks on either side. Up on a pasture hillside a few gnarled old apple trees showed touches of green, and the red buds of the tall maples were bursting with life. Rills and little brooks tumbled across the road. The soft winds soughing down from the hills held a promise that quickened the heart of a mountain-bred man.

A woodcock beat through the alders with a startled "kree-eek!" and fluttered off through the pines in crazy flight. A great gray hawk wheeled a quarter mile overhead. The rhythmic drumming of a cock partridge strutting a hollow log vibrated through the stillness, and I can still hear "Doc's" happy shout, "Drum, damn you, drum! We'll have you in a pot come fall!"

There comes a time in every life after the trail has been long and tiring when one pauses to look back on some tranquil scene poignant with memories, and that May morning will ever be mirrored in my mind: the cheerful banter of the boys, the squeaking of the big wheels of Myat's hayrack, and the smell of the earth, the spring, and sweating horsehide as we toiled over the hills to the big woods in the valley.

We built our camp four square to the great outdoors, in a clearing swamped out with our own axes in the birch and maple on the banks of the Gale—a one-room shack twenty-four feet square shingled all over with a hip roof and a ladder leading up to an open chamber under the eaves.

As "Doc" drove in the last nail he said with satisfaction, "Now we can rest."

I said, "That's the name." So we burned CAMP REST on a board and propped it over the door.

There is no satisfaction like the snug comfort of a camp, however humble, that has been built by your own hands. We lay in our bunks, tired and sore from unaccustomed manual labor, listening to the roar of the river and the gnawing of a hedgehog at the floor stringers, and I would not have swapped my bunk for the finest suite at the Alcazar. Hard work and mountain air were the tonics needed to offset the nervous wear and tear of a hectic winter.

It rained hard during the night, but when we opened our door in the morning we looked out on a golden world. A bright sun was gilding the cliffs across the valley. The Gale was running bank full after the rain, which made fishing impossible.

The very thought made my mouth water. We had been too busy building to think of trout.

Nothing is dearer to my heart than brook trout—*Salvelinus fontinalis*. All New Hampshire men feel the same. They remember, as barefoot boys, catching trout in some brook near home. Though in later years they may roam the world in quest of the regal salmon or the fighting tuna, carrying with them fishing tackle that cost thousands, their allegiance sticks to the mountain stream and its denizens.

I happened to remember that a little brook lay about three miles over the ridge, and set out alone.

The fish came from every direction. I never fished such water. From every pool and overhanging bank hungry trout rushed out to meet my bait.

I was enjoying myself too much to note the flight of time, and the sun was dropping behind the western hills when it came to me that I had better hurry back to camp if I didn't want to spend the night in the woods.

There was no trail, but I knew the country. I hurried along down through the gulleys and over the ridges. Suddenly I realized I wasn't going to make camp before dark, but I kept going until the last of the spring twilight vanished in the treetops.

Well, a night in the woods in May wouldn't hurt me, and I knew the boys wouldn't worry, as we had traveled the woods together since boyhood. I built a fire and prepared to spend the night. Soon I heard someone chopping wood, and the sound of voices. I picked up my gear and walked over into our camp. If Doc and the boys hadn't come out for stove-wood I would have slept in the open all night within sight of Camp Rest.

Hot baked beans, brown bread, and raw onions, washed down with scalding coffee, certainly tasted good, and we spent the evening cleaning the trout and telling stories.

After we were in bed there was a terrific mountain thunderstorm. Thunder cracked and rolled among the hills, and almost continuous lightning played along the ridges. I couldn't think of poor old Dennis out there in the woods alone, so I got up, lit the lantern, and went out to see him.

The storm was so violent that every time the thunder cracked and the lightning flashed he crouched down and tried to find what shelter he could under an overhanging bough. I took Dennis by the halter and led him into camp. The fellows were asleep in their bunks and if ever a horse tiptoed into a house, Dennis did. He lay down gratefully between the bunks with a snort of content, his head almost touching the cookstove.

I blew out the lantern and climbed between my blankets. I felt a great deal better! The storm blew over but the rain fell all night. I don't know of any sensation more pleasant than to lie, half asleep, in good warm blankets in a snug camp listening to the soft patter of the rain on the roof.

In the morning Doc swung out of his bunk, half asleep, and struck his bare feet on Dennis. It scared the living hell out of him. He jumped and landed standing straight up on his bunk and yelled, "How did that damn horse get in here? I thought it was a moose!"

We stayed in Camp Rest all through June. Every ten days or so we'd toss up to see who would make the eighteen miles out and back for supplies and the mail.

We loafed, fished the mountain streams, and each Sunday climbed one of the Franconia peaks. Soon it was time to get back and help Father open the Upland Terrace.

That was a grand summer! All the Bethlehem hotels were full, and life, for the most part, moved in its usual tranquil way. My friend Frank Knox of the Manchester Union was tearing all over the country in an automobile lining up the Bull Moose party for his old sidekick, Colonel "Teddy" Roosevelt. Later he was Secretary of War under F.D.R. All the new automobiles had self-starters, and a friend wrote

Father from Florida that the first Florida east coast passenger train had arrived in Key West.

We topped off the season with a big society circus, complete with parade, big top, and side shows, one of which I ran. It was Scheherazade, the trained centipede, made up of twelve girls leaning over, each grasping the waist of the girl in front. They were under a canvas covering painted to resemble the body of a gigantic centipede and the first girl carried a pole on which was Scheherazade's head. At the crack of a whip Scheherazade stood on all her left feet then on all her right.

It is a pity there are so many diversions these days. It is certainly a fact that people around resorts do not have so much fun as they used to when they had to make their own.

Father wanted me to go to Fort Myers with him that fall. By this time we were full partners. The day I was twenty-one Father made his banking account a joint one and had "Frank H. Abbott and Son" painted on the sign and printed on the stationery at Upland Terrace, after some kidding insistence on my part that it read "Karl P. Abbott and Father." He understood that I needed to be on my own. But the Florida west coast was developing fast, and he thought there was a good future there for a young man.

For my part, I was anxious to see what had happened at Fort Myers since I had seen it last, so when cold weather and the year 1913 began the Yankee cracker again started southward.

Until I arrived at Fort Myers I had not realized how many changes had occurred there. Gone was the little cow town nestling at the side of the river; instead there were the beginnings of a thriving city. Trains arrived with a certain amount of punctuality and there was a new hotel called the Bradford, operated by Peter Schutt, who today operates the famous Ormund Beach Hotel.

Many fine homes had been built, and the spirit of enterprise, egged on by a chamber of commerce, was a contrast to the sleepy atmosphere of bygone days.

There was a large addition to the Royal Palm, and a swimming pool had been built at the side of the Casino. The long dock out into the river was the same, except for the addition of four boathouses that housed long, sleek motorboats, which were very different from our old-time launches. They whisked sportsmen to the fishing grounds, and I thought back to the old guides such as Billie Bartley, George West, and Tillit Henderson, who rowed a skiff fifteen miles down the river, rowed for trolling all day, and rowed the long trip back at night, for three dollars.

Dr. Terry, Harvey Heitman, and other public-spirited men were completing a road through to Punta Rassa, and below town the riverbank was dotted with lovely estates.

The Royal Palm was the center round which all the social life of Fort Myers revolved. The hotel was full all winter and catered to a splendid clientele. A number of yachts lay in the harbor and life was carefree.

I had charge of the reservations, the desk, and the entire front of the house, which was good experience. I am afraid that I took advantage of the fact that Father was running the hotel and indulged in many social activities that I would not otherwise have enjoyed.

We had a grand young crowd that winter—a family named Harris from South Orange, with three beautiful daughters and a younger brother; the Noblit girls, Edah and Sally, from Philadelphia, whose family owned an estate down the river; and other young people from Louisville, New York, and Boston. We went on yachting parties, moonlight picnics, and held gay dances.

Soon after we opened a beautiful yacht called the *Caprice*, out of Chicago, dropped anchor in the harbor. The "grapevine" reported that it belonged to Steven Metcliffe, who, with his mother, had taken our finest suite for the winter. His father, who died when Steve was a small boy, had been a great financier at the turn of the century, and Steve was one of America's real playboys.

I will never forget my first glimpse of him! It was around eleven o'clock on a peaceful Sunday morning. Many of the older guests were sitting about the lobby and veranda, engrossed in their Sunday papers, when Steve came down the main stairs.

He was several years older than I, nearly six feet tall, and if ever the phrase "tall, dark, and handsome" fitted anyone, that man was Steve Metcliffe.

I heard someone gasp, someone else dropped a book, and there he stood, dressed in white tie and tails, a black opera cape with white satin lining thrown over his shoulders, wearing a tall silk hat, and carrying a gold-headed ebony cane. He was a picture!

Walking nonchalantly through the lobby and to the end of the dock, he carefully placed his cape and stick on a bench, pulled his high hat over his ears, dived overboard, and swam out to his yacht.

Later in the day he strolled up to the desk. He was wearing sports attire.

"I suppose those old biddies think I need a keeper," he said, with a broad grin on his darkly tanned face. "Well, I had to do something to knock them out of their chairs."

I had no inkling in that moment as to how close we would become through the years.

But I liked him. Everyone liked Steve. The guests decided he was crazy, but nothing was further from the truth. He was a normal young American with a vivid imagination, an absurd sense of humor, and more money than he knew what to do with. A thoroughly lovable guy, but restless and bored.

The peace and quiet of that Sunday morning had brought out the imp in him.

Sometimes, on moonlit nights, Steve would ask me out on

his yacht. We would run down the river and out into the Gulf of Mexico and sit out on the stern while he drank innumerable highballs and told of his experiences all over the world, and quoted Kipling, Keats, and Shelley by the hour.

With Fort Myers grown into a progressive little city and the great influx of northern people, I had been lulled into the belief that the old gun-fighting spirit was a thing of the past. I should have known better! It was still there, just under the surface.

This was brought forcibly to mind when I went on a short business trip with Father. He was the executor of an estate that owned a large tract of turpentine land and two wealthy turpentine still operators were bidding for it. He had an appointment to meet these men at Bartow.

As our train pulled in there was the sound of gunfire and great excitement on the station platform. The conductor signaled the engineer to keep going, but Father yanked the emergency cord and stalled the train. When the shooting stopped, both the men we had come to see were dead. While waiting for Dad to arrive they got into an argument over the deal and shot it out.

Twenty years later I was telling of this incident at a dinner party in the grill of the Sagamore Hotel, Bolton Landing, New York, which I was operating, and the others started to rib me for telling tall tales of Florida. One of the party was Mr. Harry D. Kirkover of Buffalo and Camden, South Carolina. After a little he smiled and said, "I have a bullet hole in my leg I got that morning on the station platform at Bartow as an innocent bystander!"

This was as great a surprise to me as to the others.

In March Mr. Robert S. Bradley, of Boston and Pride's Crossing, arrived at the Royal Palm. He was tall and lean, with a florid complexion, military mustache, and a remarkable lack of patience. He demanded instant and perfect service and was willing to pay for it. He got it too. As Father used to say, "the wheel that squeaks the loudest gets the most grease."

He hadn't been in the hotel an hour before the staff was up in arms. It was always a point of pride with me to be able to handle the most difficult guest, and by a little extra effort and a great deal of forbearance I was able to make an impression on him.

A few days before he was to leave he was in a towering rage because he could not secure a private car to take him home. He kept rushing up to the desk and sending wires to the presidents of various railroad lines, but to no avail. Finally I spoke up.

"Mr. Bradley, you seem to be having difficulty securing a private car. I think I can get one for you."

He glowered. "Young man, do you mean you can get me a private car when the presidents of three railroads can't?"

"That's what I mean," I said. "Today is Thursday. Give me a hundred dollars and I will have your private car on the siding Saturday morning. I don't want a dime for it, but a hundred dollars will work miracles in Florida with the season almost over."

He said it was the damnedest foolishness he had ever heard of, but he opened his pocketbook and threw two fifties on the desk.

Saturday morning the car was on the siding. It was not exactly a private car, but a Pullman with a drawing room at each end and a steward in attendance. Mr. Bradley was delighted.

As he left the hotel he spoke to me. "When you come to New York, come to my office at Number 2 Rector Street. I have something to say to you."

The remark meant little at the time, but I remembered it.

After the Royal Palm closed I visited Steve in New York. He and his mother were staying at the Plaza and asked me to be their guest for a few weeks. Steve was known everywhere and that is where we went—Bustanoby's on Thirty-ninth Street, Delmonico's at Forty-fourth Street and Fifth Avenue, Lew Marin's, Rector's, Louis Sherry's—all gay spots and in the height of fashion. Keen's Chop House and the Lafayette were his favorites.

Before leaving Florida Father had told me while in New York to be sure to pay my respects to Mr. Treche, the famous Oscar of the Waldorf, whom he had met many times at hotel men's gatherings. The Waldorf-Astoria was then located on the present site of the Empire State building. It seemed to me to be all red plush and bronze, and I remember the thrill of walking down the long carpet of the famous Peacock Alley. I confess I was a little self-conscious as I was ushered into the office of the famous maître d'hôtel, who was, in fact, a great deal more than that. He was the embodiment of the spirit of the Waldorf—the *persona grata* of royalty and many great personages.

This kindly man, in cutaway coat and striped trousers, was an exhalted figure in my world. With instant discernment he put me completely at ease and gave the young man from the sticks as much time and consideration as he would have some noted dignitary. It was a lesson in courtesy I have never forgotten.

In the midst of the New York gaiety Mr. Bradley's invitation was kicking around in the back of my mind. I didn't attach too much importance to it, thinking that perhaps he wanted to give me some small token for the little extra attentions I had rendered.

One morning I went downtown to his office and gave the receptionist my name.

I was greatly surprised when the door to his private office opened and Bradley himself glared into the anteroom and barked, "Abbott, come in here." He waved me to a chair, seated himself behind his desk, and stared at me for a minute without speaking. Then he said, "Abbott, I'm a damn difficult guest to take care of! I've been all over the world and stopped at the finest hotels—the Waldorf, the Barclay in London, the Ritz in Paris, Shepheard's in Cairo—I'm a crank on service. Last winter you were on the job. You anticipated my wishes! Can you run a hotel?"

"Yes, sir," I replied.

"Can you build a hotel?"

"Yes, sir!"

"When?"

"Tomorrow morning."

The merest suggestion of a smile crossed his face. "Do you know enough to do exactly as you're told?"

"Yes, sir."

"All right. The southern terminus of the C. H. & N. Railroad is Boca Grande on Gasparilla Island on the Florida west coast. It is, primarily, a phosphate loading plant for transatlantic freighters, but my brother Peter, Jim Gifford, and I feel that it could be a wonderful resort. We have a very small hotel there now—simply to house visiting directors and company officers. I got your Father's advice when I was at the Royal Palm last winter (Father had never mentioned it to me). Take this letter and go up to Boston and see my brother Peter, the president of the company. He will tell you what to do. Work hard and maybe we'll make a hotel man of you. Good day!"

I left his office walking on air, took the night train for Boston, and saw Peter Bradley. You could recognize them at once for brothers, although their personalities were exactly opposite. There did not seem to be the nervous tension and spirit of apprehension around the large, sunny offices at 92 State Street that had prevailed in Robert Bradley's office in New York. Peter Bradley was heavier set than his brother; he looked like a good sport, and had a jovial disposition.

I knew what Robert Bradley meant when he said his brother was president of the company. One sensed immediately that Peter Bradley was the dominating factor. I liked him on sight and inwardly swore my allegiance to him. It lasted for fifteen years.

My chance had come—the chance to walk up on the bridge and command the ship. I had been born in a hotel and brought up in a hotel, and it was the only world I knew. As young as I was I felt I was ready—in fact, I was a little cocky.

I was just twenty-four years old.

As the train crawled across the four-mile trestle from the Florida mainland to Gasparilla Island I knew it was the beginning of a great adventure. Across the flats and through Gasparilla Pass to the azure gulf the water seemed painted with a gigantic brush—splashes of pink, green, indigo, and saffron delicately blended, dotted with tiny white sandspits and islands. Pelicans sailed above the shimmering waters and dived for fish, and as we approached the draw and the engineer gave long blasts on the whistle, great flocks of sea birds rose screaming into the cloudless sky and circled our train.

The track ran along the beach almost at the water's edge, and in places, Gasparilla Island was so narrow that the water was close on either side. The island is seven miles long and a mile at its widest. The landscape was covered with a scattered growth of cabbage palms, sea grapes, and cactus. Here and there were shacks, a fishhouse with long racks of fish nets drying in the sun.

I was excited by the wild beauty of the island and began remembering the many stories about the pirate José Gasparilla and the treasure he had buried there. This had been his harem island, and in my mind's eye I caught glimpses of his rakish ships in the lagoons among the mangrove.

Boca Grande, as I stepped off the train, was a blinding white glare of midday sun reflected from the white sand and shell that had been pumped out of the lagoons to make fill where the town was to be. There was practically no vegetation—

merely a desolate waste where streets and avenues were marked off with stakes. Not a ghost town, but one in embryo.

The railroad station, a red-brick general store, a drugstore, four residences the C. H. & N. Railroad had built for its officers, an unpainted frame church, a schoolhouse, and the little inn made up the hamlet of Boca Grande.

God knows it was a lonesome spot, but there was plenty of activity. A large dredge was working in the bayou and men were laying out streets and sidewalks and a sewer line.

I went over to the little inn and met Mr. Fouts, president of the railroad, who was in charge of everything at Boca Grande, and he took me on a gasoline car over the railroad to South Boca Grande, three miles away, to give me an idea of what was being done to develop the island. At South Boca Grande were huge loading terminals and docks and Boca Grande Pass, with water deep enough to admit ships of any size. I met the pilots, Captain I. W. and Will Johnson, and young Kingsmore Johnson who was to be my good friend. They were fine-looking, weather-beaten men who had stood on the bridge of many a freighter and brought her safely over the bar.

About a mile from town land had been cleared for a nine-hole golf course, and as there was no topsoil for a course, it was being brought from the mainland by the trainload. All the fresh water had to be brought from the mainland also.

I met Mr. Kennard, the architect from Tampa, and all the old-timers—Jeff Gaines, the postmaster, Jerome Fugate, the druggist, a man named Gilligan who ran the general store, and John Riley, the superintendent for the company. In a little room in back of the store Louis Fouts, son of the elder Fouts, had opened a bank.

I can't imagine going into any city or hamlet on earth and not feeling completely at home in twenty-four hours. At the end of my first afternoon in Boca Grande I felt I had lived there all my life. It was to be home to me for fifteen years.

Assisting in the birth of a town seemed very exciting, and the directing of the expenditure of what was to me a vast amount of money to build the hotel, help's quarters, power-house, guides' quarters, boathouse, and bathing pavilion on the beach, also on the furniture, equipment, and landscaping, gave me a fine sense of responsibility.

Trainloads of lumber and supplies began to arrive and a contractor from Tampa, Captain Miller, took charge of construction. Using the little inn as headquarters we built the Gasparilla Inn, with a beautiful lounge and clubroom, dining room and kitchens, and about ninety bedrooms, each with private bath. These rooms were large and airy and each had a tremendous clothes closet, which, incidentally, is about the most important thing in a resort hotel bedroom and always a bone of contention between an architect and a hotel operator who knows his business.

While pumping out the water to build the hotel we came across portions of an ancient chest, but we found no pirate gold.

By fall Gasparilla Inn was practically completed. I went North to help purchase the furniture and equipment and hire my crew.

It was my first experience in this field, and before starting I had many a long talk with Father, who was in Boston making his usual winter preparations for the Royal Palm. Father was oversolicitous that his only son do well. He wanted to help pick my crew and furnishings and everything, but I wouldn't have it. The Gasparilla Inn at Boca Grande was to be all mine.

Most of the furniture was purchased at Paines in Boston and Peter Bradley insisted upon helping select it. We bought a lot of heavy mahogany bedroom suites with large four-poster beds. I held out for single beds but was promptly overruled. Mr. Bradley just looked at me. "If there is any man who won't sleep in the same bed with his wife, I don't want him in my hotel."

So the furniture was shipped with double beds, and after we opened the hotel practically no one would use them and they all had to be replaced with single beds. Along the right of way of the C. H. & N. Railroad were little houses for the colored section hands. Riding up and down the line for the next fifteen years I could look through the open shutters into these little houses and see those beautiful big mahogany four-poster beds.

I went to the Morandi Proctor Company in Boston and bought the kitchen equipment, then to Jones McDuffie and Stratton for the china. There I was guided by "Uncle Joe" Norcross, the head salesman, who had "sold" Father for years and wouldn't let me go wrong. Then down to the Meriden Britannia Company—now the International Silver Company—for all our table service. Frank Wilcox, the sales manager, treated me with so much consideration that I had a suspicion he and Father had had a talk behind my back.

In any event, I was learning fast.

Then I started thinking about a crew. They had to be New Englanders, New Hampshire by preference. I did not want employees who had worked in large hotels with the caste system and specified duties; rather people who had worked in small hotels, who were used to all kinds of duties and hours, and who were neat and conscientious and took pride in their work. I went up to Colebrook, New Hampshire, and hired almost the complete crew out of this one town—good clean Yankee help, not afraid of work. I got them down to Boston and arranged our sailings on the Savannah line for the South.

On one point Father was insistent. He was determined to select my private secretary. He wanted an efficient dyed-in-the-wool businesswoman. After much time and a great deal of pains he found what he wanted. I didn't meet her until we were on the boat. She was a willowy brunette and looked intelligent, but I thought her a trifle standoffish.

The first night she started to entertain the purser.

and by the time we reached Savannah she had worked up through the ship's officers to the captain. Two days after we arrived in Boca Grande she and one of the guides got drunk and fell off the dock into the harbor. I wired Father I'd had to fire her and asked if he wanted to engage another secretary.

Father wired back: "Hire your own. Your judgment can't be worse than mine."

When we started to put the Gasparilla Inn in order for the opening I was hard put to find cleaning help. Out in the jungle, a mile from Boca Grande, was a big unpainted frame house known as the "Titanic." It was a Negro bawdy house, frequented by the Negro laborers working on the construction crews. In desperation I went there and got about a dozen of the inmates to come up and help wash windows and scrub.

At the inn I lined them up, took a pay-roll book, and started listing their names. In the line was a big black amazon almost six feet tall. When I asked her name she fidgeted, standing first on one foot, then on the other. Then she giggled. "My name is Viola, but they calls me 'Pet!' I'm the Reverend Simmonds' daughter, but I done gone wrong!"

Soon the Gasparilla Inn was ready to open. Everything was spotlessly, beautifully new. Miss Hattie Rhoda Mead, a young lady from Sloane's in New York, had done a beautiful job of decorating. It was a wonderful feeling, walking around the new plant, a managing director at last. I remembered Father swinging around Uplands the morning of opening day, touching his fingers to the piazza steps to see whether the paint was dry.

Father, busy with the Royal Palm over at Fort Myers, telephoned to say I was not to worry about anything, just go ahead and open the hotel. He'd be over every week to see how things were going.

Everything was wonderful. There was only one drawback.

I didn't have a single booking. Gasparilla Inn had no guests.

Chapter Seven: GASPARILLA INN

THE first application for reservations for Gasparilla Inn was a telegram from a prominent Boston dowager. Thank goodness I knew my Boston! From the empty lobby of an empty hotel I wired back that I might be able to get her the accommodations she desired, and to please wire me a social reference.

That really set us off! She, how well I knew, was the dowager to impress all dowagers. She got a big kick out of my telegram and told all her friends, and we laughed about it together after she arrived at the inn.

The inn caught on in Boston. It was whispered up and down State Street that someone had discovered a little hotel on an island off the Florida coast that catered only to "the right people." The "right people" came: Frank Crowninshield and his wife; Steven M. Weld and his family; the Saltonstalls; the Russells; Mr. and Mrs. Payne; the Peter Bradleys from Hingham; the Cabots; the Frothinghams.

They found others of their ilk as Gasparilla Inn—the Drexels, Biddles, and Pauls from Philadelphia; the Duponts from Wilmington; George Eastman and Mr. Stuber, president of the Eastman Kodak Company; the George Robesons from Rochester; and John and Cora Myers from Evanston. A grand crowd, and so easy to cater to! As a rule, the more people have and the longer they have had it, the more traveled they are and the more assured their social position, the easier they are to please. Such people know and appreciate good service and good food.

When you open a resort hotel—when that first guest arrives

—it's like starting a ship across the ocean and sitting on a keg of dynamite all the way. It's a ninety-day journey and a big investment, and almost anything can happen. The market can break, the weather changes, strikes, politics, a polio scare—any one of a thousand catastrophes can wreck you.

The actual procedure of opening is automatic. Every member of a well-trained staff knows his job and does it as a matter of course. There is just so much working space to any hotel—a front desk, a kitchen, a dining room. The managing director moves in and takes over. The crew members take their places, the chef puts on his white hat and starts to cook, and the hotel opens.

I never can understand the large amounts of money often allocated by resort hotel owners, or operators, for pre-opening and closing expense. Any resort hotel should be opened in ten days and neatly closed within forty-eight hours.

It has always been a point of pride with me to lay a hotel away so that if anything happens to me before another season a new manager would find things immaculate and in order.

I learned a lot about the handling of help that first season. Problems look different when viewed from the top down. It is always easy to criticize the boss, but I had no conception of what the boss's problems were until I became a boss.

The hardest thing I had to learn in employee relations was that there are two sides to every question, and that there are few arguments that cannot be settled amicably, provided both parties are willing to take into consideration the other's viewpoint. Father used to say, "Don't give advice to people. Fools won't heed it and wise men don't need it."

Over at Fort Myers Father kept his ear to the grapevine, to learn how I was getting along. He had said he'd be over when we opened, to lend a hand. The first week he phoned that it was inconvenient to leave his own hotel. The second week he phoned again to say he couldn't get away. The third week he didn't phone at all.

He didn't visit the island all season. He knew I'd take responsibility better alone.

I was in the kitchen one noon when a hard-boiled waitress dropped a couple of dishes. I spoke to her rather sharply, and as I went through the door into the dining room I heard her remark to one and all: "Did you hear what the baby boss said to me?"

Behind my back, and I knew it, I was the "baby boss" from then on.

It was difficult to set a table that would please such a discriminating clientele, situated as we were at the terminus of a little railroad. Our meats came from Boston in huge casks that were set out on the decks of the Savannah liners to Savannah and then shipped express to Boca Grande. Our groceries came from Pierce's in Boston, and I had a man in Arcadia who scoured the countryside and shipped me fresh vegetables. All the water we used in the hotel had to be shipped in tank cars from the mainland, and the freight charges were terrific.

All the years I was at Gasparilla Inn we served an old-fashioned strawberry shortcake with whipped cream every day for lunch. Either "Mar'm" Bailey, or Mrs. Hicks (known affectionately as "Hickey"), our New England pastry cooks, used to bake these shortcakes in huge pans. They took them out of the oven piping hot, spread them with fresh butter, and didn't put on the cold berries and whipped cream until the waitress was ready to rush into the dining room. These strawberry shortcakes made me a reputation. It was not unusual to receive a wire for a reservation: "Hold one double room, two beds, bath, for the sixteenth, and save us some strawberry shortcake."

Once there was a hard freeze and I was afraid I was going to ruin my record and miss out on shortcakes, so I took a handcar to Plant City, went from grower to grower, and persuaded them to uncover their berries and pick enough to tide me over.

One man used to come up from the islands with terrapin. The first time he came he had about a hundred. He was middle-aged and barefooted, and his generally unkempt appearance made me think he was one of the usual island beachcombers. When I paid him for the terrapin, I handed him a receipt, asking him whether he could write.

He laughed, and not only signed his name but proceeded to embellish the receipt with the most beautiful example of chirography one could imagine. Handing the pen back, he grunted, "It's because I can write like that that I'm down here catching terrapin." I believe he was a forger who had signed one check too many.

At Boca Grande the natives dug scallops to use for fish bait. Up North we considered this shellfish a great delicacy. I served scallops to my guests and they loved them, but word soon got around the island that young Abbott was serving his guests fish bait!

Early impressions of Gasparilla Inn wash over me, of difficulties and humorous events incidental to the opening and operation of a fine resort hotel in such an isolated community. I remember Steve was one of the first to arrive, on his yacht, but I had little time to spend with him except for bull sessions and snacks late at night in his suite. But he amused himself; he was an ardent tarpon fisherman and went on hunting expeditions.

John Singer Sargent, the great portrait painter, was a guest, and I heard that his definition of a portrait was "a picture with something wrong with the mouth." I am told that he painted Mrs. Jack Gardener in full evening dress and lost patience trying to get her mouth right and left it out altogether, and that the picture, just as he left it, is in Mrs. Gardener's palace in Boston.

We had the Reverend Henry van Dyke staying with us. (He was afterward Minister to the Netherlands and Luxemburg during World War I.) Sundays many of our guests attended the little frame church at Boca Grande. It was an ordinary country church, complete with steeple and mortgage. The young pastor was industrious and devout but terribly underpaid, and there was never enough money for hymnbooks and repairs.

Many of the guests wanted to hear the Reverend Henry van Dyke, and he said he would preach in the little church provided the other men staying at the hotel would attend service and not just send their wives. The following Sunday the little church was filled to overflowing and people were standing in the churchyard.

After a powerful sermon the great New York divine stepped to the front of the rostrum.

"My young pastor friend and myself," he said, indicating the local minister, "have been talking things over. As everyone knows, this church is in need of money and there are repairs to be made. We have also decided to pay off the mortgage."

He looked over the congregation. It was filled with his friends. He fixed his eye on Mr. Robeson from Rochester.

"George, what business are you in?" he asked from the pulpit.

Mr. Robeson smiled. "The cutlery."

"How was business this year?"

"Very good."

"Then the Lord and I will put you down for five hundred dollars."

The congregation laughed, including the man who had been put on the spot. The Reverend Henry van Dyke called on every wealthy friend in the church that morning and raised enough money to make its repairs and lift the mortgage.

In the middle of the season Mr. and Mrs. Robert Bradley arrived. He was as proud as Punch at the way the inn looked

and at the clientele we had. He hadn't been with us long before my troubles commenced.

The roosters kept him awake at night. Now any self-
respecting Florida rooster crows all night, particularly if there
is moonlight. All would be quiet and peaceful when some old
Langshan cock would throw back his head and proclaim to
the world that he was head man of his flock. Immediately he
would be answered by his feathered brethren all up and down
the island. A crowing contest would last a good half-hour and
quiet down only to start all over again.

The first night Mr. Bradley was there he phoned my room
about 1:30 A.M. and told me to stop those damn roosters so
he could get some sleep! Of course there wasn't anything I
could do about it then. I couldn't run around in the dark from
coop to coop all over the island shushing roosters!

When he came down next morning he really blistered me.
The fact that it wasn't my fault didn't make the slightest difference. After he had gone in to breakfast I took one hundred dollars out of the cash drawer, jumped on my bicycle,
and started around the island buying roosters. I gave the owners five dollars for each if they would kill it in my presence;
then I gave the rooster back to its owner for the pot.

An old cracker woman who lived across the road had a big
light Brahma rooster with a voice like a foghorn and she
wouldn't kill him. She said, "Old man Bradley and all the rest
of them highfalutin hotel people don't have money enough to
get me to kill my rooster!"

I knew if I didn't get that rooster out of the way before
night, and he opened his big mouth, I might as well start walking over the trestle, because I would be out of a job. Robert
Bradley didn't tell you but once! After a while I hit upon an
idea. I told the lady I would have a coop built and give her
five dollars a month if she would keep the rooster in this coop
every night, to which she agreed.

The hotel carpenter built a coop just high enough to hold

the old rooster, but every time he tried to throw back his head to crow he banged his head on the top of the coop and let out a surprised squawk.

When I got back to the hotel I rushed in to tell Mr. Bradley that I had the rooster situation all straightened out. I thought he would be pleased; instead, he started taking the hide off me because his dishes were cold at breakfast and that the one thing he wanted was hot dishes. So I rushed out and had a conference with the headwaitress and the chef, to guarantee Robert Bradley's dishes being hot from then on.

That noon I was eating lunch when Mr. Bradley came into the dining room. The captain signaled Mr. Bradley's waitress and the place plates and silver were in order by the time he was seated. When Mr. Bradley's lunch was served he was conversing with some friends and absent-mindedly picked up his knife and fork. He dropped them with a startled exclamation. The crew had put his silver and dishes in the oven. He wanted them hot and, believe me, he got them red hot!

That night he phoned me that there was a spider in his room. There was, too, a great big Florida house spider, like the one I had dangled before Mr. Edison's nose. It was perfectly harmless, and old-timers in Florida like to have spiders in the room, as they live on mosquitoes and all kinds of bugs.

Robert Bradley didn't feel that way. He wanted the spider killed, so we got a couple of bellboys with brooms and they had quite a chase before they killed it. In fact, they had to move half the furniture in the room. Mr. Bradley gave each one of them a dollar. That was a mistake.

The next night there was another spider in his room, and the boys had to go through the whole procedure again. The third morning I found one of the bellboys under the baggage room trying to catch a big live spider, and I caught on. I had to break up their racket. Every one of those spiders was good for a dollar tip!

Mr. Bradley had told me that he would make a hotel man of me and he was doing it the hard way, but I will be eternally grateful to him! I was learning that a hotel man who knew even the slightest fraction more about his job than the average would always be in great demand.

The Gasparilla Inn was especially difficult to operate because many of the guests were tarpon fishermen, who fished Boca Grande Pass and on the tides. They were going out and coming in all times of the day and night and had to have early breakfasts, late suppers, and lunches to take out; as we only had one crew, this meant tremendously long hours for everyone.

We had about twenty guides and they all owned good boats. There were Mac Mickle, Captain Able, Lee Hickock, Ben Smith, and others. Once in a while, on a moonlight night, I would run down to the Pass for an hour or two in a little Gloucester dory with a one-lung engine that belonged to the hotel. Sometimes I managed a short trip with Steve on his yacht.

The Pass was about a mile wide and lay between the Gulf of Mexico and Charlotte Harbor. It was a wonderful sight when off across the pass thirty or forty little white cruisers rode with the tide, their riding lights twinkling over the water. They drifted in for two or three miles on the incoming tide, and then would "hook up" their motors and start out through the Pass again. Soon the whole fleet was headed for the Gulf, and when they were outside they would kill their motors and drift back through the Pass.

When someone hooked a fish, there was plenty of excitement. All the nearby boats got out of the way immediately to give the lucky sportsman plenty of room. Sometimes two or three boats hooked fish simultaneously and then things really happened! The sight of the great tarpon leaping like silver meteors in the moonlight and the encouraging cries of the sportsmen from nearby boats were an unforgettable experience and one that paid for all the dreary waiting and the infinite patience necessary to the sport.

Of course the tyros brought their catches in to be weighed, photographed, and admired, but the old-timers simply took a couple of measurements and turned them loose.

We organized a fishing club among the inn guests called the Pelican Club, and gave buttons and prizes to those who brought in the largest catch. We built a clubroom and scoured the island for trophies to decorate the walls. Someone got hold of an old pirate map, so we built a cofferdam at little Gasparilla Pass and dug for private treasure. We went down to the Ten Thousand Islands, the last retreat of the buccaneers, to try to find John Gómez, known as "Panther Key John, the Last of the Pirates," who was reputed to be one hundred and sixteen years old and had come to the islands as José Gasparilla's cabin boy. He had been living there, working his little farm, for almost a century. But we found no trace of him.

Someone has said, "When fishermen tell the truth, they do it well!" By the same token, when they held postmortems in the evening in the "Pelican Room," they expected, and received, a credulity from their fellow sportsmen they never would have been granted by the uninitiated. This made for good fellowship and was part of the inn's stock in trade.

Those were wonderful days at Boca Grande. Sometimes I'd go out on the pilot boat with Kingsmore Johnson, almost out of sight of land, where he'd board some big vessel and bring her in over the bar. The immigration officers intercepted Chinamen being smuggled illegally, and the story goes that on one ship that came in to Boca Grande Pass the engine-room crew had about a dozen Chinese hidden in an empty water tank, and when the quarantine boat came alongside one of the crew got panicky and turned on the valve and filled the tank with water.

A little Spaniard named Manuel was smuggling *aguardiente* from Cuba into Boca Grande, and probably taking back some other kind of contraband. Steve was always deviling me to fix it so that he could go on one of these smuggling trips, so I contacted a friend of Manuel, who agreed to take Steve for one hundred dollars cash, paid in advance.

Steve was smuggled aboard Manuel's sloop at evening and sat around drinking aguardiente and playing poker all night with Manuel and his crew. When I went down to the dock the next morning, Manuel and his boat had pulled out, but Steve was laid out on the dock in state with his hands crossed on his chest and his head resting on a life preserver. The guides had been stepping over him all morning. That aguardiente certainly was potent! When Steve finally came to, he insisted that he was in Cuba, until he rolled over and saw his yacht lying in the lagoon.

The guides were always giving us a laugh. One of the colored boys, cleaning up after a fancy-dress party, found a battered silk hat. When he started for home after work he put it on and strutted past the guides' quarters when one of them shot it off his head. Another was suspected of smuggling aguardiente, and one afternoon he boarded a train for South Boca Grande with a large suitcase. A deputy sheriff boarded the train also and when the train pulled out he insisted the guide open up the suitcase. After some argument he did, and a seven-foot black snake whipped out of the box and up and down the aisle. Anyone who knows how fast a Florida black snake can travel can imagine the riot it caused on the train.

About this time the three-day Gasparilla Carnival was originated over in Tampa to re-enact the capture of the city by Gasparilla and his pirate band. Since we lived on the island where the pirate had actually held forth, we decided to join the fun. We had a band at Boca Grande, made up of company employees, guides, fishermen, and anyone else who could play an instrument, including myself. We hired a C. H. & N. daycoach, hung big signs, "Gasparilla's Pirate Band, Boca Grande, Florida," on each side, and started for Tampa. Our costumes were pirate garb, complete with mustaches, bandannas, three-cornered hats, and red sashes.

Steve took a crowd on the *Caprice* and tied her to the dock in front of the Tampa Bay Hotel, so as to have a front seat when Gasparilla's ship came up the river. The entire city was decked out in gay bunting and imbued with a holiday spirit of carefree hospitality.

The center of much of the festivities was the Tampa Bay Hotel, operated by Father's old friend Fred Adams. He was one of our top-flight New Hampshire resort operators, a spry and nervous man, always poking into every nook and cranny of any hotel he was running and trying to supervise every detail of food and service.

As I knew Fred would be busy with many big functions during the carnival, I went to the hotel as soon as I arrived to see if I could give him a hand. He was buzzing around like a gadfly, greeting guests and stringing out orders. When I caught up with him he was in the kitchen having a hot argument with a young chef by the name of Jimmie Gavins, who was fast on his way to making a nationwide reputation.

It seems there had been a fire in a wholesale grocery warehouse in Tampa, and Fred, whose Yankee blood couldn't resist a bargain whether it was needed or not, had bought a lot of canned goods that were perfectly all right except that all their labels had been burned off. Since the hotel was feeding about fifteen hundred people each meal and serving many private luncheons, dinner parties, and late suppers, Fred thought this would be a wonderful time to use up all the canned goods. He was hovering around trying to be helpful and of course Jimmie was fit to be tied.

In about twenty minutes the dining-room doors would open for lunch, and everyone was rushing around the kitchen trying to make the deadline. Jimmie was opening one can after another. He couldn't tell what a can contained until he opened it. Just as I came in he blew up.

"You get out of this kitchen and don't come back till I ask you! How the hell do you think I'm going to make succotash out of applesauce and beets?"

Jimmie kept his boss out of the kitchen all through carnival week.

How hard those old-time resort crews worked during a critical time such as this, when the hotel was filled with seasonal guests and there were hundreds of extra meals to prepare! Pride of accomplishment, loyalty, and enthusiasm for a job well done made them put it over.

The pirate parade stretched up Tampa's main avenue—beautiful floats adorned with gorgeous girls, Spanish dons on horseback, pirates in ships, and marching bands.

Our Boca Grande band rode the replica of an old pirate ship mounted on a large truck. Also aboard with us was a case of beer. The ship was not anchored securely, and every time the parade halted, the ship rocked and threw us out of our seats, nearly knocked our teeth out, and drove our mouthpieces down our throats.

It was hot, and the Tampa population on the sidewalks were perspiring in the sun, and we started sampling the beer. Never having touched a drink before, two bottles really put me on the beam. Soon the parade took on the enchantment of a majestic pageant, and the tunes we played all sounded the same. I thought I was doing some fancy stuff on the alto horn until I discovered that someone had poured a bottle of beer into the bell and it had creamed over the top.

When the parade ended we were on our own, and the band members agreed to meet at the railroad station at two o'clock in the morning to return to Boca Grande.

What a relief to get aboard the *Caprice* and take off that

pirate outfit! I took a cold shower, put on a linen suit, and came up on deck. Steve was lounging in a deck chair with a highball in his hand. We grinned at each other. The evening was ahead.

We had all Tampa to choose from. The social life was very gay, and Steve and I knew enough people to be invited to many of the social functions—Bill and Penn Taliaferro, Todd and Collins Gillette, and Percy Culberth, who often came to Boca Grande as agents for foreign ships. We attended a large dance at the Tampa Bay Hotel and dropped in on other affairs, and along toward two met the Boca Grande boys at the station. Our private train was about to leave.

Some of the construction gang who had come up with us were missing.

We piled into a cab and went looking for them "down the line." There was a red-light district in Ybor City running wide open, and when I knocked at the first door and a woman opened the door a crack I asked: "Are any of the Boca Grande boys in here?"

The woman yelled, "My God! More of that wild gang from Boca Grande? The girls is all busy," and slammed the door in our faces.

We went to the Melville Club. In the large reception room was a player piano that was played by putting quarters in the slot. The close air held a mixture of stale beer, cigarette smoke, and cheap perfume. A doorway opened on an elegantly furnished bedroom, with the largest double bed I ever saw. It had a white satin counterpane and dozens of lace-covered pillows garnished with little white ribbon bows.

It struck Steve and me so funny that we howled.

The girls were young and wore evening gowns. One dazzling brunette looked familiar. Her transparent olive skin held a warm glow, her dark hair fell in heavy waves below her shoulders, and about her was a warmth of suggestiveness and a promise of fulfillment. She was more richly gowned than the other girls and stood out among them like an orchid in a bowl of field daisies. She was completely lovely.

She saw me staring, and came up to me.

"Don't you remember me?" she asked softly. "I'm Rickey —from the Alcazar!"

I tell you that girl was *quality!* Yes, I remembered her and the stir she and her millionaire husband had created when they arrived on their palatial yacht and occupied the bridal suite at the Alcazar Hotel. She had everything—wealth, social position, a fine husband.

"What are you doing here?" I managed to gasp.

She tossed her head. "This is where I want to be and where I always knew I would end up. Polite society bores the hell out of me. I'm a bad woman!"

The boys from Boca Grande were not there, so we drifted down to Hilda Raymond's. This was the largest and finest "house" in the district. There were a number of large automobiles parked out in front and the atmosphere was more refined—if one may use the term. I was surprised by the loveliness and amiability of the girls—they seemed no different from any other gathering of young ladies. The Boca Grande contingent was not there and we had no time to waste. We needed those men on the island.

We walked on down the street in the soft Florida evening. There was a glow of red above the entrance of the houses and the subdued tinkle of pianos and faint laughter. The night seemed mysterious, wicked, and intriguing.

As we approached the more disreputable "dollar houses" the sidewalks gave way to dusty paths and dilapidated single-story frame houses, their sordid surroundings softened by darkness. Suddenly a door burst open and a shaft of light stabbed the darkness. There was the sound of angry voices, and a group of men barged out. Against the light I recognized the fellows we were looking for—the bridge gang from Pacida and a couple of cowboys from Nocatee.

There was a noisy argument—one of the party was still in the house and they wanted to go back and get him. This met with shrill protest from the women inside. As the boys stormed back we crowded in behind them. "Big John," one of the foremen, who weighed more than two hundred pounds, was inside dead drunk.

How to get him to the station! The boys ripped out a bathtub, laid Big John in it, and everybody took hold and started marching down the street. Someone came out of a side street with a trumpet under his arm, joined the procession, and started to play "After You're Gone." A block farther along an alto and a slide trombone picked it up. This was getting to be some procession! About this time a big Tampa cop standing on a corner drawled in a pleasant voice, "You boys are sure having a high time. You'd better break it up and go on back to Boca Grande."

There was no argument. Tampa cops were pleasant dynamite, as the boys well knew. We rounded up some taxis and got back to the train.

Not everything that happened at Gasparilla Inn was amusing. Sometimes disaster threatened. One afternoon the barometer dropped and by evening the wind was blowing hell's bells. The surf was tremendous, and the tide rose alarmingly over the island. We put the guests and help aboard a train with the engine steamed up, ready to leave at any moment. This allayed all fears, and everyone accepted the emergency as a gala occasion and sang and played games in the cars. Then one of the guides came and whispered in my ear that two miles of track had been washed into Charlotte Harbor.

We couldn't get off the island now if we wanted to.

Here was a case where ignorance is bliss. The guests and crew went on playing games and singing and no one else on the train knew about this danger until all was over.

Sometimes tragedy struck at Boca Grande. People died and

I had to measure them for a coffin. The nearest undertaker was in Arcadia, and when he came down he brought the casket with him. Sometimes we had a doctor, oftener we had none.

That first season I was confronted with a crisis. Just before dark one afternoon a large yacht arrived and cast anchor in the bay behind the hotel. The weather had been cold and rainy for a couple of days and was getting worse.

I was sitting in my private office when the owner of the yacht walked in. He was a great financier and a nationally prominent figure. When he introduced himself, I was very much impressed. He bit the end off a cigar, lighted it, and came straight to the point.

"Abbott," he said, "I've been cruising down in the islands. I have my daughter on board. She is eighteen years old and a very sick girl. I want to get her in the hotel as quickly as possible and get a doctor."

I said regretfully, "There is no doctor here now; I doubt if we can get one from Fort Myers before tomorrow noon in this weather. The quickest thing would be to put her on the train going up after lunch tomorrow and send her to the hospital in Arcadia."

He agreed that that would be best. "In the meantime," he said, "we'll bring her to the hotel and make her comfortable."

As gently as I could I said: "I'm willing to do anything I can to help you, but you can't bring that girl into the hotel. I am on this island with hundreds of guests and employees. Some of the guests have children. We have no doctor and I do not know what is wrong with your daughter. You will have to keep her on the yacht."

He flew into a terrible rage. He accused me of being inhuman and without sympathy. After a terrific tirade he stormed out of my office uttering dire threats.

He knew nearly all the guests in the inn. In a short time I was visited by a group of sixteen guests, who had signed a round robin demanding that I bring the young lady at once to the hotel.

To get the picture clearly—this angry group of men crowded around my desk represented a tremendous amount of prestige and power. Each was the head of some large organization and was accustomed to having every order carried out without question. There was no softness in their demand that the young lady be brought from the yacht at once, with no more foolishness on my part!

This was a tight spot, and one which only courage and cool thinking could get me through. There was but one way to deal with men like these, and I took it without hesitation. I looked one after the other straight in the eye.

"Gentlemen, I want you to understand my position. I have been sent down here to operate this hotel. It is a position of trust. I have the responsibility of all my guests and their families as well as my employees. I'll not have the young lady here."

The man nearest me growled: "The hell you'll not!"

I retorted, "Exactly! I have twenty guides down at the guide house. I've known them all since childhood. I've a good crew in the powerhouse and plenty of other huskies in the kitchen. Every one of these men will do exactly what I ask. Push me too far and I'll have them lock all of you in your rooms. I'm doing only what I think is right, so get out and let me work this out as best I can!"

You can imagine the frame of mind in which they left.

The next twenty-four hours were as long and ugly as any I have known. Not one of the guests spoke to me. Many of the employees sided with them, and there was an air of indignation and hostility throughout the hotel.

We got the young lady a drawing room on the noon train the next day and within four hours she was in the hospital in Arcadia. It was an anxious wait for me until about six that evening a boy brought a telegram to my desk. It was from the country physician, stating that if the young lady had been in the inn he was declaring an immediate quarantine, as she had a virulent form of diphtheria.

I walked out into the lobby and with shaking fingers pinned the telegram to the bulletin board. Then I went back to my office, sat down, and laid my head in my arms. The relief was so great it left me dizzy. A few minutes later someone knocked, the door opened, and in filed the same group of guests. I give them credit, they were all there.

One of them said, "Karl, you were right. My God, I have four children here. What might have happened if you had let this sick girl into the hotel?"

Another spoke up. "I would have been in a fine pickle if I had been quarantined on this island with my annual board meeting coming up next week in New York."

One by one each member of the group apologized.

It was a lesson to me. It taught me that there are times when a crisis rises and to be worth his salt a man has to meet it without fear of consequences.

Up to now my life had been carefree. But about two-thirty one morning in March I was awakened from sleep to see the form of old man Batty standing at the foot of my bed. He had come over from Fort Myers in a fast motorboat. The night was bitter cold for Florida, with a strong wind blowing, and he looked pinched with cold. He told me that Mother was desperately ill and he had come for me. How that wonderful old man took his motorboat across Charlotte Harbor and through the long, narrow reaches of Matlacha Pass in the pitch-black night, skirting oyster bars by a matter of inches, I've never been able to understand. Dawn found us on the broad expanse of the Caloosahatchee River and we arrived at Fort Myers soon after sunup, but we were too late.

Father and I started the long trek to the White Mountains to take her home. During the years that I had gone North and South with my parents as a child I had often heard Mother say, "Frank, there will be a last time." And this was the last time for her! Somehow I felt that after the many years of traveling back and forth that she would be at peace in the little mountain cemetery under its deep blanket of snow.

That spring Father sold his lease at the Royal Palm Hotel to Barnett and Parent of the Martinique Hotel, New York.

Hereafter he would be with me, summers in the mountains, winters at Boca Grande. I went back to Gasparilla Inn to close it for the season. More than ever before, at the end of a hotel year, I wanted to get away. Steve was still there. We decided to take the *Caprice* and idle down the mangrove coast for a month, fishing for tarpon in the Ten Thousand Islands.

WE BROUGHT the *Caprice* to the Ten Thousand Islands, the largest mangrove plantation in the Northern Hemisphere, extending down Florida's coast for miles and interlaced with a veritable labyrinth of waterways where none but native fishermen and Indians could go without getting hopelessly lost around the first bend.

Besides the captain and the crew we had with us two fishing guides. They had worked for Father at the Royal Palm and I had known them all my life. So we were four close friends off on a holiday, and the work was share and share alike between us.

We had with us a couple of flatbottomed skiffs that drew very little water, so we could get up into the shallows.

Steve and I had been night fishing and were asleep below when we ran up Shark River as far as the *Caprice* could go. When we came on deck for breakfast the broad gray-green river stretched away through dense growths of dark green mangrove with roots like grasping terra-cotta fingers to which great clusters of oysters clung. We knocked off a peck, and they were delicious.

We loafed through the day and amused ourselves casting for ladyfish off the stern of the *Caprice*. These little silver streaks of dynamite are like miniature tarpon, though larger and slimmer, and put on a great show.

In the two skiffs the next day the two guides, Steve, and I, started on an exploration up through Tarpon Bay, fly-fishing for small tarpon. In the skiffs were blankets, mosquito netting, camp utensils, axes, a rifle, food, and fishing tackle.

We entered the Everglades by a narrow river, went to the very end, and camped that night in a thicket of cypress. We could go no farther. There were several inches of water underfoot, so we cut down small cypresses and built two platforms, cooking and eating on one, sleeping on the other. With darkness the mosquitoes arrived in clouds and we gave up, doused the fire, and crawled in under our mosquito bars.

I lay on my hard bed of cypress logs, looking up into myriad stars that seemed to shimmer just above the treetops. Steve and the guides were sleeping the sleep of utter exhaustion. But sleep was not for me. It was all too wonderful! Too exciting! This enchanted land of the Everglades, called by the Indians "Pa-hay-okee," or grassy waters, was a great primeval swamp, or rather a sea of floating grassy islands—islands of hyacinths and water plants dotted with hammocks and stands of stunted cypress.

At sundown on the mangrove coast a quiet hush prevails. Not a leaf moves, and from the depths of the jungle comes a quiet that one can feel. Great birds glide into the treetops on silent wings, and not even the breaking of a twig betrays a single wild creature astir. But when darkness falls, as it does in the semi-tropics, like a great black blanket enveloping the world, the stillness is rent by the scream of a great panther cat, or the bellow of a bull alligator on some far-distant point, and the jungle comes alive!

The scent of wet bodies mingled with the smell of kerosene, with which we had soaked our clothing to keep off red bugs. The air was heavy with the smell of rotting vegetation.

Under it all was the dread ground-swell humming of the innumerable mosquitoes that meant certain death for one caught unprepared.

Mist seeped through the trees from the waterway, blotting out the stars, and dew fell from the branches like reluctant rain, to rise again to meet the fog.

One of Jack London's characters came out of his blankets every morning with the cry of "Burning daylight." And so did Steve!

A sharp warning from one of the guides stopped him as he started out from under the mosquito bar. The guide pointed to a purple plume of smoke that rose above us through the uppermost branches, undulating gently in the breeze—mosquitoes following our body scent.

The first slanting rays of the yellow rising sun glinted through the trees and the mosquitoes disappeared. We slid from beneath our mosquito bars and sloshed over to the other platform and prepared breakfast.

As we were drinking our second cup of coffee a dugout canoe paddled by an Indian, with a white man in the bow, glided noiselessly up the little waterway. We waved a friendly greeting and invited them into camp. The white man was a "plume hunter," which he readily admitted, as he knew the guides and they vouched for us. The dark eyes of the Indian lit up when I told him that I was an old friend of Stanley Hansen and had known John Brown, the old Indian trader.

Over coffee the plume hunter told us how the birds were slaughtered, shot off the nests, or caught with copper-wire snares. The nuptial plumes brought fabulous prices. A guide could make as much money in a week on the rookeries as he could pulling at the oars of a fishing boat all winter, so the temptation was great. He told of the bloody work of cutting the feathers and plumes out of the backs of the birds, and of the hawks and buzzards and crows feasting on the young at sundown. It made me sick!

The vanity of American women for three generations had made devastating inroads into the birdlife of south Florida. Hats in the fashionable millinery shops along Fifth Avenue, and their counterparts throughout the nation, sported all manner of plumes, feathers, and tiny stuffed highly colored birds.

Ornithologists and bird lovers had raised a feeble hue and

cry from time to time against this slaughter, and the Florida Legislature had passed laws against it, but the wily plume hunters were a law unto themselves.

This pair knew the jungle waterways as other men know their neighborhoods.

Steve was wild to venture farther into the Glades, and it was a golden adventure for me. We had been unable to go because there was no one to guide us; but now good luck and generous cash considerations all around settled that.

We could not proceed farther with the skiffs, so we loaded the dugout with the barest necessities, and with the Indian leading the way crossed a few yards of muddy slough and came out on yet another fresh-water lagoon that meandered in and out through the trees and saw grass.

The day was breathless. The sun blazed down on the water and blinked off through the saw grass. We skirted great hummocks engulfed with trees and throttled with vines and the strangler fig. Far off to the westward green masses of mangrove marched along the horizon. We came to the end of the waterway and there seemed no way out, but a sharp turn under a great overhanging bough brought us into yet another, and so on and on and on. In the cypress trees at the edge of these fresh-water lagoons were nests of great blue heron ("Poor Joe" to the Florida cracker) and other half-dead trees, their trunks splashed with white killing guano, held hundreds of cormorant nests.

Water turkeys flapped off stumps in hysterical haste, their snakelike necks stretched forward, wings beating wildly on the water before they got under way. They disappeared around the bend and circled back over our heads, flying down in the waterway with great speed, their glossy bodies glistening in the sun.

Marsh hawks and the great red-shouldered hawks sailed in lazy circles just over the top of the grass in their persistent quest for frogs and mice. Swallow-tailed kites, usually in pairs darted and swooped gracefully, drifting on the air currents. Flocks of Florida crows flew lazily by, their soft-voiced cawing subdued in contrast to the raucous voices of their northern cousins. Huge black vultures, their ragged wing tips silhouetted against the blue, never seemed quite able to attain the great heights of the buzzards in the sky above.

The Indian silently poled the dugout through a long green tunnel of overhanging branches interlaced with vines that blotted out the sky so that not a single ray of the probing sun filtered through. The Indian said, "*Allapataw!*" and began a soft grunting call. A huge alligator, at least fourteen feet long, slid off the bank and swam out into the stream. He was all but invisible in the brown water, and only the tip of his round snout, his two eyes, and the tip of his tail showed above the surface.

Otters slithered down their slides and cavorted in the water. The courageous little otter has always seemed to me to be nature's clown and possessed of a rare sense of humor. Like the northern mink, he is the busybody of the wilds, always sticking his nose into other people's business, and knows the jungle gossip for miles around. He fears nothing, not even the great alligators, and flashes by them in the water kicking spray in their faces as if to say, "Catch me if you can."

We watched the otters as they romped and frolicked, their long, lithe bodies undulating. They swam on their backs or, treading water, stood up in midstream and looked at us with shiny black shoebutton eyes, eager and inquisitive.

We came out of this world of leaves into the blinding midday sun and a veritable domain of birds. Coots and ducks paddled sedately through the rushes, and gray clouds of sandpipers lifted from the meadows. Black man-of-war or frigate birds, one of the most marvelous fliers in the world, with a wingspread of more than seven feet, swept in from the sea; high in the heavens they looked like graceful black swallows flying without perceptible wing motion.

Long, wavering lines of white ibis, weaving up and down like a white roller coaster, passed us and disappeared across the dim horizon. Big black-and-white wood ibis, like storks right out of Hans Christian Andersen, flew in, making teetering landings in the treetops. A pair of osprey were fishing in a cypress pool where our Indian guide turned the bow of our dugout and we landed on a sandy beach to "boil the kettle" for lunch.

The sand was covered with the little handlike raccoon tracks and a deer path led off through the saw grass. A caracara (Mexican hawk) sat on a nearby stump and blinked its eyes at us. While gathering wood for the fire the Indian ran onto an alligator's nest—a large mound of wet grass and rotting water plants—and uncovered a couple dozen of its oblong-shaped eggs.

The savory smell of frying bacon and filet from a small snook Steve had caught plug-casting in the shallows whetted our appetites to a ravenous edge.

I took a nap and was awakened by the sound of the wind sighing through the saw grass, the rumble of distant thunder, and the roar and crash of a sudden downpour. The spring rains had begun. The deluge swept over us, blotting out the landscape, drenching us to the skin, The squall passed off to the westward as suddenly as it had come, whipping the surface of the lagoons to a frothy spume. The sun blazed out again.

As near as I could figure, we were in the upper tributaries of White Water Bay as, according to the sun, we had been traveling south for a long time. Sometimes, standing up in the canoe, I could look out over a thousand square miles of saw grass. I shuddered to think what would become of us in this great morass if anything happened to our guide! As the dugout had only a few inches free board and was none too steady, Steve called it a "trust in God," an old "Geechee" saying from up Charleston way.

One afternoon we went up a river alive with fish and

camped on a sandy windswept point away from the mosquitoes. It was hard by a great hammock that our guide told us
was his favorite spot for alligator hunting. We built a fire and
I fried some "hush puppies," those toothsome little patties of
corn meal and onions, crisp and palatable, that are so dear to
a cracker's heart. Father was fond of them and told me the
first time he ever ate any was when he and several friends
sailed down the Indian River in a catboat in the early eighties.

We lazed around the fire, and our native guide regaled us
with local legends. He told us of two plume hunters who got
drunk on aguardiente and lay out in their skiff all night and
were killed by the mosquitoes. He chuckled at the story of
the two white men who were hunting in the Glades with his
cousin. At noon they camped on the shore of a grassy little
pond. The water was crystal-clear and the men decided to
go in swimming. They asked the Indian if there were any
alligators in the pond and he replied, "No alligators." So they
waded out. A long, sinewy shape glided toward them and they
rushed in panic to the shore. One shouted, "I thought you
said there were no alligators in here?" The guide grunted,
"He no alligator, he crocodile."

He told us of the great black panthers in the hammocks
near by whose skins were the prize-winning trophies of the
young braves, of the "green corn dance" and the "hunting
dance" of the harvest moon, and the belief of his people as
to the creation of the world. The first peoples, he said, were
raised from seed scattered by the Almighty in a great and
fertile valley that was bisected by a river; and how many of
them went down to the river and washed until they were
white and weak; and how others who, because they did not
wash so long, were bronze and strong, and were Indians; and
then of still others who were lazy and would not wash at all
and remained black, and were Negroes.

Steve was planning an alligator hunt. I had hunted 'gators
at night in my boyhood and I knew what a kick he was going

to get out of it. The Seminole stepped into the brush and came back with a wire fire basket attached to a pole that he had cached in the hammocks, and set it up in the bow of the dugout.

We knew the mosquitoes would be unbearable, so although the night was hot we took our hunting jackets and each of us tied a scarf around his neck so he could pull it up over his nose and mouth to keep from actually inhaling the insects. The Indian was impervious to them.

We chopped some dry wood into chips, filling the fire basket to overflowing, and put a pile in the bow so that we could replenish the fire from time to time. Finally we pushed off, and it was uncanny to see the way the Indian threaded the labyrinth of waterways in the darkness. We seemed to glide through black nothingness between earth and sky.

For a time we drifted. Then the Indian whispered, "Now, light fire." Steve lighted the torch. The flames leaped up, turning the surface of the water into a black mirror. All about us were eyes—pairs of little eyes close together; big eyes far apart; red, angry, blazing eyes glaring in the firelight! They winked and blinked, disappearing and reappearing, like red coals. Alligators lay on the surface as thick as logs, their deep, throaty hissings and horrid bellowings, as they fought among themselves, turning the night into a primeval nightmare. It was dangerous business floating in a "trust in God" on the darkened lagoon surrounded by thousands of giant reptiles. A cold chill ran down my back as I contemplated what could happen.

Mosquitoes, attracted by the light, descended in clouds, almost extinguishing the fire in our dugout.

A crash of gunfire shattered the night! Ahead of us the surface was lashed to a foam by the mortal writhings of an ancient leviathan. Steve had hit a grandfather 'gator smack between the eyes! He shot only two, as we had no need for more. We wanted to procure a couple of extra-large skins for trophies. Then we returned to camp. No use looking for the dead 'gators for a few days, as it would take some time before their bodies rose to the surface where we could find them and skin out the hides.

Several days later I left my feather-weight hunting jacket over a stump, and then I slipped it on without giving it a thorough shaking. I should have known better! Three cute little lobsterlike scorpions—two in the collar and one in the sleeve—bit me on the back of the neck and on the left hand. I was sick all night.

In a day or two it was plain that the bites had become infected, so we started back to the *Caprice*. In another twenty-four hours the swelling was terrific, and I insisted that Steve open up my neck and hand with a razor, which gave me almost instant relief and some scars to carry for the rest of my life.

When we got back where we had left the guides, we found one skiff and a note telling us that they had gone for food. Steve and I parted with our Indian friend and began the long row back. I could row with only one hand.

The banks were alive with moccasins; they lay twisted over the tree roots sunning themselves on the banks. As we passed under a great limb that reached out over the water, one of these—about six feet long—slid off the bough and fell into the bottom of our skiff. Steve and I were both barefooted. Before Steve thought what he was doing, he grabbed the ax and cut off the snake's head with a well-aimed blow. He also cut a hole in the bottom of the skiff which, no matter how we tried to plug it, let in a considerable amount of water, so that by the time we got to the *Caprice* both of us were pretty well tuckered out.

We needed a bath, food, sleep, and some clean sea air, so the captain got the *Caprice* under way and we started for the Keys. When we awoke the next morning we were at anchor in the beautiful harbor of Islamorada.

Here was fishing at its best. We cruised up and down the Keys for the next two weeks—the fishing was so good that we hardly took time out to sleep. We waded quietly in the shallows for bone fish, speared crawfish—those succulent Florida lobsters—using a light fish spear and a wooden bucket with a glass bottom through which we could locate our game. We gathered large conchs, the meat of which, after being well pounded, makes delicious sea-food patties.

We went outside to the banks and the stream and trolled for everything from sailfish to grouper. They were all there and all hungry—amberjack, barracuda, kingfish, wahoo, and all the finny tribe.

We drifted over the big reefs and our gaze followed the sunshine down into the inverted jungle of a marine fairyland. Ocean growths of every hue, mingling with the coral, undulated gently in the current; highly colored fish, singly or in schools, swam through a luminous blue in which huge jellyfish lay suspended. There seemed to be an unending variety: parrot fish, crimson and jade; many varieties of grouper; African pompano; black angelfish; brightly colored red snappers; and many more.

We trolled along old railroad trestles for tarpon on moonlight nights and ate midnight lunches on pale silvery beaches that were almost crowded into the water by tropical growth. A million moonflowers shimmered in the night. Now and then a crocodile coughed in the jungle at our backs and a big loggerhead turtle trundled off the beach, swimming away in a glow of phosphorescent fire. It was a lotus land, and though I had to leave it, I knew I would return whenever I could.

There are no lotus blooms in a hotel lobby. I had to get back to work.

Chapter Nine: FIRST LINK

AFTER the Everglades trip I arrived home in an automobile bought in Boston. It was the first car any member of our family had ever owned, and strange to say it was an Abbott. I brought it up into the White Mountains with only a few miles of driving experience, and when I pulled up before the hotel stables I had to do some fast talking to convince Father that I had not lost my mind.

By knocking out the stalls, we converted the stables into a garage, and the buggies, surreys, and spring wagons were soon replaced by Hupmobiles, "flivvers," and Stanley Steamers. Our old horse, Dennis, was retired to a farm Father owned back in the hills, where he lived to a ripe old age, a respected member of the family to the end.

Another change at this time was a habit of referring to motion pictures as "movies." One warm evening after the hotel opened "Doc" Clark and I were stretched out on the lawn above Main Street bewailing the fact that Bethlehem had only one small and slightly primitive theater. The vacant lot across the street at which I happened to be looking suddenly took on a vision—before my eyes rose a modern movie house with electrically lighted marquee.

I reared up and pointed. "Doc, let's build a theater on that lot!"

Back of Hen Smith's drugstore we found some old boards,

and we painted a sign that we stuck up that night on the vacant lot. It read:

THE COLONIAL THEATER
Will Open Here
July 1, 1915
Abbott and Clark, Owners

By the time we had our sign painted it was about half-past three in the morning. Going home, I cut across a field of new-mown hay and lay down on one of the haycocks to dream about our new venture. The next I knew, the bright sun was in my eyes and the newsboy was coming up to the hotel with the morning papers. I took one, and sat in the hay pile in the hot sun reading the big black headlines in the New York *Tribune* that told what had happened in Europe the day before:

AUSTRIA DECLARES WAR.

It was July 29, 1914.

I read without much interest that Austria was rushing a vast army into Serbia and Russia was massing 80,000 men on her border. On the hotel piazza early-rising guests were rocking and reading the same news. No one paid much attention to it at first. Some of those crazy European countries were starting another of their comic-opera wars. What had that to do with us in Bethlehem, New Hampshire?

No one realized that our snug security was tumbling about our ears and that this July headline heralded the beginning of an era that would put a violent end to the peaceful living we had known.

Headlines followed headlines. Great Britain issued her ultimatum.

I remember T. C. Taliaferro, the Tampa banker, standing by the desk of Upland Terrace in conversation with Father and E. M. Statler, the hotel man, who was our regular guest for so many years, and Taliaferro was proclaiming fiercely: "This will end it! England will sweep the seas in ninety days!"

That spring "Doc" Clark and I completed the Colonial Theater. It took all our cash and a lot of slow notes, so we thought we might as well go overboard on pictures. We bought an all-Paramount program with picture changes daily, which policy we pursued all the years we ran the theater.

Doc and I took turns running the hand-driven machine and rewinding the films.

We played all the "firsts" as they came along, *Cabiria, Ben Hur, The Birth of a Nation.* It was my first venture outside of hotel business and exciting; besides, we made a handsome profit.

I was all steamed up by reports of the Panama-Pacific International Exposition in San Francisco, and when the season closed persuaded Father to take the trip with me. I had our tickets written the longest way out and the longest way home, and when they were handed to me, they were about five feet long. The trip was a wonderful blur of memories—Medicine Hat and the Rockies, Vancouver, Jack's in Seattle, hearing my first Hawaiian band playing "On the Beach at Waikiki," and our suite in the St. Francis Hotel in San Francisco where Father practically collapsed. He told me to go out and see the Exposition and not come back for a week.

I remember Father strolling up to the rim of the Grand Canyon.

"Gee, that's a big hole." Then as the tremendous scene grew upon him, "My God, that *is* a big hole! You could put the whole Presidential Range into it and never miss it!"

It was good, later, to have that trip to remember.

Father was sixty-five. He stayed in Bethlehem that fall in a little cottage near the closed hotel. One minute he was a tall, husky man, vital with life, and the next he was not expected to live. An acute heart attack left him unconscious for weeks. They sent for me, and when he opened his eyes his first words were: "What are you doing here? Don't you know you have a Florida hotel to run?"

We called in a nurse. "I hate taking these short cases," she said.

She was to be with him almost twenty-five years.

If he could only get to Florida, Father told me, he was convinced he could get well.

After weeks in the hospital we took him on a stretcher and put him aboard a southbound train. Twelve of our leading citizens were down at the station to see him off as a mark of special esteem—the president of the bank, leaders of local organizations, and so on. With the doctor, the little group comprised thirteen upstanding, healthy-looking men.

As the train pulled out one said regretfully: "There goes the last of Frank."

In Florida, Father was soon sitting up in a wheel chair. He lived to be nearly eighty-nine. He outlived every member of that group, including the doctor.

How he loved Boca Grande! Once I found him in his chair out in the open when the heat was terrific. "Aren't you hot in this sun?" I asked. "Don't you want to move back into the shade?"

He grinned up at me. "Son, after thirty years in a pung sleigh in New Hampshire, do you think these old bones will ever get warm?"

It was the end, for him, of active if not for mental living. From this time on the partnership consisted on his side of good advice and encouragement given from the vantage of a wheel chair.

Someone has said you know a nation's history by its songs. In 1916 we had a song, "I Didn't Raise My Boy to Be a Soldier," and a slogan, "He Kept Us out of War."

War was declared that year.

By 1917 we had food pledges, sugar slackers, beefless and wheatless days, and we sang "Over There," "Good-by, Broadway, Hello, France," and "How'ya Gonna Keep 'Em Down on the Farm After They've Seen Paree?" And 1917 saw the pioneering of the night clubs and Sophie Tucker's melodied "Some of These Days."

By 1918 we were singing "Dear Old Pal of Mine," and "Hello, Central, Give Me No Man's Land." November 11 was our first Armistice Day, celebrated in America's hotels in a fashion that began a trend of big hotel parties.

During the hectic war years I did what thousands of other young American men were doing: I joined the Navy. I got married.

The cycle continued after the war: North in the summer, South in the winter, head of a family now—new faces, personalities, scenes, events, interests. Monotony had no part in it. Memory jumps from high light to high light, with here and there memories that bring chuckles and others too poignant to recall.

I can see now, looking back, that the year 1918 was the dividing line in the American way. Nothing was the same as it had been before Armistice Day. The speeded tempo and sense of anxiety were new. Anything to escape reality! We listened to Eddie Cantor, the original Dixieland Band, Paul Whiteman, Ted Lewis, the Black and White Melody Boys, and on the screen, entranced, we watched the jerky emotings of Charlie Chaplin, Mary Pickford, Douglas Fairbanks, Sr., Wally Reed, Charles Ray, Lillian Gish, and Marguerite Clark.

Hotel men and hotel life changed.

The Armistice Day celebrations started an era of royal entertainment to the hotel profession by its members, and a keener rivalry. On December 19 "Oscar" gave a dinner to all hotel men, at the old Waldorf. "The dinner was, as usual, a masterpiece," one report ran, "Oscar having laid himself out to give the hotel men something they would long remember."

This was his menu, every dish piping hot or icy cold, as required, and faultlessly served:

Grapefruit

Chicken Gumbo à la Creole

Celery   Olives   Salted Almonds

Filet of Sea Bass   Lobster Sauce

Château Pacheteau Sauternes

Potatoes Parisienne

Mignon of Lamb Oporto

Château Pacheteau Lafitte

Green Peas Sautéed in Butter

Breast of Guinea Hen à la Tyrolienne

Hearts of Lettuce, French Dressing

Gold Seal Burt Vintage 1907

Paul Masson Vintage 1907

Paul Garrett Extra Dry

Fancy Ice Cream   Assorted Cakes

Coffee

Saratoga Geyser Water

Briarcliff Water

White Rock—Clymic

Perrier

H. Anton Bock & Co. Havana Cigars

Pall Mall Cigarettes

So a fabulous era of hotel entertaining began that was to reach its crescendo in the booming twenties.

The hotel operators and owners who were leaders in this dramatic era were not standardized. Chain hotel operation was something new under the sun. A hotel operator had to be prepared to make instant on-the-spot decisions involving $100,000 on his own authority. (A few more years and he would almost be obliged to call a board of directors meeting to buy half-a-dozen towels.)

Being in independent positions and having made a success of their hotels through their individual efforts, these men, like their hotels, were colorful. Most of the better hotels were noted for some particular advantage that no other hotel featured.

The hotel chains were in turn developed by the individual initiative of some leader in the industry, such as Ellsworth Statler.

Statler, to my mind the greatest of hotel men, was our guest for more than twenty years. He enjoyed his holidays in our hotels, where he had no responsibilities. No hotel man can relax in a hotel of his own. In Florida or New Hampshire, wherever we might be, he was a guest first of Father's, then mine. During those years I came to know him well and admire him greatly.

Statler was a dynamic little man with unbounded energy, and ability stuck out all over him. In his twenties he was a bellhop. In his thirties he owned a small basement restaurant in Buffalo, with a turnstile at the door and a sign, "All you can eat for twenty-five cents." In 1901 he built his first hotel, the Inside Inn, a three-story structure adjoining the fair grounds of the Pan-American Exposition in Buffalo. President McKinley's assassination during the Exposition ruined the celebration and Statler's business venture.

Three years later he built a temporary hotel on the grounds of the Saint Louis Exposition and made money with which, in 1908, he built the Buffalo Statler.

This was the first hotel in America to have a bath with every room. Circulating ice water, telephones, and a newspaper at every door each morning were innovations. He had two hundred and fifty people working for him. As I write this his company employs nine thousand members of one hundred and fifty different crafts, professions, and skills.

Other hotels followed rapidly—in 1911 the one-thousand-room Detroit Statler at a cost of $4,200,000; in 1912 the one-thousand-room Cleveland Statler; in 1917 the Statler in St. Louis.

That winter he was my guest at Gasparilla Inn and I remember discussing with him the building of his Saint Louis hotel. He wanted to send me out there as assistant to the managing director, Dave Lober. I walked around Boca Grande a couple of hours before giving him my answer. Such a move, I knew, would be a turning point in my life. Finally I went back to him.

"Mr. Statler, I'm not going to take that job," I told him. "I'm not cut out to be a cog in a big organization."

The twenty-two-hundred-room Pennsylvania in New York, now the Statler, and owned by the company, and the thirteen-hundred-room Statler in Boston were later added as links to the rapidly growing Statler chain. Every hotel was built shining and new and of the most modern design. Statler once told me, "The secret of hotel business depends on three things: location, location, and location." His chain was to be one of the few that withstood the crash of 1929 and the depression that followed.

He was simple and direct. I went to several of the big hotel dinners with Mr. Statler, and he would rarely if ever occupy a seat of honor on the dais, but would steer me off to a corner table where he would tip the waiter to ignore the sumptuous menu and bring us bacon and scrambled eggs.

The other day I was lunching in the Boston Statler with D. B. "Burt" Stambro, its genial manager, who started with the organization as Statler's secretary, and we were reminiscing about the grand old man. He told me that one night when Statler was staying at the New York Statler (then the Pennsylvania) he phoned downstairs, very late at night, for an apple.

Kitchens and room service were closed and there wasn't an apple in the plant. Statler phoned his night manager.

The manager came up to his room, and Statler—a little fellow sitting on the bed, looking up at him—asked: "How many hotels have I?"

The man answered promptly, "Half a dozen, Mr. Statler."

"And how many hotels have you?"

"I don't have any."

Statler smiled. "I have a half-dozen hotels and I can't get an apple, and you haven't any hotels and I'll bet you can get a whole bowlful of apples."

Statler got his apple.

In this same era John McEntee Bowman, who came to New York from Canada as a boy and worked at a riding academy and started at the Biltmore as an assistant manager, was building up the great Bowman chain—the then new Commodore, the Atlanta Biltmore, the Miami Biltmore, the Oklahoma Biltmore, the Westchester Country Club, and so on. Jack was building a $4,000,000 hotel every few months!

They tell me that within the past forty years the Statler company had reinvested about 79 per cent of its profits into building a bigger business. After Statler's death the business went on to the glorious future he had anticipated. The hotels in Bowman's chain were largely financed by people in the localities in which they were built and when Jack died the chain disintegrated.

These two men, who were leaders in the great building era of new hotels, show a marked contrast in the way in which their hotel chains were put together, but they exemplified the personal care that went into individual hotel building. Each hotel was given loving supervision, from the floor plan up.

Today we have a different method, as exemplified by the Hilton chain, which is fast becoming pre-eminent. As there is no necessity at the present time for new hotel construction, the company has acquired many of the better hotels in the large cities through purchases of real estate or securities and, in turn, the Hilton stock is on the Big Board.

Another of the great hotel men I used to meet at the big hotel parties was George C. Bolt, builder, president, and managing director of the old Waldorf-Astoria and the Bellevue-Stratford Hotel in Philadelphia. He was known as "The Creator of the Modern Hotel and the Man Who Revolutionized the Hotel Business in This Country." He was the first to introduce European service to America.

In this period of great hotel men and greater changes, in 1918, I formed a syndicate and purchased the Forest Hills Hotel in Franconia, New Hampshire, not far from Bethlehem. This was my first venture in acquiring hotel property by ownership, and although I did not know it at the time, it was the beginning of chain hotel operation so far as I was concerned.

The Forest Hills was a little hotel of about sixty rooms, situated on a bluff facing Franconia Notch, with a gorgeous view and beautiful surroundings. It had been closed for some years, so taking it over entailed not only its reconstruction and refurnishing, but the building up of an entirely new clientele.

This was good schooling. It also gave me experience in running more than one resort hotel at a time and was my initiation into the art of delegating authority, inasmuch as I was operating Upland Terrace and couldn't be in two places at the same time.

Don't think I didn't try!

Before this I had thought that I had to see to everything myself. Father and Mother had been the working force of the hotels they ran. So, up to this point, had I. But with the knowledge that a man could run more than one hotel and still have time on his hands came the discovery that he could also have a life not entirely dominated by his guests and their needs.

From this time on my family lived in a cottage near the hotel, whichever one it might be, and home was a place where a hotel man could shed his formal attire and relax.

The first season at Forest Hills was so successful that the next year we built a large addition, practically doubling the size of the hotel, and in the third season another, also a nine-hole golf course, and a swimming pool.

We were beset by the usual difficulties, which, for some reason, succeeded in being unique. A gang of men dug the pool in a meadow across from Franconia Hills, and to speed matters I conceived the idea of blowing the hole out with dynamite. There was none to be had in the vicinity, but a company in Littleton was expecting a carload that would be sold first come, first served. Leo Nolan, my assistant manager, who is still with me, set out in a Fiat touring car we had built into a truck that would go like blue blazes, to get as much dynamite as possible before it was sold out.

Leo streaked back to Franconia from Littleton with a load of dynamite at eighty miles an hour. A motor cop tried to stop him from speeding, but when he learned what Leo had on board, he gave the car a wide berth. After we had two or three loads Leo and I placed the dynamite in the center of the excavation, cut a very long fuse, and touched it off.

The explosion made our swimming pool all right, but black mud was flung over trees, shrubbery, and landscape for hundreds of yards in every direction, and it took all the summer rains to wash it off before we could get near enough to use the pool.

The golf course was in charge of a colored greenkeeper named Don. I had a Walker foxhound bitch with six almost-grown puppies, and I'd soak a coonskin in water, tie a string around it, and drag it through the woods on horseback, then turn Winnie and her puppies out and let her take the trail to train the pups. One day Don had some spare time, so I asked him to drag the coonskin.

After lunch, as I walked over to the barn, I noticed with satisfaction that the golf course was filled with players. Not knowing where Don had dragged the coonskin, I turned the dogs loose.

It was Don's habit to walk over the greens each day during

lunch hour to see if they needed attention, and on this particular noon he had walked from green to green, dragging the
coonskin.

Winnie and her pups picked up the trail at the barn door
and started out in full cry—straight to the first hole and on.
There was no stopping the rush of baying hounds across the
greensward, and the course was uproarious with flying putters
and profanity.

Forest Hills went a long way toward giving me the confidence and experience I was to need now.

Chapter Ten: BIG TIME

COLONEL CHARLES GREENLEAF was president of the Profile and Flume Hotels Company that owned and operated the Profile House in Franconia Notch, and had sent word that he wanted to see me right away.

Speeding over the five miles of mountain road from Forest Hills, I recalled trundling over this very road as a small boy behind old Dennis, when, with Father, I had visited Charlie Greenleaf at the Profile House, and he had asked me if I planned growing up to be a big hotel man.

This afternoon, on the broad piazza of his hotel, he asked me almost the same question again.

Profile House was strictly "big time," comparing favorably with such famed resorts as the Poland Spring House, the Mount Washington at Bretton Woods, the Homestead at Hot Springs, and the Greenbriar at White Sulphur.

The property consisted of some eleven thousand acres, stretching through the Franconia Notch for miles and extending from mountaintop to mountaintop.

The Profile House, a most attractive four-story frame building, was situated at the height of land where two little brooks start from springs only a few feet apart, one to run north and find its way into the mighty Connecticut, the other south to seek out the Merrimack and on to the Atlantic.

From the front piazza we looked across the wide driveway, spacious lawns, and tennis courts, toward Profile Lake and the entrance to the Franconia Notch. Near by the sides of Cannon Mountain and Mount Lafayette rose almost sheer.

On either side of the hotel were two beautiful mountain lakes, the Echo and the Profile. Two thousand feet above the crystal waters of Profile Lake, and mirrored in its depths, the majestic granite features of the Old Man of the Mountain jutted from the living rock.

And now Colonel Greenleaf was asking me if I would like to own the Great Stone Face. He was offering me the management of Profile House and all these magnificent properties, with an option to purchase.

Such an offer, made to a man of my age by Colonel Greenleaf, was very flattering.

There had been two previous Profile Houses on the site of this hotel, the earliest dating back before the Civil War. Both had been destroyed by fire. This one had been built under the direction of Colonel Greenleaf, who was without doubt one of the finest resort operators of his time.

I went over the hotel from roof to basement and marveled. Because Colonel Greenleaf had conceived the building with an eye to the comfort of his guests and from strictly a service standpoint, it was one of the most workable resort hotels I had ever seen. The public rooms were gracious and ample, the service areas adequate, and the rooms and suites sunny, airy, and beautifully furnished.

The kitchens were particularly spacious, having been built at a time when square footage and per-cubic-foot costs were inconsequential. There were upward of four hundred rooms in the main building and twenty-nine so-called "cottages" of from eight to seventeen bedrooms each. These "cottages" were arranged on terraces and were connected to the hotel proper by covered runways with red carpeting.

The little community also comprised employees' dormitories to house more than three hundred, large stables, a two-hundred-car garage, laundry, powerhouse, and other buildings of various nature pertaining thereto. There were also souvenir stores and tourist attractions scattered through the Notch, which I would have to operate if I took over.

I could not have been put on a worse spot than having to follow a man of Colonel Greenleaf's ability in running this fine property, while carrying on the operation of three other resort hotels at the same time—quite an undertaking for a young hotel man at the age of thirty-two. It was particularly difficult in that I had to cater to a distinguished clientele many of whom had been guests of the Profile for two or three decades. Some of the older generation had been included in Ward McAllister's Four Hundred.

After my experience with catering to the clientele at Boca Grande, however, nothing daunted me—it was merely that the Profile was a larger operation.

A syndicate was formed to acquire the property and I took over the Profile in what we then considered the "dark days of the depression" of 1921. A few years later everyone found out what a depression could mean.

It was a busy spring. I had about six weeks to assemble a crew and complete the usual spring rehabilitation. This entailed a flock of painters, a carload of paint, 10,000 rolls of wallpaper, and the cleaning up of the Notch from one end to the other. There did not seem to be hours enough in the day. As Mr. Wakefield, our superintendent at the Profile, told some traveling salesmen who were waiting for me when I tore by in my car, "Sometimes he comes through local and sometimes express."

I was hard pressed to see that all the men kept at work. I remember passing the Profile one afternoon and seeing a half-dozen painters asleep on the roof. I slipped up in the attic and locked the trapdoor. Wakefield heard them calling for help about nine o'clock that evening and had to go up and let them down.

One carpenter was a colored boy I brought from the South.

I'd go out, furious over something he hadn't done, and he'd see me coming and start walking fast around the building. "If I can just get around it once, before he catches up with me," he used to say, "Mister Abbott gets over being mad."

We opened July 1, 1921, and I remember my striped trousers and cutaway coat which typified the pomp of a formal opening of a resort hotel in that era. All of the staff were youngsters. Al Pettengill, my chef, was a year younger than I and has since been chef at many famous resort hotels. Later he was catering manager at the Roney Plaza in Miami Beach. He had a remarkable crew. A green kid named Eddie Welsh, just out of the Navy and serving his apprenticeship on the broiler, later became the distinguished chef des cuisine at the Boca Raton, Florida. Arthur Turner, our roast cook, was recently chef des cuisine at the Hollywood Beach Hotel, Hollywood, Florida, and Leon Aiken, our waffle cook, was steward there.

Father summed us up with the comment: "You're just a bunch of fresh kids who haven't any more sense than to think you can run a hotel, and for that reason you probably will, unless someone comes along and tells you different."

Leon had what we believe was the first electric waffle kitchen in any resort hotel in America. It comprised thirty-six little home units fastened to a table, as we were unable to find any institutional units. It had been said that no resort hotel could serve waffles to four hundred people each morning, so we built this kitchen to meet the challenge.

We had a young pastry cook who was an excitable prima donna of Italian descent. He made the ice cream. One morning I went by his shop and said, "Joe, how are you feeling this morning?" He said, "Meest' Cal-abot, I feela mean, an' when I feela mean I make-a da lemon ice cream. Nobody like. Nobody order. Nobody eat. So I make!"

I don't think I ever had a greater thrill or took more pride in operating any property than I did the Profile, my first really large command; it ran as smoothly as a luxury ship, because it was built to be run that way. The Profile House was worthy of its clientele.

The driveway in front of the hotel was used strictly for carriages and saddle horses, and the porte-cochere on the east end of the building was for automobile traffic.

Guests drove under the porte-cochere and alighted from their cars to proceed up a flight of broad steps into the main lobby. This was a very large room, about two hundred and fifty feet long, and extending down both sides were massive plate-glass picture windows with Irish lace curtains draped across, reaching from the ceiling to the floor. One of these curtains was destroyed and it cost twelve hundred dollars to replace it. The walls and carpeting were Pompeian red, the room was trimmed in white with huge white columns down the center and white pilasters to match between the windows.

The room could seat five hundred people easily and in one corner were accommodations for the orchestra composed entirely of musicians from the Boston Symphony who gave concerts every afternoon and evening.

The main dining room was a separate building, built in the shape of an octagon with tremendous plate-glass windows in each wall. The domed ceiling was some thirty-five feet above the floor with not a column to hold it in place—just this magnificent arch. The room had ample seating for six hundred, was carpeted throughout, and the Irish-linen napery and silver service gave it an air of old-world refinement seldom encountered in a resort hotel.

Knowing the clientele, Father was a little more apprehensive than I. "If you can't lick them, you'd better join them," he reminded me. He had in mind a story that was going the rounds of the resort field about a resident manager—let's call him Jones—Charlie Greenleaf had employed a couple of seasons before. Being most anxious to please the Profile clientele, it was alleged that he walked up to one of the dowagers whose family had been at the Profile for many years and said, "Excuse me, I am the manager here. I like to know my guests and I like to have my guests know me." The dowager adjusted her lorgnette, casually looked him up and down, and walked off. Not to be discouraged, the manager went into the kitchen that evening and had a splendid plank steak prepared. He sent it to her table by a captain with the message that "Mr. Jones personally had gone into the kitchen and had the steak prepared." The dowager sent back word: "If Mr. Jones is in the kitchen, let him stay there; it is exactly where he belongs."

To my mind this was a most humorous anecdote inasmuch as it shows that this man hadn't the faintest conception of the psychology of that special type of patronage.

When I opened the Profile I made it a point not to speak to one of the old guests. I saw to it that the food was fine and the service beyond reproach, but I religiously refrained from any contact whatsoever with any except the new guests I had brought to the hotel. I knew I was being "weighed in the balance."

One day, as I was crossing the lobby, I heard a commanding voice, "Young man! I've been in this house three weeks, and all I've seen is the back of your head going through a door." I turned around. "Madam, my office is just off the lobby, and I'm there every morning from nine to twelve. I will be delighted to receive you at any time and do anything possible to make your stay pleasant."

She answered, "I have an appointment with you in your office tomorrow morning at ten o'clock. Be there!" Knowing that she was one of the leaders of the "cottage set," I made it a point to be there.

The next morning she came in under full sail. "Young man, will you come to my cottage for tea this afternoon at four-twenty?" I told her I would be delighted.

When I arrived at her cottage that afternoon she had assembled about thirty of the most prominent guests of the Profile and we had a most delightful afternoon. From then on I belonged. I had known that if they were going to accept me at all, they would accept me on their own terms and in their own good time, and after considered judgment.

Opinion now prevails that these old dowagers were stuffy and stupid, but they were far from it. They were women of the world, with merriment in their natures, but they brooked no foolishness. They believed that society was built upon the conventions and that when they were broken, society suffered.

Bless their hearts, I can see them now, walking down the long corridors after dinner. They forgathered in front of the fireplace in the lobby, where each grande dame had her favorite chair, with a solicitous bellboy tucking a hassock under her feet. A captain and waiters from the dining room would wheel in the table with their after-dinner coffee. No woman had ever been allowed to smoke in a public room at the Profile. One evening, shortly after my acceptance as their official host, I took a terrific chance. I approached a group of dowagers having their coffee after dinner and offered them cigarettes. They were delighted. One said, "Do you mean to say we don't have to go way off to our rooms to smoke, as we have been doing? This is wonderful!" They were human, after all. Times were changing in the resort world. The younger set were going around humming "I'm Just Wild About Harry," and young girls without corsets and with skirts ten inches from the floor smoked cigarettes and played the new game of ping-pong while their elders enjoyed mah-jongg. People came to the hotel in "closed cars" and brought their new "radios" that had our engineer, Sawyer, putting floor plugs in like crazy. Sawyer presided in the engine room at the powerhouse which was so immaculate that he had red carpets on the floor in front of the boilers, and many is the night I have seen leading financiers in evening clothes holding an impromptu talk fest there.

Electric irons appeared in the bedrooms for use by the

personal maids, and we were seriously considering the installation of one of the "new-fangled" beauty salons that were becoming the vogue in the cities.

There may have been a sharper demarkation between the guests and the employees than there is now. There was, on the other hand, more friendship and understanding between the two groups, and upon arriving most former guests would make it a point to ask after the welfare of many individual members of the staff. Some of the employees of long standing were characters and amused the guests no end. We had one truck driver by the name of Jim Hawkins who used to take the garbage from the hotel each morning on a large truck down the long three-mile hill to the Profile farms.

One morning he was coming down with about twenty barrels of garbage on the truck when he burned out his brakes and the truck ran away.

He and the truck ended up in the middle of a rock garden with garbage scattered down the hill for a quarter of a mile and Jim lying on his back in a bed of oriental poppies. At this moment one of the dowagers was passing in her chauffeur-driven Rolls-Royce. She had the car stopped and ran over to Jim. "Oh, Mr. Hawkins, are you hurt?" Jim replied, "Great God, no, lady! I bring the swill down this way every morning."

Cannon Mountain derives its name from a rock formation at the top shaped in the form of a cannon. An Indian guide came around once or twice in the season weighted down with ropes, knapsack, an ax, and a lantern. Then all the old guests went to the new guests and made up a collection to hire Joe to climb the mountain and "fire the cannon at sunset." At sunset the new guests assembled on the front piazza to listen for the salute which never came.

My old friend, E. M. Statler, once told me that appearances are sometimes deceiving. He said, "You never know who the old gentleman in the wrinkled suit and straw hat is. He may be a senator from over the ridge." I had this brought home to me when an assistant manager stepped into my office one morning and said, "Mr. Abbott, a seedy-looking individual at the front desk who looks like a tramp is asking to see some of our better accommodations." I walked out to the desk, greeted the man cordially, and personally showed him around. He picked out our finest suite, and I went with him to the automobile entrance where another rough-looking character was waiting in a new runabout which was splashed with mud.

The new guest smiled and said to the man in the car, "Bill, you can keep this car; you have given me a wonderful two weeks of fishing." Then I woke up to the fact that he was talking to his Maine guide.

The next afternoon two expensive touring cars rolled in—one with his family and the other with baggage.

The operation of the Franconia Notch was an additional experience. We had souvenir stores at Echo Lake, the Old Man of the Mountain, a photographer at the "basin" and at the Flume, where we also maintained a toll road to take people up into the chasm.

Prior to my coming to the Profile the company had somewhat questioned their right to maintain this toll road and had made very little to-do about it. They had a man at the entrance with a little green bag who charged five cents to go into the Flume. I saw a chance to increase the company's profits and built a large gate at the entrance of the tollgate, put in automatic turnstiles, and hired pretty girls as gatetenders.

As I remember it, we increased the revenue from this source from some two or three thousand dollars a season to thirty thousand dollars the first season I was there.

Frank Brace was our most efficient manager of the Notch concessions. Frank was very ingenious and was always thinking up gimmicks and gadgets to sell to the tourists. One season he started wrapping five-cent maple-sugar cakes in cellophane and sold literally tons.

It was all interesting, operating the Notch, rebuilding and enlarging the stores at Echo Lake, the Old Man, and the Flume, rebuilding the toll road, and figuring out ways and means of extracting the fast nickel from the pockets of the traveling public.

Within three years ideas had raised the general income from fifteen thousand to one hundred thousand dollars a year, and the number of post cards sent out changed the little post office from third to second class.

We kept a weather eye out for any publicity that would bring the Notch and the hotel before the public.

One morning Miss Billie Burke (Mrs. Florenz Ziegfeld) and her lovely little daughter Patricia arrived in a chauffeur-driven Rolls-Royce phaeton. They were on their way to a hotel at Bretton Woods. Miss Burke decided it would be nice to lunch at the Profile House, but the certified milk for Patricia had been shipped to the other hotel.

I had my fastest driver, Frank Brace, race the eleven miles to the station and back with certified milk in time for the little girl's lunch.

While we were waiting a line of about thirty burros ambled through the Notch. I stopped the caravan, picked out a gentle burro, and put little Patricia in the saddle and had her photographed beside the car in which her beautiful mother was sitting. The resulting picture, showing the newest and one of the oldest methods of transportation, made all the Sunday supplements.

The tempo of my life was picking up and memories became as the blur of the landscape when one looks out the window of a streamliner. Those years, to my mind, were best portrayed by show business—the arrival of the night club and Texas Guinan's "Hello, Sucker!" the team of Clayton, Jackson, and (Jimmy) Durante; Rudy Vallee playing a saxophone in a college band; George M. Cohan in *Little Nellie Kelly*;

Vincent Lopez and his "Kitten on the Keys"; and Paul Whiteman's immortal melodies. The clouds of our little depression were lifted and we were entering what staid bankers called "a new era," where history meant nothing and the future was rosy.

Little did we realize that it would be an era of boom or bust!

The Profile was on the Boston Road and therefore in the thick of the bootlegging streaming down from Canada. I made so many night trips between Boston and the White Mountains that I came to know most of the bootleggers. We had property on both sides of the road for miles through Franconia Notch, and this was a favorite place for the liquor authorities to set traps for the rum-runners. I wanted no part of it, as I was always afraid that the bootleggers would think I had tipped off the authorities and would set our timber afire in revenge. Many times we were warned that liquor was coming through, and one of the funniest things I ever saw in the Notch was "Big Red" dressed in a long black coat and black hat driving a hearse, filled with liquor, which was followed by three limousines complete with undertaker, mourners, and more liquor.

Another time I saw Red racing through the Notch with a carload of liquor like a bat out of hell with the law on his tail. It was haying time, and the big doors of the Profile barn were open. Red saw his opportunity—he made a shrieking left-hand turn and drove onto the barn floor and the men working inside pitched hay all over his automobile. Two minutes later the officers arrived, but Red was out of sight, car, liquor, and all.

It's a pity the full story of prohibition can't be told. A blind man could have seen it wouldn't work. You can't legislate tolerance into a man's heart or morality into his mind. The bootlegger and the moralist worked unknowingly together to maintain prohibition—vice money and church-pillar money joined.

The results we know—a half-hundred speakeasies to one New York block, a vice king taking in his millions a month and ordering his boasted murders.

But no one dares tell the complete story.

The effect on hotel business was evil. Instead of a quiet drink in a bar or restaurant with his girl, a guest smuggled girl and bottle into his room.

Bellboys, waiters, everyone was bootlegging. You couldn't stop it.

Driving to Boston by night behind the bootleggers' cars was an experience. The bootlegger was king of the highway and had the right of way.

In the middle of my second summer at the Profile I went to Boston to pick up a roadster I had on order. I took the sleeper out of Littleton, and when we reached Woodsville I was awakened by someone getting into the berth across the aisle, and recognized the voice of my friend, Jack Eames, talking to the porter. Jack was president of the Interstate Amusement Company. The thought hit me—here is the fellow to run the Colonial Theater in Bethlehem! While it was a very successful operation, it was just one more thing for me to look out for. So then and there in that waking moment, as Jack was dropping off to sleep, I called across to him:

"Jack, why don't you buy the Colonial Theater?"

"Oh, hello, Karl," he mumbled. "How much?"

I told him. "Done," he said, and we both went to sleep.

When I returned to Bethlehem, I had the deeds made out and sent them to Jack through the mail, and when he received them, he called and asked me what it was all about. He had been so sleepy he had forgotten the entire matter. After refreshing his memory, he laughed. "Okay, I'll send you a check. It is too much trouble to undo the paper work."

What little success I have had in different business transactions has invariably come from the casual deal made on the spur of the moment, something that landed in my lap out o nowhere or that I stumbled over where it lay calling for a quick decision. Anything I have had to plan for, strive for, or pursue, and gain by a great deal of effort, has turned to ashes in my mouth.

Of course it isn't so simple as it sounds. In Jack's case, I knew my man.

One morning in July 1923 I was in the hotel barbershop being shaved when Colonel Harry Balfe of New York, one of our guests, sat down in the next chair. Colonel Balfe was president of a corporation that owned the Kirkwood Hotel at Camden, South Carolina. It had been operated by my good friend T. Edward Krumbholtz, one of the finest of the resort hotel operators, who died the preceding winter.

Colonel Balfe and I started discussing Mr. Krumbholtz and Camden in general, and suddenly the colonel, looking over from his barber chair, asked: "Why don't you buy the Kirkwood?"

I had never seen the Kirkwood Hotel. I had never been in Camden. But I recalled having seen pictures of the place in its booklet and knew that the property comprised the hotel, stables, polo field, and two golf courses. Through the hotel grapevine I knew approximately what its earnings had been.

Before leaving the chair I had bought 56 per cent of the Kirkwood for $300,000.

This was the first deal I had gone into absolutely on my own and the whole procedure didn't take five minutes.

When I got out of the chair the colonel looked up at me and his eyes twinkled through the lather. "Look out, young fellow," he said, "you're playing with blue chips!"

The next day I arranged a $30,000 down payment with Colonel Balfe and left on the train for Camden to look over my new property.

At the Kirkwood I found my good friend Mike Whelan in charge. He is now managing director of the Dallas Park in Miami. The hotel sat on Hobkirk Hill, commanding a fine view of the beautiful South Carolina countryside and the little town of Camden, and I was delighted with it. I remember sitting out in the sun on the brick wall of the hotel discussing with Mike how good a deal I had made and privately worrying where I was going to get the money eventually to buy in all the minority stock and have an extra $100,000 available for rehabilitation and operating capital.

After spending a couple of days with Mike at the Kirkwood I took the afternoon train for New York. I stepped off the train in Pennsylvania Station the following morning, picked up a newspaper on my way out, and hailed a taxi. After giving directions to the driver, I settled back on the seat and casually glanced at the headlines.

There was one big black headline I read over and over and still it didn't make sense.

PROFILE HOUSE AT FRANCONIA NOTCH, NEW HAMPSHIRE, TOTALLY DESTROYED BY FIRE!

It had burned while I was on the train.

I was so stunned I could hardly think. But I told the taxi driver to rush me to the Grand Central.

At the information window I learned there were no quick connections to the White Mountains. The stationmaster said that an immigrant train was leaving New York within a few moments for Canada, and would pass that afternoon through Concord, New Hampshire. I wired Frank Brace to meet me there and caught the train. That was a grueling ride, my imagination running riot—how, when, what had happened? Hotel guests injured? Loss of life?

The newspaper account had been brief. A million fantastic possibilities rushed through my mind.

Frank was waiting at Concord. I tossed my bag into the car and slid behind the wheel, and Frank asked rather anxiously if I didn't want him to drive! Worried as I was, I couldn't help but grin, knowing Frank would have given anything to escape the ride ahead. The year before I had been given a state trooper's commission by the Motor Vehicles Commission, and I had a siren under the hood. That siren didn't stop all the miles over the narrow, twisting black-topped roads.

Beyond Newfound Lake we ran into a shower and slippery pavement. The car skidded twice around and shot off the road through a fence and into a pasture. The car didn't have a dent in it, believe it or not, and we drove out through the same opening we made when we went in.

A few miles farther on we hit a detour sign, where a gang of about forty Italians were repairing the road. We tore through, leaving picks and shovels suspended.

Frank was looking green about the gills but he was piecing together the details of the catastrophe of the day before. I remember the date very well—August 3, 1923, the day President Harding died in San Francisco.

Some guests who were playing tennis had happened to glance up at the main roof and saw a thin spiral of smoke rising in the still air. By the time they had sounded the alarm and Mr. Wakefield and his crew reached the attic, it was an inferno. No one to this day knows the cause of the Profile House fire.

A few minutes more and the entire top floor of the main building was a roaring mass of flame. The fire spread rapidly to the dining-room wing. Al Pettengill told me afterward that it was an awe-inspiring sight to look through the great plate-glass windows and watch that splendid dining room with all its snowy Irish linen and gleaming glass and silver set up for the noonday meal, with the bright flames playing through the dome.

There was no panic. The entire crew turned to the work of saving all that could be saved. I will never be able to forget the many acts of heroism and sacrifice that that loyal group of men and women performed; their only impulse was to get the guests out of the hotel bag and baggage. They gave no thought to their own personal belongings or even their own safety, and the miracle is that not a single person was hurt nor a piece of baggage lost.

Bellboys and kitchen crew carried baggage and even furniture down the grand front staircase. Chambermaids and waitresses emptied the contents of bureaus and saw to it that every child was safe.

Mertie Baker, my secretary, stuck to the telephone switchboard with water running around her ankles until all the lines went dead. Just before leaving she emptied all the cash and jewels out of the office safe into a blanket and carried them out of the building.

The heat, the roar and crackle of flames, turned the scene into a holocaust. Fires sprang up everywhere, apparently by spontaneous combustion. The help's dormitory went next, and fires started in the stables and garage a quarter mile away. Cottages at the far end of the terrace burst into flames that raced through the long corridors toward the blazing main building.

Furniture which had been carried out of the buildings and deposited on the road caught fire, and the furniture which had been taken from the cottages and placed out of harm's way was looted by the sightseers who came from miles around, some even with trucks, like vultures to the kill. The roads north and south of the hotel were blocked with traffic so that the fire companies from the surrounding towns were unable to get through.

The entire entrance to the Notch was a blazing inferno against which the puny efforts of man were inconsequential.

By the time I arrived our beautiful little mountain community was an area of smouldering ashes.

A state of chaos prevailed in the ruined Notch. I noticed a crew of telephone linemen repairing the telephone lines in the Notch and persuaded them to set up an emergency telephone on a cracker box beside the road. I sat on that box and started calling up resort hotels throughout New England—the Mountain View House, the Mount Washington, Poland Springs, and so on. I asked the same question of each: "How many guests can you care for? How many bellboys can you use? Waitresses? Chambermaids? Cooks? Housemen?"

Before dark I had all the guests in rooms and every member of the staff in a new job and automobiles lined up to take them to their destinations.

I remember sitting there by the road signing checks, and that I paid off the entire crew their full summer's wages—they had earned it all in the past twenty-four hours.

Father drove up from Forest Hills just before sunset. He sat in the car and looked at the ruins without a change of expression.

Finally he said quietly: "Karl, I expect you to take this as we Abbotts have always taken adversity. Always look at the rising sun, never at the setting sun."

Then he drove off.

But that, from Dad, was enough.

My first thought was that a new Profile House should rise on the site of the old. That evening, after I had the guests and crew settled and before the ashes of the hotel had cooled, I started work on the new one. I telephoned Harold Field Kellogg, my architect friend in Boston, and told him I thought a huge Swiss chalet would look well in the Notch. Harold worked straight through the next twenty-four hours and arrived at the Profile site with a rough drawing.

After two or three days' discussion it was decided not to go ahead with the project.

It was then that Father began his argument that the Notch should become a state park. He had done so much for me, the least I could do was to accede to his wishes.

After some negotiations the Notch was finally sold for $400,000, the state of New Hampshire furnishing $200,000 and the Society for the Protection of New Hampshire Forests furnishing the additional $200,000.

Of this amount Mr. James J. Storrow of Boston furnished $100,000 and the remaining $100,000 was raised by the society with the aid of the New Hampshire Federation of Women's Clubs. If it had not been for Father's dream for a Franconia Notch State Park, the Notch never would have been sold. Its earnings at that time justified an investment of a million dollars, and it is my opinion that it could not have been taken over by eminent domain for a lesser figure. We had contemplated the building of the tramway that was subsequently built by the state, as well as a number of other improvements, which have not been built. In fact, I traveled to most of the national parks throughout the United States to get ideas on the subject.

The Franconia Notch Forest Reservation and Memorial Park was dedicated September 16, 1928, with an impressive service. The Hon. Huntley N. Spaulding, governor of New Hampshire, said in his dedicatory speech:

"And in this connection it gives me pleasure to say that the attitude of those in whom the title vested toward its acquisition by the state was at all times friendly, fair, and public-spirited. The owners were men thoroughly acquainted with the situation; fully aware of the public necessity for preserving the Notch and the Profile; and as desirous as any of us for having this property brought about."

I took to myself the words of Mr. W. R. Brown, chairman of the State Forestry Commission, who presided at the dedication, in his opening address:

"Lift up your eyes to the hills from whence cometh your strength is ingrained in every New Hampshire boy and girl, and in after life returning perchance to this spot, these men and women of New Hampshire have revived their souls at the sublime solitude and unchanging constancy of the Great Stone Face and the mountains of their youth."

What was it Daniel Webster said of the Great Stone Profile?

"God Almighty has hung out a sign to show that there He makes men."

It is a source of satisfaction to me that this beautiful property is in the hands of the state, where it will be safe for all time. The Franconia Notch State Park was the biggest of Father's dreams, and he made it work from a wheel chair. Daniel Webster was right—New Hampshire makes men.

Chapter Eleven: CAMDEN

AFTER the Profile burned other hotels came along, a new one every year or so. For the next twenty-five years four or five hotels in the North and four or five in the South kept me reasonably busy.

In August 1923, a few days before the fire, I had bought the Kirkwood at Camden, South Carolina, and that fall headed a group that purchased the Vendome in Boston, my first city hotel.

I secured a two-weeks option on the Vendome for $1,200,-000 and promptly came down with the flu. But I borrowed $700,000 on a first mortgage, took $400,000 that was left over from the Profile deal, and with the aid of five slow notes for $10,000 each, signed by myself and four of my friends, gathered together $1,150,000 by the time my option expired.

When I went down to complete the deal I was $50,000 short, but a check for $1,150,000 is hard to refuse.

There was some discussion about a thousand-dollar revenue stamp to affix to the papers. I was glad the owners didn't ask me to buy it, as I didn't have a spare one hundred dollars in the world—not even for working capital. They brought it in —a little yellow stamp with no glue on the back, and I put a paperweight on it so it would not blow off the table.

When the papers were signed and I left the room, a representative of a leading hotel company in Boston was waiting. He offered me $50,000 for my deal, which would have been $25,000 a week for two weeks' work, but this only confirmed my judgment that I had made a good buy. Of course all this seemed a whale of a deal to me in those days, and, as Harry Balfe had said, I was playing with blue chips.

Father often wondered why I was willing to deal with the bankers without the aid of a broker, attorney, and auditors. It was perfectly simple as long as they confined their conversation strictly to hotels. When they started talking about anything else I left.

With the deed to the hotel in my pocket, I rode to the Vendome. As I hurried through the front door I almost fell over a rubber mat, and a supercilious doorman snickered behind his gloved hand, instead of springing to my assistance.

My first act on taking charge was to point my finger and say, "Fire that doorman!"

As in most cases when one takes over a new hotel there were a lot of changes to be made in order to have it conform to a new policy of operation. We gave the old place a face lifting. I changed over the main dining room to an empire ballroom and I remember a slender young brunette in slacks standing on a stepladder painting a mural. This girl is now the proficient painter Maria Liszt. Harold Field Kellogg built the Nippon Room. Again following Charlie Greenleaf, who had long operated the Vendome, I had to be on my mettle and live up to our new slogan.

For more than twenty years we advertised: "Abbott Hotels—Service with a Smile."

As far as I know, we were the first to use this slogan that has since been put to national use by many industries.

The Kirkwood was different from any resort I had known before. Unlike Florida or Pinehurst, Camden was truly antebellum South, a sleepy little town surrounded by many old-time plantations and steeped in tradition and historical lore. It was a horseman's heaven, where bridle paths and hundreds of sand roads wound through great stands of longleaf pine and across sunlit cotton fields. "Nothing Can Be Finer Than to Be in Carolina in the Morning" is not only a song title but a fact, demonstrated by a brisk canter on a good horse across country or along a winding path in some shady dell where cardinals dart like vermilion arrows through the foliage and mockingbirds proclaim their ecstasy.

The Kirkwood sat on a hill surrounded by green golf courses and polo fields. It was a white frame structure of two hundred rooms, the central part of which had originally been the old Canty Mansion. Its massive white columns and winding entrance stairways gave it an air of stately dignity.

The great doorway, with its beautiful fan and side lights, opened upon an interior of spacious rooms designed by gentlefolk for gracious living. The doors were flanked on either side by huge fireplaces where pitch-pine logs had burned these many years. It seemed the beautiful rooms were doing their diffident best to give a warm welcome of southern hospitality to the northern guests.

We brought many of our staff down from the North but also employed a large number of colored people, who lived in Camden, as bellboys, chambermaids, kitchen help, yardmen, and caddies. Many of these people had been employed as butlers, maids, and cooks in southern homes and were especially well trained.

A Christian colored gentleman named William Gamble who has been my superintendent of service in many hotels over the years once asked me, "Mr. Abbott, do you know why we colored people love you? Because you are one white man who realizes there is an aristocracy among the colored race much more sharply defined and of more importance than in the white race."

I once heard an old southern gentleman remark that he "would raise a monument to pierce the skies to the integrity of the old southern Negro." And this was the rich heritage that had been handed down to the Negroes employed in those days at the Kirkwood.

Many of the townspeople bore the names of South Carolina's aristocracy, and while a few were "unreconstructed," most of them got along with the northern people on a very friendly basis. Sometimes, however, the old southern spirit flared, often culminating in an amusing incident. I remember attending a polo game and was seated in the grandstand near an aged southern colonel whose son was one of the players. There was a collision on the field and the young man was thrown from his horse. The colonel pounded with his cane and roared, "Robert, come here! Robert!"

When his son came up to the box he demanded, "What did he do to you, Robert?" His son replied, "Why, Father, he knocked me off my horse."

"What did you say to him, Robert, what did you say to him?" demanded the father.

"Why, Father, I called him a Yankee son of a bitch!"

The old colonel beamed. "Did he hear you, Robert? Did he hear you? Go back and tell him again!"

The fast money and huge profits of the 1920s had given many a broker, investment banker, and business executive the means to disport themselves upon the American scene and to conduct their business on a basis that allowed them much leisure winter and summer. After a couple of seasons at the Kirkwood or other mid-southern resorts where they played golf, rode horseback, and tried their hand at quail shooting, it became the vogue to buy old plantation houses and become landed gentry, however synthetic.

The first step was to buy an old plantation house from a local real estate man who gave them a beating only to be compared with that given the Union Army at the first battle of Bull Run. The house was always in a terrible state of disrepair so that the local contractors had a field day.

The next step was to staff the establishment with trained Negro servants who smiled and bowed and rendered perfect service, albeit with much amusement and secret disdain.

The third step was to try to ingratiate themselves into the good graces of the old southern families which, I suspected, they rarely did. I felt closer to the Southerners than most Yankees inasmuch as I had lived in the South half of each year since childhood and grown up with them. I knew the process of their thinking and understood their pride.

Once while attending the races at the Springdale course with a state senator, the governor of South Carolina came along and the senator introduced me. As I walked away I heard the senator remark, "Yes, Governor, he's a damnyankee, but he's been down here so long he's practically civilized." A very fine compliment!

It was a fascinating and complex situation, this intermingling of three different groups: the Northerners, the Southerners, and the Negroes, each with their different habits, psychologies, and traditions. Watching the interplay of ideas, prejudices, and personalities among these people was, to me, a source of never-ending interest.

One morning I stopped to speak to a northern lady on the veranda of the Kirkwood, who said she was leaving Camden and sorry to go, but "her mission was completed."

"Are you down here on a mission?" I asked.

She explained she was writing a treatise on the Negro race.

After learning that this was her first trip in the South, and that said visit had consisted of a two weeks' sojourn as a Kirkwood guest, I demanded, "Do you mean to tell me that after spending two weeks in a southern resort hotel that you feel qualified to write an article on the Negroes?"

She smiled loftily. "Certainly."

I started in to say, "Madam, I've lived in the South since infancy and I would no more think myself qualified . . ."

But I stopped. There wasn't any use.

Just then Jim, a colored carpenter I had employed for years, ambled past the veranda. I went down to meet him. I thought the lady had gone into the hotel.

"Jim," I said, "you stand right on that spot and look up at that roof. Remember yesterday I sent you up to fix a hole in it? You didn't think I'd climb up and look, but I did, and that hole is still there. Now you go straight up that ladder and fix it."

Jim had a hatful of apologies. "I sho' will, boss. I s'pected I wasn't goin' to get away wid it. I was jest in a hurry to get into dat crap game over to Dusty Bend."

He took his tools up on the roof and I removed the ladder.

"You stay up there till you get that roof fixed," I ordered. "When you finish, holler, and I'll let you down."

Down from the veranda sailed the northern lady who was writing the treatise on the Negro.

"Don't let Mr. Abbott talk to you like that!" she told Jim indignantly. "Don't you know this is a free country, and you're just as good as I am, and just as good as he is?"

Jim looked down over the edge of the roof in astonishment.

"Lady, I know this is a free country, and I'm just as good as you is, but don' you talk like that about Mr. Abbott. He's quality!"

It was a point of view that she would never understand. Loyalty and respect must be earned over many years.

I belonged to a small hunt club that had leased a ten-thousand-acre hunting preserve outside of Camden which was run by a white man born and raised in the locality. He lived in an ancient unpainted house with his wife and four children and owned the little patch of ground he cultivated, a horse, cow, some hogs, and a few chickens. We paid him sixty-five dollars a month.

One member from Connecticut was fond of this gamekeeper, as we all were, and offered him a position up North. That spring the gamekeeper moved his family to Connecticut, where he was given a beautiful vine-covered cottage and one hundred and twenty-five dollars a month, all the milk and cream he could use from his employer's dairy, plenty of fresh vegetables from the garden, and his children had the advantage of a modern school.

But next fall I found him back in Camden in his old house and ready to take me quail shooting.

"What happened?" I asked. "Didn't you get along up North?"

"I got along fine," he said. "Everybody did everything for me and for my children, but, Mr. Abbott, I just can't live in a country where they eat their peas green!"

He was used to the hot, sun-dried peas, hominy grits, and fat back of South Carolina, and to the satisfaction of being his own man. No amount of money, luxury for his family, or educational advantages for his children could compensate.

The Northerners never fully understood the average South Carolinian's love of his land, which was more important to him than the material standards by which they judged success.

Camden became the accepted winter home for my family. The Gasparilla Inn remained a favored point in my line of duty, but I was always glad to return to the Kirkwood.

These were some of the happiest years of my life. We catered to a splendid clientele from the North and middle West; happy, energetic people—sportsmen all. Golfers, horseback riders, and quail shooters forgathered in this sunny clime for carefree vacations. We lived in a contrasting environment —a weird intermingling of the languid life of the old South and the vigor of modern living.

I used to stand on the wide veranda of a morning and look down across the golf course at the smoke rising in a blue haze from a hundred little chimneys which was colored town. Dogs barked, roosters crowed, and from here and there came the faint rattle of pans and cooking pots and the shrill cries of children. I heard the melodious singing of the Negroes as they wended their way up the long path to the hotel to begin their day's work and was, in fancy, whisked back to ante-bellum days.

The carefree life of Camden got under your skin. It was like a perpetual house party. There was a fine spirit of camaraderie between the guests and everyone connected with the place, and there was always something interesting to do.

A couple of miles from the hotel was the Springdale Hunt Club backed by Ernest Woodward and presided over by that internationally known sportsman, Harry D. Kirkover, both of Buffalo, New York. Here once a year the Carolina Cup was run—three and a half miles over timber—and attracted some of the finest horses in America.

Back of the hotel were the golf clubhouse and riding stables. The latter were presided over by Luce Bramlett, a wonderful character who came down out of the North Carolina mountains every fall, bringing with him a string of sixty or seventy beautiful "peavine" horses and several North Carolina mountain boys who acted as riding instructors and grooms.

Most of the fun centered around the stables. After breakfast on a sunny morning many of the guests would saunter down to the barn, most of them in riding clothes, all set for a morning canter. Luce was usually sitting outside the barn in a cane-bottom chair tipped back against the barn with a group of guests standing around listening to his conversation.

The boys kept a lot of gamecocks, brought down from the North Carolina mountains, and "walked them" on the little Negro farms around the country. They would take a fine gamecock and drive out into the country about five or ten miles and stop at a Negro's hut where they kept chickens. They would buy the Negro's rooster for five dollars, kill it, and give it back to the Negro family to eat, then put down their gamecock with the hens. They must have had a hundred gamecocks throughout the countryside. Every once in a while they would have a main or tournament in a pit about fifteen miles down the country. Men from all over North and South Carolina and as far as Virginia would bring their gamecocks and sometimes the fights lasted two or three days.

The cocks were matched according to weight and they had to weigh into the pit side to a fraction of an ounce. If Luce wanted to enter, say eight fights in one day, he had to have eight cocks that made the exact weight of their class and he had to have eight or ten cocks of each weight so as to have one that would make the exact weight and be in top condition on that particular day. No prize fighter was ever trained to a finer point than Luce trained these cocks to make the necessary weight and condition.

The pit was a squared circle like a prize ring in an old shed, with bleachers on all sides and coops for the birds in the rear.

Of course this was all strictly against the law, and I always got a great kick out of the humor of it because when you went through the gate and paid your admission a gatekeeper stood with the ticket taker and remarked:

"Now, boys, this is a-goin' to be a quiet and law-abidin' chicken fight. Check your artillery at the gate and don' use any profanity."

I never liked cockfighting, but it was interesting. The tense moment when the two handlers crouched in opposite corners of the pit with arm raised bringing it down with the word "pit"; the flashing of wings and the muffled tattoo of the steel-gaffed spurs as the birds met breast to breast and fought and fluttered above the ground until one drove a gaff into some vital spot and leaped upon his adversary with a crow of victory, gave me an unwilling thrill. The great fighting heart of these wonderful birds aroused unbounded admiration and, in a way, made me feel apologetic or ashamed of the human audience.

My greatest pleasure in Camden was the quail shooting. I had the pointers which we had raised from puppies and they were a joy to shoot over—well trained and thoroughly finished, steady to wing and shot, and good retrievers. To my mind the average sportsman who has the opportunity to shoot over his dogs only a maximum of thirty days a year seldom has a well-broken animal.

There was always much controversy in sporting magazines as to whether a high-bred, fast pointer, with plenty of heart, particularly a field-trial type of dog, is good on anything but quail.

I think it is a matter of experience. Our dogs were hunted six months every year and were shot over either by Nolan or myself or some sportsman staying at the hotel every day hunting was possible. They became veterans, or professionals, if you please, and there is no teacher like experience under a good handler.

Every summer I shipped the dogs North, and about the middle of September Leo Nolan and I took them to eastern New Brunswick where we worked them every day and all day on woodcock and grouse. After a season or two the dogs seemed to know what it was all about, worked their cover carefully, and rarely ranged more than twenty-five or thirty yards ahead.

For some reason, unknown to me, I have never seen a dog that enjoyed retrieving woodcock. Sometimes they pick them up by one wing and bring them in with their heads turned in seeming disgust.

About the middle of October we would move down to the White Mountains of New Hampshire for a short sojourn and then over into the Lake George region of New York until the snow was too deep.

By the time the dogs arrived in Camden they had a full two months' hunting behind them and were in fine form to start the quail season.

Here their tactics changed completely. They started ranging wide, taking field after field, instinctively hitting the birdy places and ignoring barren ground and unlikely cover.

Some of them had remarkable memories, and when they entered a field that we had shot over the year before would strike out for the spot where they had formerly located a covey.

Is there any greater thrill than to see a fine pointer crossing a field at top speed, freeze slam! bang! into a point, and stand as if etched in marble, frozen solid by the scent?

I have hunted quail all my life and never reached the point where the hair did not rise a little on the back of my neck as I flushed the first covey of a morning. The explosion of the birds from the ground—the little brown bombers fanning out through the trees and the satisfaction of making a clean double. The retrieve and the leisurely stalk of the singles, maybe one or two, so as not to cut down the covey unduly, and then on through the sunshine to the next field.

I enjoy the leisurely stop at noon with a little fire to boil the coffee; the dogs lying about; a filling lunch; post-mortem conversation on the morning's hunt; and afterward my inevitable nap of thirty minutes stretched out on the bare ground. Then the long afternoon, and the good, clean, tired feeling; a fresh brace of dogs; and the last covey located in a cornfield as the big red Carolina sun disappears over the pines; the long walk back to the wagon with the tired dogs at heel; the smell of the wood smoke from the darkies' cabins; and the ride home through the soft night with well-filled game bags. Truly a man is king in his own right after such a day.

Are you wondering what this has to do with hotel business? My answer is—everything! The hotels I ran were home to me and their backgrounds were mine. I learned, and loved, the best they had, and it was this I gave my guests. Every corner of our United States has something wonderful and distinctive to offer. Camden had charm and conviviality and sportsmanship.

As long as Nolan and I have hunted birds, some twenty-five years, we were amateurs compared to Harry Kirkover. To my mind he is the master. He had a lovely home in Camden, with stables in the rear and a kennel where he kept couple dozen bird dogs—both pointers and setters—of the finest breeding and trained to the nth degree. Harry had a bell in the dog kennel and push button by his bed, and if the dogs got noisy and started to bark of a morning, Harry would ring the bell and the dogs silenced immediately.

He would line them up at feeding time at what he called his Sunday school, and each dog would step forward and eat his dinner in turn.

A grand old gentleman of Camden by the name of George Little had a fine pack of foxhounds. Luce Bramlett, in charge of the stables, Leo Nolan, and I had a pack that we kept in a kennel back of the Kirkwood.

Our type of fox hunting was entirely different from the traditional English fox hunt. We did our hunting at night. We took the dogs back in the hills of a moonlight night and turned them loose, then we'd build up a fire, make a few side bets, and await developments.

It wouldn't be long before one of the dogs would strike, and away they would go in full cry, their exciting music echoing through the night. When the pack was almost out of hearing we took our station wagons and followed along through the woods on the sand roads.

Sometimes the dogs ran all night and until after daybreak. This was the sort of fox hunting that the native mountaineers of North and South Carolina have pursued for generations, and they line-bred their hounds for speed, stamina, and endurance.

My hounds were pure-bred Walkers, long-legged, clean-limbed black-and-white dogs with keen noses, bugle voices, and a tremendous natural will to hunt.

When we had been in Camden a few years the northern winter residents organized a hunt club which was most exclusive. They purchased a fine pack of English foxhounds and once or twice a week sallied forth dressed in full regalia. They made a very fine showing: all the ladies and gentlemen in black coats with orange collars and cuffs and with their horses groomed until they flashed in the sun.

Everything was done according to Hoyle. They laid out a hunting course over the surrounding countryside. At first they merely had drag hunts, where they sent out a groom on horseback who dragged a well-soaked fox pelt or a bag saturated with the oil of anise, and soon they were away, galloping across the country and over the jumps with the pack in full cry.

These affairs culminated in a hunt breakfast given by some member in his or her manor house.

After a few weeks they decided that they should have a live fox, so they bought one that had been caught down at the state convict farm below Camden.

On a fine morning they forgathered in impressive array on a little hill. The entire membership was present. The master of the hounds was in command. The whippers-in were on the job, and the English foxhounds were lined up in military precision. The fox was released and sped over the hill. Those elegant English hounds moved forward, sniffed at the trail, and looked at one another in bewilderment, as much as to say, "I say, old chap, are they spoofing us?"

This was something new, and they would have no part of it.

Harry Kirkover telephoned me and asked whether Luce Bramlett and I would bring our hounds over and give them a hunt. I explained that our hounds were night-hunting dogs and if they got after that fox they'd run him straight through to Canada. Of course Harry knew all this, but I suspect he wanted to see some fun. I selected about eight brace of dogs, put them in a truck, had a pair of horses saddled, and Luce and I went over.

When we arrived the members were impatiently milling around on their horses and Harry Kirkover was sitting astride his fine hunter, grinning. He had hunted with the gentry of three continents and I could see that he was getting a great kick out of the situation.

I dismounted, took Winnie and Walker, my strike dogs, led them up to the brow of the hill, and turned them loose. They took one sniff at the trail and lit out for parts unknown, tonguing with every breath.

I knew nothing about the etiquette of crying "Tallyho" and riding behind the master and the whippers-in and staying with the hunt, so when the dogs sighted the fox, I yelled, "There goes the bastard—now!" and set forth on my own.

The pack disappeared over the brow of the hill and away went the hunt club on their fine horses, a brave sight indeed.

Luce and I listened to the dogs, and I said:

"With all the steam that fox has got behind him he's going to make for water, and quick. Let's go cross-country to Sander's Creek, where we will probably find him."

When we reached Sander's Creek the dogs were down in the tall grass, standing in more or less of a circle, sniffing something on the ground, with their tails erect and wagging. Sure enough there lay the fox the dogs had killed. Still ignorant of the nuances of fox hunting, but having heard vaguely of the "brush," I cut off the tail and we started back for the Kirkwood stables.

About halfway home we met the Camden Hunt galloping aimlessly in the general direction of where the dogs had gone, and in my naïve ignorance I gaily waved the brush at the gathering as we raced by. I noticed Harry Kirkover was enjoying the situation immensely, but I didn't give it a thought until he arrived at the Kirkwood stables a few moments later.

It was my first and last experience "riding to hounds." It seems I had broken every rule of fox hunting. Incidentally, a groom was sent over to demand the "brush."

Nothing about the operation of the Kirkwood Hotel distinguished it from any other resort hotel I had known except that the social activities, sporting events, and resort life generally were exactly suited to the locality. I was running it in the booming days of the twenties, when the mid-South was very popular, and the hotel was always filled to capacity. The tempo of the times made for "dizzy" living, and managing an exclusive resort hotel was like operating a Ferris wheel.

Everybody was playing the stock market. We had a brokers' office in the hotel and many stock manipulators as guests. Several had private wires to New York in their suites and gave tips to their favorite employees.

A friend of mine who owned a hotel came down to breakfast one morning looking so blue that his headwaiter asked him what was the matter. He told the headwaiter that the mortgage on his hotel was due and he couldn't pay it, and that the headwaiter and all the rest of the help might have to look for other jobs.

"How much is the mortgage?" asked the headwaiter.

"Fifty thousand," answered my friend.

The headwaiter beamed. "Oh, I can let you have that much!" And he did.

We had a stock brokers' office in the clubhouse adjacent to the first tee, and once a guest, walking out to tee up his ball, called back to the manager:

"Jack, buy me a thousand shares of radio."

He played the course, and as he sank his putt on the eighteenth green he called in to the broker:

"Jack, sell my radio."

The stock had gone up ten points and made him a profit of $10,000 while he played the eighteen holes.

The rates that seemed terrific then are commonplace now. I recall my good friend, the late Ward Belcher, came down from New York without a reservation. The reservation manager did not have a vacant room so he cleaned out the shoe-shining parlor, put in a double bed and a dresser, and there Ward slept until someone left and we could move him. At the end of the week he received a bill for twenty-five dollars per day, which he paid willingly, and then turned to me and said with a grin, "Karl, Jesse James had to have a horse!"

With AAA steaks selling at thirty-five cents a pound, wages one third as high as at present, and Uncle Sam more modest in his demands than now, a resort operator could really make a profit.

In one of our southern hotels a visiting "professor," who was only five feet tall and a marvelous magician, came every year, put up banners, and gave a show in the ballroom. One rainy afternoon when he came on the stage only two little boys were in the hall. But he was gallant—he doffed his high silk hat and went through the entire show not to disappoint the youngsters.

Toward the end of the performance an elderly guest tiptoed in and sat at the back. After it was over he joined the professor and his audience of two. "I want to thank you for not disappointing these children," he said, and wrote out a check for one thousand dollars. Handing it to the professor, he added, "They are my grandsons."

Another guest at this hotel developed delusions of grandeur, and I sent for his brother, who, not wanting to have him committed by the sheriff and the law, secured the commitment papers himself and took his brother away for psychiatric treatment. They went by train, and when the sane brother went to sleep sitting in the Pullman, the insane brother stole the commitment papers from his pocket.

The next day they were met at their destination by a group of physicians and a closed car. The insane one pointed to his brother.

"He's out of his mind, poor fellow," he explained, and produced the papers.

Of course the sane brother made a big scene, which helped convince the medicos that he was crazy. It took a lot of disentangling before they committed the right brother.

I remember a party at the Kirkwood that reflected the times, given for the governor of South Carolina by our northern guests after one of the Springdale races. My staff was busy for days preparing for the dinner, which was a sumptuous affair and not designed for profit. I was on my mettle to show these gentlemen the finer points of the boniface's art.

During the cocktail hour preceding the dinner colored servants passed among the guests bearing large silver salvers of hors d'oeuvre. I noticed one senator never let a waiter pass him by, and I was aghast at the amount of hors d'oeuvre he was able to consume. Just before we were to go in to dinner he came up to me.

"Mr. Abbott, suh, I would like to take this opportunity to tell you this is the best banquet I have ever had the privilege to attend."

He put out his hand to say farewell, and at that moment the big door to the grill was thrown open, and there was disclosed the glittering banquet table set for one hundred guests.

On the table, resting in a bed of asparagus fern and sweetpeas, framed by a thousand roses, was a tremendous centerpiece measuring fifteen feet, an authentic reproduction of the Springdale Steeplechase Course, complete with miniature hurdles and gallery, toy horses, and riders. Our efficient maître d'hôtel, Maurice St. Clair, had worked on this creation for two weeks, and he told me "it took twenty waiters and busboys with their shoes off to place it on the table."

The rest of the evening was glowing with mellow candlelight, mellow laughter, and mellow bourbon freely flowing. Prohibition was on, but there was always private stock.

These were the boom days of the hotel business throughout the country, and the hotel men, flushed with money and success, were trying to outdo one another in royal entertainment, especially to the other members of their own profession. Lavish entertaining was the finest type of publicity and advertising, and it tended to enhance their reputations, and, I suspect, flatter their egos.

Some of the hotel parties in the twenties rivaled the splendor of King Solomon's court and the fabulous scenes of the Arabian Nights. They were never chronicled in public print, but they made history.

Dazzling affairs were hosted by John McEntee Bowman of the Bowman chain, at the Hotel Commodore in New York. One was his "Open House," given in the fall of 1921 in honor of five or six hundred hotel men who came to the United States to inspect the marvels of our newly constructed American hotels and study at firsthand the many innovations.

The Europeans arrived en masse on one of the luxury liners —I think the *Ile de France*—and from the time they landed on the dock until they re-embarked some two weeks later they were the guests of the American hotel men and were not permitted to spend one cent on accommodations, food, liquor, taxis, flowers, et cetera.

We sent them by special train to Chicago, where they were entertained with a lavishness calculated to outdo anything they could look forward to in New York, then by special train to Washington, where they were feasted, wined, and dined, then by special train to Atlantic City, where they were again entertained royally, and back by special train to New York, where they were housed in the city's finest hotels.

As they arrived back in New York the hotel show, lasting a week, burst into full swing in the Grand Central Palace, where the leading purveyors, equipment people, furniture dealers, decorators, and so on, showed their wares.

The climax of the week was Jack Bowman's "Open House."

About five hundred leading American hotel men were invited to the Commodore in addition to the European guests. Jack's short welcoming speech ended on the note, "On with the show." After cocktails and hors d'oeuvre served in a large foyer we were ushered into a larger room, metamorphosed into a circus side show, with all the attractions of Ringling's—the beautiful half-ton fat lady, the wild man from Borneo, the midget troupe, and such prize-yielding amusements as the Wheel of Fortune, Potting the Nigger, Ringing the Sticks, and Coaxing the Monkey (a live one), and a feature attraction—the Agglomeration with a huge caption reading: "MULTIFARIOUS, multigenerous, myelemiopopolous, agglomeration of astonishing anomaly, annihilating, apocalyptic, witching world wonder—FIRST AND FINAL PERFORMANCE!"

We were disporting in the side show when the clanging of bells summoned us into the ballroom where Ringling's Circus tent had been set up, complete to the last clown. Under the big top men and women swung in aerial acrobatics and into the rings trooped clowns and magicians, strong men and funny men, singers and dancers, the Queen of the Fairies, the Dusky Princess—all stars of the three-ring artistry. Adding to the general fantasia were cavalcades of trained dogs and horses, darting bareback riders, and, probably on their first visit to any ballroom, Ringling's trained elephants in majestic promenade.

We must not forget the dinner, served impeccably, with the circus in full cry, to a thousand hotel men used to the finest in Europe and the United States, who exclaimed in wonder as course followed course, each with its proper wine. I don't think our European guests were allowed to learn about our dark secret called prohibition.

Seated on the dais was Jack, surrounded by other notables, among them Sir Thomas Lipton, who had come to America to win back the racing cup with his famous *Shamrock IV*.

At the height of the evening there was a terrific commotion at the entrance. Headwaiters and captains were struggling to keep out fifty leather-lunged newsboys who burst into the ballroom with their arms filled with New York papers shouting "Uxtry uxtry, morning paper," and distributed copies to all the guests. The lead stories were authentic, but scattered through the columns were other stories of the most ludicrous, witty, or embarrassing kind, concerning those present.

In our immediate party were L. R. "Lit" Bolton, Fred Adams, and A. B. Ricker of Poland Springs, who, I honestly think, was the most loved man in our profession. After we had wined and dined to suffocation and the last dessert had been served, A. B. pushed himself away from the table and remarked thoughtfully, "God, I wish I had a doughnut!"

Before writing of this affair I checked with John McCall, banquet manager of the Hotel Commodore, who was instrumental in its staging. While talking with him I tried to imagine the tremendous responsibility and untold detail such a function entailed. Once a press agent became famous by smuggling a lion into a hotel. Jack Bowman brought an entire circus into the Commodore.

Another of Jack's fabulous parties was strictly stag, given to Ye Members of Ye Tavern Club on December 18, 1925, in the ballroom of the Commodore.

In the ballroom that night was an old English inn, complete in every detail, with a mounted master of hounds and a full pack of hounds outside and people in ye old costumes at the door in a standard English coach complete with driver, footman, and four horses.

There were only twenty-six places at the dinner table, including those of the two guests of honor, Mayor Jimmy Walker and Governor Al Smith.

The genial Thomas D. Green, one of the members of Ye Tavern Club, was among the guests. Tom Green fathered the American Hotel Association, as we know it now, and was its president from 1925 until 1940.

He told me the cost of this party for twenty-six guests was reported to be upwards of $40,000.

Chapter Twelve: FLORIDA BOOM

*D*URING the summer of 1925 all my friends and neighbors in the White Mountains began to talk Florida Boom. They questioned me about Kelsey City, Utopia Beach, Enchanted Gardens, and hundreds of places I had never heard of; they had invested in these enterprises.

The man who had delivered milk at Forest Hills drove up in a new Cadillac. He had gone to Saint Petersburg and become sales manager for a small subdivision known as Celestial Isles—or some such place—and to hell with the milk business, brother! He said, "You must be nuts, plugging along in the hotel business with all this easy money to be picked up in Florida! You mean to say you've been down there all your life and haven't got wise?"

I asked myself: How long has this been going on? and decided to find out.

I had a good crew and the hotel was full, so I turned it over to the resident manager, and on the last of July started for Florida.

As the train sped through the Carolinas and Georgia I looked out of the window and saw the highway crowded with cars—"tin Lizzies," purring limousines, trucks, open touring cars, and coupés and motorcycles—some piled high with tents, farming tools, suitcases, pets, and children—a never-ending stream flowing South in the summertime.

I hadn't any idea where I was headed—simply Florida.

I got off the train at Jacksonville early in the morning and went into the station for breakfast. As I went up the ramp

I remarked to the redcap, "I hear you're having a boom in Florida."

"Yes, sir, boss, we sure has. These northern people comin' down here so fas' we can't hardly take care of 'em."

"Where is the most excitement?"

"It don't rightly matter, they's people ever'where—Miami and Saint Petersburg are going strongest."

"When are the next trains out to Miami and Saint Pete?" I asked.

"They's one for Saint Pete in 'bout twenty minutes."

I bought a ticket for Saint Petersburg and boarded the train. Walking into the smoking compartment, I edged onto the little side seat near the door. Everyone was talking real estate.

"Bought a lot in Aladdin Acres near the boulevard last week for nine hundred dollars and sold it yesterday for thirty-two hundred dollars. I took an option on three more . . ."

"I made forty-seven hundred dollars in commissions in the last ten days."

"What's Osceola County acreage quoted today?"

"I bought eleven thousand acres of Hernando County last week and was going up to see it but I sold it to the Wilson boys for sixteen thousand dollars' profit."

I was in a daze. This wasn't the Florida I knew. I had been through two previous booms—the orange land boom of the nineties and the truck-land boom later—but nothing like this.

I remembered Saint Petersburg as a quiet little town with a few modest hotels in front of which elderly people sunned themselves on green benches. When I got off the train I was surprised to find a modern city with large office buildings and modern fireproof hotels. The traffic was heavy and the streets were lined with hundreds of real estate offices, some of which had barkers outside, like a sideshow, haranguing the passing crowds, "Hurry, hurry, buy now! The Mangrove Estates Realty Company has the best buy today. You'll never get rich working for somebody else. Resale profit a hundred per cent a month."

Next door a vacant store of twenty-five-feet frontage by a hundred feet deep, fitted out to represent the Hanging Gardens of Babylon, sported a three-piece orchestra and a barker who spieled: "Build a dream house in Spanish Acres! Here, far from the madding crowd, find solace from this workaday world—palm-fringed two-hundred-foot boulevard . . ."

I checked in at the Princess Martha Hotel and asked the clerk to give me a room high up, as it was hot as hades. After supper I walked around and kept pinching myself to see if I was really awake and that this was not all a dream.

Next morning, looking through my window and across the city, I saw the steel frame of a structure built upon a sand spit that jutted out into the bay. It was painted with red lead and looked enormous. When I called a bellboy to take a suit out to be pressed, I asked him what large building was going up over on the bay front. He said:

"That is the new Vinoy Park Hotel."

"Who's building it?"

"The Lockner Enterprises."

"Where are their offices located?"

He told me they were down on the bay front near the Soreno Hotel and that the president of the company was Mr. Ima Lockner. After breakfast I went down to call on him.

Mr. Lockner was in a board meeting, but I prevailed upon the receptionist to take in my card, and after a short wait I was ushered into the meeting room. I met Mr. Lockner and Baird Cook and the other directors. I liked Lockner immediately. He asked me what he could do for me.

I remarked that I had come down to operate their new hotel and added:

"You may never have heard of me, but I'm the second generation of Abbotts in the resort hotel business. To save a lot of conversation, I'd like to have you call two or three people who know me."

One of the directors leaned back and said, "We don't know just what we are going to do about a managing director. We've had a number apply. We don't know whether we want a blond, a strawberry blond or a brunet."

I laughed and asked him what his business was. He replied that he was a surgeon.

I said, "Well, Doctor, you probably don't take on work in competition with other surgeons. By the same token I wouldn't go into competition in applying for a position. I'll be up at the hotel."

That afternoon Mr. Lockner phoned me and the next morning we closed the deal and went over on the bay front to inspect the property.

It was a beautiful location and the architect was doing a fine job.

This was no project to play around with. The hotel had to be completed, equipped, and furnished and the grounds landscaped by the first day of the new year, which gave us about five months.

To make things more difficult, there was an embargo on all building material, equipment, and furniture into the state of Florida. Freight cars were backed up on sidings miles into the country. Labor, particularly skilled artisans, was scarce and demanded high wages.

After going over the hotel with the architect and mentioning a few things that would improve the building from a service standpoint, I went North to arrange for the purchasing of the furniture and equipment.

Buying the furniture and fixtures for a new three-hundred-and-seventy-five-room hotel is a complicated job requiring a thorough knowledge of the market and market conditions, but when it is further complicated by the fact that the owners in the venture are new to the hotel game and are, understandably, concerned as to whether their money will be wisely expended, it is a task.

It takes time to stop and explain the use to which equipment will be put—the difference between underglazed and overglazed decoration on china; why a bed sheet should be one hundred and eight inches long; or the thread count in a square inch of linen. I knew that I was not going to be able to drag the board of directors around from salesroom to salesroom or from factory to factory, so I hit upon a plan which saved a lot of traveling.

I went to the Commodore Hotel in New York City and got in touch with my good friend George Howard. We took the furniture out of many of the bedrooms on one floor, except a suite for the directors and one for myself. Then I started calling the heads and sales managers of the firms we had always done business with.

It was as hot as the devil and I sat on my bed in britches and undershirt telephoning for a couple of hours, and when I finished I had a bill for more than a hundred and fifty dollars in toll calls. We arranged with each firm to send its sales manager, demonstrators, and artists, to be there on a certain date to meet the Vinoy owners and bring with them whatever samples were necessary.

Each firm was designated a bedroom or two, as needed, in which to set up its merchandise. As I remember it there were Mohawk, Bigelow-Sanford, and a couple more carpet concerns; Wallace, Gorham, and International Silver Companies; Berky and Gay, Widdicomb, and other furniture people; Syracuse and Lamberton China; Baker Linen Company, and my good friends from the Kenwood Mills with their blankets. There were also kitchen equipment people, printing equipment people, drapery people, elevator people, lawn furniture people, fire-fighting equipment people, refrigerating people, piano and organ people, safe and vault people, office fixture people, bar fixture people, Venetian blind people, lamp and lampshade people, plumbing fixture people, and just people, people, and people.

They milled around the corridors in their undershirts through a haze of tobacco smoke, barged into one another's rooms, flattered the owners, flattered me, poured drinks, told stories, and talked shop. These were the days when competition was keen, not when you had to be "in the know" and have a pull to get supplies. I could have done the job alone in a week, but it took much longer under the circumstances.

The top salesmen entertained the owners at dinners and leading "hot spots," so everyone was a little slow in getting under way mornings.

I can see Frank Wilcox now, the sales manager for International Silver, trying to get the owners to twist the top off a silver coffeepot, or throwing it on the floor and stamping on it with his heel. What a showman!

An artist at his easel in a carpet exhibit designed a Pompeian carpet for the main dining room with bright-colored chalk while I sat in the next room and chain-smoked innumerable cigarettes, sweating over long columns of figures to see whether our budget was coming out right.

It is inevitable that the budget for equipment, furniture, and fixtures of a new hotel *never* comes out right for the simple reason that there is *never* money enough available to do the job as it should be done. To understand this it is necessary to go back to the time when someone somewhere gets a bright idea to build a resort hotel; someone somewhere has land to sell; someone would like to sell stock and bonds; somewhere there is an architect who would like to design a building and a contractor who would like to build one.

In due course the owner or owners of the land calls in the architect, who makes a set of plans and a beautiful wash drawing in color, and they take it to the contractor, who gives them an estimate. They then go to the man who is to do the basic financing to see how large a mortgage they can get and from there out into the highways and byways, using one of the many known devices to raise the equity money.

When this is accomplished, they start building the hotel. Not by the wildest stretch of imagination would they call in a first-class resort hotel operator who has spent his entire life exploring the ins and outs and the pitfalls of hotel operation until the building is so near completion that it is practically impossible for him to correct the mistakes that he sees the first time he looks at the plans.

People who build steel plants always get a top steel man. People who build railroads always get an experienced railroad engineer. Why, then, do people who build resort hotels never get a top resort hotel man until it is too late? This is a classic example of a little knowledge being a dangerous thing.

An experienced hotel man might point out to them that a resort hotel built parallel to a beach has half of its rooms facing the water and half back rooms; whereas if it is built at right angles to the beach, half of the rooms look down the beach and half of the rooms look up the beach, and everybody's happy; or that a two-hundred-room hotel, designed by a good operator, can be more efficiently operated with 25 per cent less employees than one poorly designed—the finest hotel architects in America notwithstanding.

By the same token he could point out that irrespective of the contractor's estimate resort hotel construction *always* runs higher than contemplated, which leaves the owners out on a limb when the time comes to purchase the furniture and equipment, the things that the guests actually see and which create the atmosphere of comfort and luxury necessary to the successful operation of the hotel. It is exactly the same as a man being well dressed to attend a party except that he has not money enough for a shirt and tie. If I were going to build a resort hotel I would first ascertain what it would cost to furnish it lavishly, allocate the money for the purpose, and put it where no one could get at it until it was ready to be spent for the purpose for which it was intended. So I beat my brains out over the budget.

I will say this for the Vinoy directors—they were a most understanding and resourceful group and when the time came they produced the funds to do a beautiful job. But even when funds are available it is a terrific job to explain to the uninitiated that it cost so much for furniture and equipment; items such as $90,000 for carpet, $75,000 for stainless-steel equipment in the kitchen, and $30,000 for linen. The owner may become intrigued with a trick corkscrew for the bathroom wall that costs only two dollars and sixty cents. Well, one for each bathroom times four hundred rooms equals $1,040, plus $200 for intallation, making a total of $1,240 for corkscrews.

The owners are likely to overlook the fact that it is one thing to order the furniture and squeeze within the budget and quite another thing to have this furniture and equipment delivered and installed ready for use. Truly there are many surprises!

Generally speaking, at this point, for some reason that I have never been able to understand, the owners build up a resentment against the operator and begin to look at him reproachfully, as if it is his fault that it cost so much to furnish adequately a resort hotel, whereas if the truth be told it is the additional 10 per cent spent *foolishly* and for added *showmanship* that makes a resort click.

Having let the contracts for the furniture and equipment, I then bent my efforts on a few other items contingent upon starting a resort hotel, such as opening a New York office, press relations, advertising, contacting some three hundred tourist bureaus, organizing a convention sales organization, getting out an attractive brochure of the hotel and other printed matter, arranging for music and other entertainment, contracting for the bulk of the food and liquor needed, hiring three hundred employees, buying their uniforms, arranging for their transportation, and arranging for concession rentals. When these items were taken care of my headaches really began.

I have said that there was an embargo on all goods shipped into Florida. Equipment that should have been delivered from the North and Middle West in a matter of days took weeks to come through. We wrote, wired, and telephoned factories; put tracers on shipments and tracers on the tracers; opened freight cars at junction points, took out the goods, and forwarded it by express.

The middle of September I went to the mountains to close the Forest Hills Hotel for the winter, drove down to Boston and took a look-see at the operation of the Vendome Hotel, gave it a lick and a promise, hired a crew for the Gasparilla Inn, and prepared to leave for the South.

An automobile salesman friend of mine drove up in a pea-green roadster. It sounds terrible, but it was really very smart. Nothing would do but that he sell it to me, so I drove it to Camden, South Carolina, non-stop, in practically nothing flat!

The Kirkwood was undergoing extensive repairs and re-decoration, and we were building a large garage and additional stables. After supervising this work I went on to Florida to see how the construction of the Vinoy was going.

It was a treadmill, a rat race, and I was like a squirrel in a wheel going round and round.

Speeding down the United States Highway Number One, I pulled into a filling station; as I was leaving I asked the attendant what the speed limit was, to which he replied, "This time of year you can just take the bridle off and let her graze!" I did just that for the next twenty-five years.

When I arrived back in Saint Petersburg the Vinoy project was alive with men inside and out—laborers, roofers, carpenters, plumbers, masons, tile-setters, electricians, elevator men, refrigeration men, painters, steam fitters and landscape men. They milled about and got in one another's way. Laborers walked over freshly laid cement and masons threw their trowels in the air.

With the best of management steam-fitting crews got in

the way of plasterers or vice versa, both crews got into juris-
dictional disputes with the plumbers, carpenters, and electricians, and all quarreled over time schedules and over who was
holding up the other.

It was a rush job and a madhouse, and the amazing thing
was that the contractors pulled a miracle out of chaos and
completed one of the finest hotels in the state practically on
time.

Contractors in Florida were sought after, wheedled, and
kowtowed to like potentates. Workmen were prima donnas,
ready to quit at a moment's notice if it was suggested, even
with great deference, that they take a little less than an hour
and a half for lunch.

Monday mornings were nightmares! Many of the best
workmen didn't show up, as there was pirating of labor all
over Florida. No one had a place to sleep, no one had a place
to eat—neither tourist nor workman.

Across the street, back of the Vinoy, another hotel was
going up—a hotel to house our three hundred employees, complete with kitchen, dining room, and social rooms. Few realize
that in a large resort hotel there must be help to take care of
help—help's cooks, help's waiters, dormitory matrons, watch-
men, et cetera.

We checked progress reports with one eye on the calendar,
hunted up materials that hadn't arrived or got in touch with
the architect and substituted others, argued with sub-contractors, cajoled foremen, chewed our fingernails, swallowed
our wrath and our pride, and gave bonuses to others who had
us out on a limb.

This mad scene was being duplicated all over Florida.

There were developments everywhere, some large and some
small, some promoted by men who kept their word, some by
fly-by-night shysters out to gyp a gullible public. And they all
wanted to build something—hotels, casinos, stores, swimming
pools, residences.

Rumor had it that there were 2,500 real estate offices in Miami and 30,000 agents selling real estate, and the sidewalks were cluttered up with men in shirt sleeves looking at maps, talking of binders and options, and perspiring under the hot summer sun. From Jacksonville to the Keys the entire state was in a ferment. Arguments raged as to the advantages of the east coast versus the west coast, and central Florida had its converts. All one heard was climate, climate, climate.

Canals were dug, land reclaimed and pumped in from the bay. Golf courses, casinos, yacht clubs, and hotels sprang up overnight.

Davis Island, near Tampa, sold $3,000,000 worth of lots the first day from a blueprint on land literally to be pumped from the bottom of Tampa Bay.

By 1925 Carl Fisher had spent millions of dollars in Miami Beach and was still pouring it into the "city built on sand." Addison Mizner and George Fryhoffer were developing Boca Raton with sales beyond man's wildest dreams. Joseph W. Young had arrived from California and invested millions of dollars in the development of Hollywood, Florida. Eugene Elliott and many others were developing projects around Saint Petersburg. So it went all over the state.

Before the main building of the Vinoy was completed the furniture and equipment began to arrive—carloads and car-loads of it—which all had to be stored under cover. We brought them from the railroad sidings in trucks, by mule teams, automobiles, and taxicabs. The main ballroom, lobby, dining room, and corridors were piled high with furniture with painters and decorators working all around and over it.

The kitchen equipment arrived together with men to install it when the weeks of leeway had shrunken to days.

There is an old axiom among resort hotel men that no man is stronger than his crew. No matter how much a manager may know about the business, if he has a poor chef he will have a poor table, or if he has a poor housekeeper things will be slipshod abovestairs. That is why it is necessary that a good manager know who the good help are, where they are, what they can do, and know more about their job than they do. This he must do to gain their respect.

I was anxious to do a first-rate job in the operation of the Vinoy, and it behooved me to secure the best crew obtainable. I wanted to stage one of the finest openings of any hotel in Florida. That was a big order! Many fine hotels had opened in Florida through the years, some with a flourish.

The opening of a new large resort hotel is like the first night of a big musical show, such as the *Follies*. Everyone is keyed up to the breaking point, and it takes experienced people, or old-timers, in the hotel vernacular, to stand the gaff. Things may not work properly in a new resort hotel, and there is no opportunity to take it out for a "shakedown" cruise as is done with a battleship or a luxury liner. For that reason I chose my crew for the Vinoy with infinite care.

The kitchens were in charge of Toni Delimano, a top-flight chef; the headwaiter was Frank "Slickey" Sawyer, the finest resort headwaiter of his time; the superintendent of service was Tom Kennedy, known throughout America as "the king of bellboys"—and so on, throughout the house. Of course these people were on their mettle as well as I, as they had reputations to maintain.

I will never forget how I hired the chief house officer. He was a fine-looking young man by the name of Dan Cooley and a New Hampshire State Trooper. I was breezing along in my green roadster between Manchester and Concord, New Hampshire, with Jack Eames, a friend, when we heard the wail of a siren. I turned to Jack and said, "This is it!" and pulled over to the side of the road. Dan came alongside on his motorcycle and took out his book to ask me for my driver's license.

I was in my shirt sleeves; I had taken off my coat and

thrown it in the rumble seat and slammed down the cover. My licenses were in my coat pocket and so were the keys to the rumble seat, so I couldn't get the cover open to present my license. I looked up at the trooper, saying:

"Where's the fire?"

Dan said, "That's what I was going to ask you. Let's see your license."

I told him it was in the back seat and we would have to drive into town and find a locksmith to get it out. Then I said,

"What do you do all winter?"

"Stay up here and eat snowballs," he replied.

"A big fellow like you would look swell in a powder-blue uniform as my chief house officer in Florida. Let's go up to see the Motor Vehicle Commissioner at the State House, and find out if we can get you a four months' leave of absence during the wintertime."

Dan went to Florida with me.

I had promised the owners that we would open the Vinoy Park Hotel with a New Year's Eve party. That was a mistake! The deadline was drawn too fine. Three weeks before the hotel was to open the crew arrived to get the place ready. It wasn't ready to get ready! The dormitory to house and feed the help was not ready, much less furnished. The help camped out wherever they could, and we fed them in the main kitchen amid a clutter of uncrated equipment. The hotel help kept getting in the way of the installation men, and decorators, carpet layers, and furniture people who were supposed to have been long gone—they also got in our way. The fact that we had about one hundred and twenty-five female help didn't make things function any smoother—the plumbers, painters, et al., thought they were wonderful! For forty-eight hours before the hotel opened I never closed my eyes once. The last twenty-four hours the dining-room and housekeeping crews worked straight through, setting up the dining room and guest rooms.

Thirty thousand dollars' worth of linen had to be laundered and put on the shelves. The hall carpets arrived by ship in such large rolls that we didn't have a door wide enough to get them into the building, so each carpet had to be unrolled outdoors and pulled up with a block and tackle through the windows.

Forty-eight hours before the hotel opened there was no refrigeration ready. We bought about ten tons of ice and stacked it on the floor and along the walls of a storeroom in the basement and I wish you could have seen the cooks skating around over this ice with huge pots of jellied soup or quarters of beef.

The Vinoy was due to open for dinner at exactly seven o'clock in the evening. At five-thirty men were still laying the oriental rugs in the lobby and electricians were feverishly trying out the lighting system in the huge ballroom, while groups of housemen were giving the last cleaning up to the public space.

At five-thirty I went to my room, took a cold shower, shaved, had a short nap, put on my evening clothes, and was back in my office at six-thirty. The owners wanted a show, and they were going to get it. Every light in every room on the front of the entire building was lighted. The great hotel that had been in darkness all these months sprang suddenly to life. I looked out of my office window and it seemed to me that there were great crowds gathered on the plaza in front of the hotel and down the water front looking up at the brilliant new Vinoy.

It was now twenty-five minutes to the deadline.

I rushed down to the kitchen, and Toni Delimano, the chef, had thirty-five or forty men in white coats lined up at attention in one long row and he was going along shaking his finger at each one of them in turn, and giving out with a torrent of excited Italian. When he reached the end of the line took him aside.

"Toni, what's the matter, have you got troubles?" He said mildly, "No troubles! I just tell them what to do."

I went over and glanced at his bulletin board. He had five hundred Shriners and their wives to feed in the main ballroom; he had the main dining room sold out and thirty-six dinner parties to serve, ranging from eight to forty people, all with different menus, and Toni was simply bored.

At five minutes to seven, the four tall, handsome doormen stepped out to the main entrance. They wore black boots with white kid tops, white trousers, long powder-blue coats, and tall silk hats with a cockade on the side. At exactly seven o'clock they opened the doors, and the great crowd entered the sparkling new, beautifully appointed hotel and milled around in the lobby and public rooms.

There was not an employee in sight except one lone clerk on the front desk. Everything was timed to the split second.

After allowing the crowd to oh! and ah! for five minutes, the clerk on the front desk pressed a buzzer. Out from the west wing marched Tom Kennedy, the superintendent of service, with the entire uniformed force—about fifty of them— bellboys, pages, elevator operators, porters, and housemen, all in new powder-blue uniforms. Their shoes shone, their uniforms were pressed to a razor's edge. He brought them up to attention, company front, in the main lobby and gave them "dismiss."

The bellboys took their stations, the elevator men manned the elevators, the two little pages—about four and a half feet tall, in blue trousers and vermilion jackets—started to page mythical people. The clerks, cashiers, and office force took over the desk.

The show received an ovation from the crowd.

Those who had dinner engagements proceeded to the dining room. Here again no one was in sight except tall, suave "Slickey" Sawyer in white tie and tails standing in front of the velvet rope stretched across the entrance.

At precisely seven-fifteen Sawyer pressed a button, and the entire dining-room staff walked in: captains, wine stewards, waitresses, bus boys, and cutest of all, six pretty little brunettes with slanting eyes and plucked eyebrows, dressed in beautiful Chinese robes and with their hair dressed high on top of their heads with huge black combs. They were to pass the relish trays, rolls, and later the petits fours. I had searched New York for those robes and combs.

At seven forty-five the entire crowd was dining at its leisure and the hotel was functioning as if it had been open for months. This is what I mean by opening a hotel with a crew who know their business.

Toni Delimano was about six feet tall, with wide, square shoulders, wavy black hair, and a florid complexion; when he smiled, he showed even teeth so white they glistened; he made a splendid appearance. In the middle of dinner he walked through the dining room in full evening dress, wearing one of the tallest white chef's hats I had ever seen. He was inspecting the food as it arrived in the dining room. It was a European touch that added to the éclat.

After dinner, while the guests were lingering over their coffee and cigarettes in the main dining room, we did a hasty job of clearing the ballroom and preparing for an evening of dancing.

The Vinoy ballroom was one of the largest and most beautiful in Florida. There was a stage with a proscenium arch at one end and a cove that ran around three sides of the room with hundreds and hundreds of colored lights hidden behind it, controlled by rheostats. We had a whole room full of them in the basement. The operating controls were in the wings of the stage, and by manipulating these controls the room could be flooded with different-colored lights and spectacular effects, from sunrise to moonlight, could be achieved.

I had hired a twelve-piece dance band from Paul Whiteman and it was under the direction of Joe Lucas. Being a dance "nut" myself, I had gone to a great deal of trouble to give the west coast something new in dance music. The great room was made glamorous by women in multicolored evening gowns and gentlemen in formal dress dancing to beautiful music in the ever-changing light.

My private office was on the mezzanine overlooking the lobby. There was a companion office for my secretary, and our desks faced through an open doorway. I had given her orders to be at her desk the entire evening in case of an emergency, but when I had an emergency and I looked through the door to see if she was at her desk, she had gone to the ladies' room. Now wasn't that just like a woman? The one time I needed her, she had to be in the ladies' room.

The emergency was in the form of a hundred-and-ten-pound brunette about twenty years old and very attractive. Where she came from I will never know. I just looked up, and there she was before my desk.

Florida was overrun by all kinds of crooks and gyp artists during the boom, and the minute I saw her I smelled danger. The girl said in a low voice:

"Mr. Abbott, there isn't a thing under this dress but just me." Putting her hand up to the low neckline of her dress, she said, "I want a hundred dollars or I'm going to tear this dress off."

I said, "Now let's not get excited. Let's see if I have a hundred dollars on me." I got out of my chair, reached into my pocket, and leaned across the desk, peering into my pocketbook. She leaned over to look, and I got my hands on her. She fought like a little fury, but I shoved her through the door onto the mezzanine, and just by luck the chief house officer was standing on the mezzanine looking over the crowd. I told him to put her on the sidewalk and turn her loose. We were just too busy to fool with her.

A managing director sitting at his desk on an evening like that, even with the best hotel force in the world, is like a man sitting on a volcano. Anything can happen, and usually does. The only thing he can do is to relax and meet a crisis when it occurs.

About thirty minutes after this episode one of the pages stepped into my office and said, "Mr. Abbott, the orchestra has struck."

I said, "What do you mean, struck?"

"They just ain't goin' to play any more."

I said, "I'll murder that band leader."

When I reached the ballroom five hundred people were standing on the floor waiting for music. I walked through the crowd and up onto the stage and said, "Lucas, what's the matter?"

He looked at me and shrugged. "Mr. Abbott, I cannot do anything with these boys, they are tearing my nerves to pieces. That damn piano player thinks he knows more about leading a band than I do. He wants to change the instruments all around. He's crazy that way."

I said, "You can't keep all these people waiting; let him try it. We'll settle this later."

The pianist got up and took the drums, the drummer the saxophone, the saxophonist the piano—all the musicians changed instruments. They played a number. It was marvelous! As soon as the number was over, again everything was confusion in the band. No one liked the instrument he was playing; they all wanted to play some other instrument! So they changed again. They played another number. It was wonderful! And then I caught on! So did the crowd. It was a gag. But what a gag! Every man in that band could double on two or three instruments.

I had had a hard time selling the owners on the expense of that music, but it certainly paid dividends.

As I was on the stage I took the opportunity of welcoming the elite of Saint Petersburg to the Vinoy.

Leaving the ballroom, I passed through the terrace between

the ballroom and the main lobby. On this terrace we served food and drinks. It was staffed by a force of a dozen tall Swiss waiters under the command of one of the most finished grill captains I have ever known.

There was a late dinner party of about forty people in progress. The host had drunk too much. Nothing irks me more than to see a man drink too much, especially in public and before his friends. We had some especially beautiful potted palms along the edge of the terrace and he thought it would be fun to tear them up. He tore one to shreds, and the captain remonstrated with him; thereupon he tore up another, and the captain was about to send for the house officer when I noticed what was going on. When the guest approached his third palm I was there.

"Hello, Mr. Bryant (which wasn't his name), having fun?"

"You betcha, lotsha fun, tearing up palmsh in potsss."

"Sure, go on and tear them up. They only cost thirty dollars apiece." If you want to hit a man a solar-plexus blow, hit him in the pocketbook. It really cuts him down to size. "Mr. Bryant" made a pass at the palm but didn't damage it, and, mumbling something, walked back to his table. I went to the cashier and had a bill made out, "two palms—$60," and took it to him, and leaned over confidentially. "Just initial this, please, before the next course is served." With forty of his friends at the table there was nothing he could do but initial the bill and toss it off as a joke. He was a good patron from then on.

A very fine old lady once said to me, "Some men's remorses are other men's reminiscences."

After the crowd left I assembled all the help in the ballroom. Toni Delimano brought sandwiches and the bar boys came up with cases of beer. The crew had come to the Vinoy as strangers; they went to bed that night as a closely knit hotel crew.

*T*HE top of the stock market boom was in 1929. I was commuting between New Hampshire, Massachusetts, New York, South Carolina, and Florida, and added to my activities the operation of the Savannah Oglethorpe in Savannah, Georgia, and promoted the building of the Sagamore on Green Island in Lake George, New York.

In the Kirkwood Grill in Camden one morning Everett Bacon, of Spencer, Trask and Company, New York, told me of the beauties of Lake George in upstate New York and of the island, which was owned by a New Yorker, Dr. William G. Beckers. On the island was a club with about thirty rooms which Dr. Beckers wanted me to operate.

That spring Dr. Beckers came to Camden. I told him I was not interested in so small a place and that he could not afford to hire me to operate it, but I made him a sporting proposition. "I'll run the club for one season on a bet, and if we make as much in that season as it lost the season before, you will have to build me a two-hundred-room hotel!"

Having tossed this suggestion out of a cold deck, I drove up to see the island. It was April, rainy and cold, and without getting out of the car I could see that the little clubhouse was not big enough to make any money out of rooms.

But I operated the club that summer of 1929. We took up a French chef and started a party business (catering to private parties and functions) and this, plus the rooms, made enough money to win my bet.

That fall I called on Dr. Beckers in New York. "When do we start building that hotel?"

He was game. I engaged Harold Field Kellogg as architect, and we worked together forty-eight hours without stopping and completed a set of plans for a two-hundred-room hotel.

Our idea was a resort unit laid out strictly from point of service and economy, and, built around that, a pleasing structure.

Green Island in Lake George is a mile long and about a half mile wide. We planned to build the hotel on a promontory about one hundred yards from the water's edge where this most beautiful of lakes, dotted with three hundred islands, reflects in its depths the verdant hills.

We wanted the building to appear as small as possible, so Kellogg designed it with four wings jutting from a common center. For once a resort hotel would be built with public rooms, lounge, dining room, and grill large enough to care for a full complement of guests without crowding and give the general air of spaciousness so necessary to the interior in a hotel of this sort.

We broke ground October 1, 1929. Our opening was set for July 1 of the following year—nine months in which to build a modern resort complete with help's dormitory, garage, stables, water systems, sewerage systems, landscaping, furnishing, decorating, staffing, and equipping the building ready for service!

Quite an order, especially with the winters on Lake George so rigorous, the temperature dropping at times to twenty-five degrees below zero!

We began work with all the optimism in the world. This was to be everything I'd dreamed a hotel should be.

The frame was up when the crash hit Wall Street.

I went to New York, where the millions everybody had owned were melting in all directions, and Dr. Beckers told me the hotel would have to wait.

After a long talk he went ahead. He had a lot of courage, and I had an agreement with the architect and builders holding them to ship material on my order. I put in orders to ship all the material I dared, without the faintest idea where the money for the freight was coming from, let alone for the material.

Meanwhile I took my licking in the crash along with the rest. I had a long sheet of paper with red typewritten items of all the notes coming due, called the "misery sheet." I carried it around in my pocket until the edges wore off.

The year 1929 took everything but my health and know-how and a large acquaintanceship. However, these are not bad assets with which to start anew.

After the crash I found myself with nine hotels to carry and another a third finished on Lake George.

From Florida to New Hampshire I talked with bankers, but couldn't raise a dime. You know how a banker is—loan you an umbrella, and when it starts to rain he wants it back?

I was standing in the lobby of the Commodore in New York wondering what I was going to do when a fellow came up to the porter's deck and said, "Get me a ticket to Saint Louis." Call it a hunch or a click of the memory, but I told the porter, "Get me one too." I had remembered Bill Bixby lived in Saint Louis and that Dr. Beckers had planned to see him.

Mr. Bixby didn't say no. He didn't say yes, either. He said, "Come back tomorrow."

I bought a box of aspirin and went to bed. The next morning Mr. Bixby gave us the money to complete the Sagamore.

Shortly after this Dr. Beckers transferred his interest in the hotel to the Essex Investment Company of Saint Louis, which was controlled by the Bixby family.

About a year after the bank holiday I was in one of the big New York banks asking for a loan. I knew the president well, and when I went into his office the president of another bank was there. When I made my request the president leaned back and eyed me coldly.

"Karl," he said, "I am not impressed with the way hotels in America have been run for the past few years."

I smiled. "They never had to close all the hotels in America for three days to find out which ones were solvent."

The visiting bank president burst out laughing. "Joe," he told his friend, "you'd better give that boy his loan!" And I got it.

We had started the Sagamore in October, and all that unhappy winter of twenty-nine I was commuting between Lake George and Florida, between sun and freezing snow. Bill Bixby's loan finished it, but there was still a little matter of money to furnish the place. I ran all over New York trying to finance the furniture. One morning I was in Glens Falls, sitting in the lobby of a hotel and wondering where to try next, when a strange man sat down beside me. He said he had a little furniture store across the street and would like to furnish the hotel.

"You can't," I told him bluntly. "We haven't any way to finance the furniture."

He went out, and I asked the clerk who he was. By the time he got through telling I realized I had just met the man who had the means to furnish a number of hotels. I tore across the street to the furniture store and admitted I had made a mistake.

Martin Wilmarth furnished the Sagamore and proved to be the best of friends.

We opened July 1, 1930, with practically no bookings. What a time to open a new hotel! The crash of twenty-nine had put a blight on the entire industry. The majority of America's hotels were going into receivership.

The Sagamore had this advantage—it was the only fine resort hotel built that year.

Toward the last it seemed we would never finish. The day

before the opening the painters' shack was still standing on the lawn. A ten-ton truck came along and I had the driver hitch a cable to the shack and haul it away. It sailed over the hill with two painters and barrels of paint still inside, spilling paint and profanity.

A guest came downstairs on opening night. "I just love my room," he said, "but I wish you'd take that cask of lime out of it."

We had one hundred and sixty-four guests the first night, and the hotel was comfortably full for the remainder of the summer. We made a good profit that season, at the start of the depression.

It is not often that a resort operator has the privilege and finances to start absolutely at scratch and build a resort hotel exactly as he wants it, but this was the case of the Sagamore down to the last detail, and for this reason it was the most economical unit I ever operated.

Our first season's successful operation gave the Sagamore a splendid reputation, and through the depression years and on it continued to make money.

We inaugurated many innovations to make it ever more popular. We built a large ring with bleachers and held yearly horse shows that brought devotees from as far as the Midwest. We held official dog shows, with three hundred dogs in huge circus tents on the lawn.

My son Frank was thirteen and serving his apprenticeship in the kitchen when I called him onto the piazza one day to be introduced to Chief Justice Hughes.

"How did you like your roast beef?" Frank asked, man to man.

"And how did you know I had roast beef for lunch?" demanded the famous judiciary.

"I was working in the kitchen when your order came in, so I cut you the very best slice."

An old dishwasher stopped me in the Sagamore kitchen to

ask for the next day off. Commencement exercises were being held at Vassar, and his daughter was graduating *cum laude*. He dried his hands to take out her picture, and with it came another of a daughter in Smith. He had put them both through college washing dishes. I looked at those gnarled old hands and a lump came in my throat. You find many like him on hotel crews.

The second season we opened the Sagamore with three conventions. Our first was a large gathering of bankers followed by an undertakers' convention. This was held before the season opened, and they had the whole hotel and island to themselves, so that the embalming fluid odor didn't bother anyone except the help. About fifty caskets were in display in the main lounge, and floral exhibits and burial gowns, and I nearly lost my colored bell row when some of the delegates told the boys with perfectly straight faces that they were going to embalm a cadaver in the main lobby. The display was a weird sight, but I never entertained a finer group, nor men who had more fun and were better spenders.

The undertakers' convention was followed by a real estate convention. In my welcoming speech at the opening meeting I told them that the bankers had been taken care of by the undertakers and now the real estate boys could provide a place to bury them. In 1930 this was a grim joke. After that we had a variety year after year. Once the psychiatrists came, and one leading speaker was a very excitable man who used the longest words I had ever heard. One night after a meeting I found him pacing the porch.

"What are you doing out so late?" I asked.

"I am expecting to commit suicide," he answered, "and I'm trying to keep from going down and jumping off the dock."

I gave him a good talking to and sent him up to bed.

Another convention we had was sponsored and paid for by a large and reputable firm. Its president, other high officials, and salesmen came from all over America. The firm requested that we send room waiters to each room every morning with a breakfast tray, rap on the door, and say cheerfully, "Good morning, I have a surprise for you."

The first morning one of our room waiters rapped on a certain door and said, "Good morning, I have a surprise for you."

The man inside, who thought he was funny, answered, "I have a surprise for *you!*" He put his arm through the transom and poured a pitcher of water over the waiter.

That evening, at the banquet, the president addressed the assemblage. He told of the early struggles of the organization and how through the years they had worked to build its fine reputation in the country, and how every man present was the guardian of that reputation. Then he related the incident of the waiter, who had only been trying to do what he had to do—in other words, earn his living. He emphasized the way all the other employees of the hotel must feel about the matter.

He finished his talk by saying:

"The man who did this is no longer with us."

In these words he fired the practical joker, who was not only a salesman but a district manager holding a highly paid position. It was an object lesson to the members of a great business.

A friend of mine who had a hotel on the east coast discovered during one convention that his elevator operators were charging the delegates—men from the deep South—ten cents every time they rode on the elevator.

One evening during a big convention at the Sagamore a college football player who ran the soda fountain rushed into the crowded grill and grabbed me by the shoulders as I stood talking with a group of delegates.

"My God, a man just died at my counter!" he babbled.

"Take your hands off me!" I ordered. I had to startle him back to his senses. "Is the man in front of the counter or behind it?" I asked. He told me behind it, out of sight.

He hurried back to his post. I telephoned the house physician to rush to the fountain, and Nolan, my assistant, and I ,joined him there. The man was lying under the counter. The boy was standing over him with shaking hands serving sodas to the customers, who knew nothing of what had happened. The doctor went quietly behind the counter, kneeled down with his stethoscope, and shook his head.

We were able to cope with the unfortunate situation with sympathy and dispatch.

The next morning, about five, I discovered that the toilet in my bathroom wasn't flushing. I telephoned the night clerk. He was a green man and unused to emergencies. "I don't know what's wrong," he answered, "the water hasn't been running since midnight." I doubt if he even heard my groan of exasperation. "My God, man, three hundred guests and you didn't let me know!"

Here was trouble that could empty the house at the peak of the season. I telephoned the fire department and they put a pumper down on the dock to start the water supply flowing, while my superintendent located the leak in the pipe. It was fifteen feet under water between the island and the mainland. We telephoned New York and ordered a diver sent up by plane to weld the pipe under water; meantime the pumper kept working.

About four that afternoon I came back to the hotel and sat down in the lobby to rest. I was all in—I thought. In a few moments Nolan came up to me and said confidentially: "One of our canoes is missing."

A woman guest had taken a canoe out on the lake that morning and hadn't come back. That could mean almost anything!

We sent men out in motorboats to comb Lake George and its islands. I had to let others carry on the search. A big dinner was scheduled for that evening to be followed by a revue, and I had promised to take part.

After dinner I went back to the lake. The woman was still missing. I came back to the hotel to learn that it was time for the show and I hadn't rehearsed or thought of what I was to do. On the way through the kitchen I stopped to borrow a uniform from a waiter and a waitress's lipstick. It had occurred to me to impersonate Leon Errol in his *Follies* drunk scene. I got into the uniform and reddened my nose as the music cue started. While crossing the darkened grill I nearly stepped on a man lying on the floor. Nolan was standing there on guard. "He's from the fourth floor," Nolan explained; "he just dropped dead of a heart attack and we're taking him to the morgue."

Two in one day, and still we didn't know what had become of the woman in the canoe! I hurried into the next room and into my act.

Hotel business. Show business.

When I came off Nolan was waiting. They had found her. By this time it was midnight. She had taken forty barbital pills and gone out in the canoe to die, but the pills nauseated her and she had tumbled into the water, which revived her, and they found her lying, weak but alive, on a sand bar.

Don't think this sort of thing goes on all the time! It was to happen once more in a city hotel I was running. The assistant manager, looking up from his desk, saw a guest in evening clothes walk down the stairs and keel over at the foot. The doctor came and pronounced him dead. The assistant manager had to go upstairs and break the news to his wife.

Later that night the guest woke up, stark naked, on a slab, scaring the attendant nearly to death, got back into his clothes, and returned to the hotel. It was about four in the morning when the night clerk looked up and saw the late guest standing before his desk and he fainted dead away. When he came to, he telephoned the manager, who had to go upstairs to explain once more to the "widow."

For fifteen happy years I ran the Sagamore. My family spent the summers there and wintered in the South. The dozen or so other hotels I ran in those years were fun and I was having a wonderful time. A few hours' sleep at night, a cat-nap during the day, kept me fit.

For twenty-five years I averaged 35,000 driving miles a year. During the boom I really indulged a passion for fast automobiles. "What, another car?" Father would say. Once I answered indignantly, "Why, I've had twenty-nine hundred miles out of this one!"

A reputation for making time between two points was something I tried to live down. Once a hotel man's meeting was held at Poland Springs in South Poland, Maine. Leo Nolan and I drove over from the Sagamore, a long run, and just before we hit the Springs I dropped the speed to thirty and we drove up before the hotel sedately.

About one hundred hotel men were sitting on the porch and the association president came down the steps to welcome us. "Well, I see you've been driving like the devil," he said.

I said, "That only shows how ill deserved my reputation is. We had plenty of time and took it leisurely."

He raised his eyebrows. "Then why don't you take that white Leghorn off your radiator?"

I walked around in front. A big white rooster was spread-eagled across the front of the car.

As a rule I'd leave the Sagamore at sunup, lunch in Baltimore, dine in Washington, catch an early movie in Richmond, and roll into one of the southern places in time for coffee and scrambled eggs. A seasoned operator can oversee a well-organized hotel in a short time. In my estimation there is no such thing as a busy executive in hotel business—if he's busy, he isn't an executive.

Impressions of the little things make up hotel operation—was the breakfast bacon cooked in advance and put in the oven to turn limp, is a light bulb out in the hall, is dust on the table in the lobby? I observed automatically. Wherever I go

I notice everything—in other hotels, railroad stations, and trains. I try not to notice, but I do.

My boy, Karl, Jr., is like that. A few years ago, when I was operating the Flamingo at Miami Beach and Karl was about twelve, he came down from boarding school for his winter vacation. He rushed into the lobby and gave me a hug, saying, "Daddy, how many bellboys do you have here?" I said, "A dozen. Why?" To which he replied, "Well, you'd better send half of them out to pick up those cigarette butts under the marquee."

I always tried to reach the Savannah Oglethorpe in time for one of the golf tournaments and oyster roasts put on for Al Smith and Rascob and Judge McCooey. I was a great admirer of Al Smith.

The hotels took on the problems of their sections. Savannah was old South. An oilman was to ship our gasoline down the Wilmington River by barge, but the harbor master wouldn't let it clear. The oilman telephoned to say he would have to bring it down by truck, and our assistant manager, a new man, down from the North, responded, "Sure, that's the trouble with you folks down here—bring it by truck so you can raise your price a half cent a gallon."

After a short pause the soft southern voice came again over the wire. "I'm coming down, and when I get there, you'd better be out on the front porch apologizing!"

The oilman hung up. The manager came to me and repeated the conversation as a big joke. It was no joke to one who is half cracker.

"Brother," I said, "get out on that front porch, and when you see the car drive up, start apologizing!"

Prior to the Roosevelt era some of the "braintrusters" began coming to Lake George. I saw quite a bit of George Foster Peabody who had a summer home there as well as his famous estate at Saratoga Springs. It was called "Yaddo" because his small granddaughter gave this pronunciation to "Shadow." He was interested in Warm Springs, Georgia, with Franklin D. Roosevelt.

About six weeks after Roosevelt became President Mr. Peabody asked me to Warm Springs to see him at the Little White House.

They were considering building a fine hotel at Warm Springs and opening it up as a great resort entirely separate from the Warm Springs Foundation.

I stayed there for a few days mulling the idea over but couldn't see any possibilities, and told them so. It didn't seem to me we could get very far in four years.

If I had known he was going to be President four terms . . .

We knew repeal was coming, and the date was set. A friend of mine who was president of one of the largest liquor purveyors in America telephoned. "Who do you know on the governor's board?" he wanted to know.

He named a nearby state where, he said, about fifty liquor salesmen were sitting on the statehouse steps waiting for prohibition to be repealed. It was rumored that the state would have state stores—a big account.

The governor had appointed three leading citizens as a sort of board to visit the distilleries and breweries and decide which had the best liquors and beers.

By a coincidence their first stop was to be a city where I was running a large hotel.

It happened that I did have a friend on the governor's board, and he had them look me up when they came to town. The party started with a double room and bath and progressed until we had eleven rooms en suite, one with a baby-grand piano. The genial sales manager for the liquor concern introduced the boys to the city and filet of sole *bonne femme* with champagne. They were in the hotel three weeks, which was the entire time allotted for their survey.

One member wandered out one night and called me on the telephone. "I'm lost," he said.

"Where are you?" I asked.

"If I knew," was his answer, "I wouldn't be lost."

I never knew what sort of report they sent in, but my friend got a whale of an order, and still has it.

There was a sequence to this interlude. I'd worked for three weeks, day and night, amusing the board, and when the big order came my friend wanted to pay me. I refused even the money I'd spent on entertainment. But fifteen years later, in wartime, I had a big hotel opening and needed five hundred cases of scotch, and there wasn't any scotch left in the world. I called him up.

"Remember repeal?" I asked. "Well, I need five hundred cases . . ."

I could see his grin across the wire. "Karl," he said, "it's on its way."

No sentiment in business? It's all sentiment!

During the last war one of our resort hotels attracted a group of high-ranking Nazi sympathizers. A captain in the dining room told me he had seen one of the men rise and propose a toast to Hitler at a private dinner party. We were keeping our eyes on them when one afternoon a costly car pulled up at the entrance and a strikingly beautiful blonde got out. She registered and went to her room, and an hour or so later two F.B.I. men came into my office and showed their credentials.

One said, "Is my face red! When I came into the lobby your head bellman nudged the boy next to him and I saw him whisper, 'F.B.I.!' "

That was Willie Gamble.

The blonde sat alone in the lounge that evening, listening to the music. A guest I had not seen before was sitting near by reading a copy of the *Saturday Evening Post*. I noticed he sat a long time without turning the page, so I strolled casually back of his chair. I saw that he had a piece of drawing paper pasted in the magazine and was sketching the young lady—full face and profile.

It seemed she was a famous German spy so highly placed that the government did not want to arrest her on American soil.

She stayed on at the hotel, and so did her Nazi-sympathizing confreres. They made no noticeable efforts to communicate with her, but an eligible young bachelor did—he asked the hotel hostess to introduce him. What a shock it would be when he discovered that the summer flirtation they struck up was conducted under the watchful eyes of the F.B.I.! Dancing in the grill, murmuring in the summerhouse, the pair were never out of the agents' sight.

One day the woman seemed to sense something was wrong and left hurriedly. We learned afterward she was arrested the moment she left the country.

Among the annual groups of husband hunters that sometimes frequent resort hotels I remember Vanilla. Without exception she was the dumbest blonde on record. She was a natural platinum, without a trace of expression or a glimmer in her eye, and the nickname "Vanilla" pinned on her was perfect. She arrived at one of our summer resorts in mid-season and found herself thrown in with several designing women who were pursuing a couple of wealthy bachelors. Vanilla said in her mild, helpless fashion that she'd like to get a rich husband too.

Of course everyone laughed.

But dear little helpless Vanilla got her man and the pick of the crop, and the other women almost went crazy with envy. I knew something they did not—Vanilla was a manicurist from one of New York's best barbershops! She had seen a Grade-B movie where a stenographer saved enough money to buy smart clothes and went to a swank hotel for two weeks and got a husband.

Vanilla saved her tips for three years and gambled all on a two weeks' vacation. Every time I see her pretty, expressionless face in the society columns I have to smile.

At this point let me illustrate what a gamble hotel business can be and how quickly the lightning can strike. We had one fine old resort hotel up North that turned into a white elephant. We had a mortgage on the place and foreclosed it, advertising in the papers that the property would be sold at public auction. When Nolan and I waded through the snow that February morning there wasn't another person in the streets. The auctioneer arrived in his tall hat and Prince Albert and set his two red flags on the porch of the empty hotel and we opened the auction—just Nolan and my attorney and I and the auctioneer—not another soul in sight.

"What am I bid?" announced the auctioneer. "Once. Twice. Three times. Sold."

He took down his flags and left, and we had the damn hotel on our hands again.

The Kirkwood in Camden was lucrative and very successful. I had purchased the minority stock and owned the property outright. In 1926, a banner year, I was offered $600,000 for the property, but I could see no point in selling, as the earnings were so great. It represented a large segment of my estate, and I saw to it that this hotel was well operated.

Two years later the cult of sun worshipers began. We heard of cabanas and beach clubs, and the fast trains rolling through South Carolina, Florida-bound, were loaded to the roof with winter tourists. None got off at Camden. We had the same hotel, climate, beautiful surroundings, service, but the Kirkwood was practically empty.

We kept on operating as if expecting a full house. A little larger band, a little better service, a little better table—but these were the strivings of despair. Only a few of the old guard remained, and they became increasingly more difficult to handle. Guests took advantage of the fact that business was desperately poor and demanded added service and lower rates.

A feeling of deep despondency permeated the staff, as their tips, on which they depend so much, became practically nil.

Any responsible resort operator comes to love a property and take pride in it. It is a heartbreaking experience to see a beautiful business disintegrate through no fault of your own. A blight covered the mid-South. All the resort hotels in Camden, Somerville, Aiken, and Augusta suffered alike. Through many a sleepless night I lay in my bed at the Kirkwood listening to those Seaboard trains roar through to Florida and trying to find a way out. I borrowed money to keep going.

After a couple of years I disposed of the Kirkwood by paying a $19,000 deficiency judgment. It was the same beautiful property for which I had been offered $600,000 a few years before. Ho, hum! Another day, another dollar. The tide of luck flowed in and out and there was no use brooding.

The vocation I had inherited was an incurable disease.

Late September was beautiful at the Sagamore, after the season closed.

In the late thirties we started the custom of closing the hotel for a couple of days to give the staff a rest and then re-opening it as Ye Olde Sagamore for a week-end house party. We excluded automobiles from the island and met our guests with horses and buggies. The entire staff dressed in the costumes of the nineties, and the pen on the front desk was stuck in an Irish potato, the way Father kept it in Bethlehem. The clerks on the desk were in their shirt sleeves, sleeve garters and all, and sported handle-bar mustaches.

We closed down the elevators and made the guests walk to their rooms, and insofar as we could reverted to the hotel life I had known as a boy. The electricity was turned off; the public rooms were lighted by oil lamps and candles; the ladies' powder room had a sign: Water Closet; the dining room was set up with tables to seat sixteen each; and the chef and his crew came in each night to help serve the harvest supper in the old tradition.

A New York theatrical costumer came up with many trunks of costumes and a make-up artist to assist the guests. A guest was not allowed in the hotel without a costume, which he wore all day and evening. We held hay rides, barn dances, and played charades and old-fashioned games like "drop the handkerchief." And each night after supper we held a community sing in the main lounge and popped corn in the big fireplace.

We had progressive whist and euchre parties and I "punched," just as I did as a boy. My daughter Gladys, dressed in the "leg-o'-mutton" shirtwaist and skirt of the gay nineties, wearing her dark hair en pompadour, looked so much like my mother that just to look at her turned the years back for me.

The guests were so keen for these parties that they made their reservations early in the summer and returned from their homes to attend them each fall. We started the Gay Nineties parties for the guests, but the crew got into the spirit, and loved them.

Such parties just don't happen. They take planning. One year I gave a two weeks' house party to a couple of dozen friends at Lonesome Lake, which lies high up on the side of the mountain near the Old Man of the Mountain. I sent a number of the girls in the party out for daily mountain-climbing trips. They rode burros I had brought from Colorado and were accompanied by French-Canadian guides. I told the girls that the guides couldn't speak English and warned the guides not to. So the girls spoke freely among themselves and when, after two weeks, the guides bade them farewell in perfect English, the girls were ready to strangle me.

The last night of the house party I suggested that we go

down to the water's edge and build a fire and toast marshmal-
lows. The little lake lay like a dark mirror framed by the
black mountains. The cheery blaze turned the nearby waters
to burnished copper. We sat around the fire toasting marsh-
mallows and engaging in quiet conversation. Soon the great
full moon rose above a cliff, painting the scene with silver.

Off across the waters drifted the melodious notes of a saxophone playing the first bar of the "Indian Love Call." From
the other side of the lake, under the pines, a trumpet softly
picked up the melody. A clarinet whimpered in echo from
under a cliff.

Then through the moonlight they came drifting—fourteen
musicians in fourteen canoes, each maneuvered by one of our
guides. The music rippled and joined as the canoes converged,
and on a burst of melody the "Love Call" ended.

It is a great satisfaction to build, open, and direct a successful hotel. The fifteen years at the Sagamore were wonderful.

There were sad memories too. Father died there. He loved
Lake George, and some of his happiest summers were spent
observing the resort's activities from his wheel chair.

A few days before his death he summoned me, pounding
his cane. His head was thatched with snow and his countenance still had a look as stern as that of the Old Man of the
Mountain. People thought him austere, but underneath he was
bubbling with fun.

On this day he banged his cane with special emphasis.

"Karl, have you seen these girls with their painted fingernails and painted toenails?"

"Why, yes."

Dad winked one bright blue eye.

"Great, isn't it!"

In 1945 we closed the Sagamore as usual. Closing is a happy
event, and this was no exception. Our young Karl, Jr., has

given us an expression, "I like it best when there's gravel on the lawn"—when the last wheels spin and the gravel flies on the grass and nobody cares until next year.

The guests were gone, the rugs rolled, each piece of silver cleaned, counted, and put away. It was like all the other years. The help were happy, with money saved, and eager to be on their way. Everyone was weary of being polite, patient, always smiling. The casual good-bys were like other good-bys: "Be seein' you."

So we closed the Sagamore, not knowing it was for the last time. Only later did a letter arrive, saying the hotel was being sold.

In hotel and show business one learns to love and let go. The big adventure is always the job ahead.

Chapter Fourteen: PARDON MY OPERATION

Anyone not interested in resort hotel operation may skip this chapter. This is not intended as a technical chapter on resort hotel operation per se, but merely a glimpse "backstage" for benefit of the layman.

The resort hotel business is delightful when things go right. The manager lives amid beautiful surroundings in a marvelous climate, occupies splendid accommodations, and eats fine food. But when things go badly the business is desolate.

Few people realize the huge investment involved and that the overhead goes on three hundred and sixty-five days a year, although the hotel may be open only a fraction of that time.

An old story in the hotel world is, "How to Build a Bat Roost." One has a popular hotel. Because of a slight depression or some other cause outside of the hotel field, the hotel has a short run of poor business. The owners get nervous and demand that the managing director drastically cut expenses. The managing director, to please the owners, cuts out all repairs and refurbishing, cuts down on his advertising, and cuts his pay roll to the point where the service is curtailed. The next step is to cut out the expensive items of cuisine. Because of these curtailments the business is a little poorer, so the managing director, in order to attract business, cuts his rates. Because of the cuts, added to a lower occupancy, the income from the hotel is much less than it was before, so the whole vicious circle starts again. This goes on until there is no business left, and then one need only break out all the windows to have a first-class bat roost.

A conscientious managing director who knows his business does not allow this to happen. His first loyalty is to the capital invested in the property. Two courses are open to him: one, to be able—out of long experience—to convince the owners that they are taking the wrong road; two, to resign.

There is no short cut to experience in fine hotel operation, and, more particularly, fine resort hotel operation. A number of hotel courses in several universities and colleges, such as the one pioneered by Professor Lois Meek of Cornell University, go a long way to prepare a man for this profession, but a lifetime is not too long to acquire the ability and experience necessary in this the most bewildering and diversified of careers.

Some of the requirements are: the ability and experience to meet any serious crisis instantly; the knowledge of the overall layout of a hotel from the standpoint of economy, service, and showmanship; the ability to prognosticate trends; the price structure and the timing thereof, which require almost a sixth sense; the matter of construction and construction costs; the working of a sewerage system; the ventilating of public rooms, lighting, decoration, and what to do about noise; the layout of a kitchen; the knowledge of where to obtain things, when, and how; the purchasing of foods; the relation between the setting of a fine table and the garbage can; the comparison of the American plan to à-la-carte service; the benefit of friendships built up throughout the years with other hotel men and the purveyors; the successful handling of help so as to maintain discipline and earn their respect and loyalty and profit by their best efforts; the knowledge of where to obtain good help, who they are, and what their capabilities and specialties are and their faults; liquor costs and the drinking habits of different types and races of people; the eating habits of the public, their likes and dislikes; entertainment, the type of music that your particular clientele desires; the psychology of working with large groups of different nationalities; the handling of conventions, banquets, and social functions; a knowledge of specialized advertising and business promotion; the ability to write letters that carry conviction; guest relations; the knowledge of hotel accounting and of hotel law; the entire field of housekeeping and the opening and closing of a hotel in relation to the time and money involved; and knowledge of literally hundreds of other subjects. Whole books could be written about any one of these.

It is a queer psychology that the operation of a hotel seems such a simple matter to most people, and when owners go about procuring the services of a top-flight man to operate their hotel they usually begin the interview as follows:

"Now, we do not pretend to know anything about the operation of a hotel, but . . ." From then on, until the contract expires, they are forever coming up with bright ideas they would like to try out, that the operator or his father tried out in the hotel business and discarded long ago. The managing director may accede to their requests against his better judgment, which invariably costs the hotel money.

Not long ago I was operating a resort hotel of some five hundred rooms. The owners and their wives decided it would be helpful if they gave a cocktail party for some of the guests. I advised against it, unless they included all the guests of the hotel. This they could not understand, and gave their party for about forty.

Like most cocktail parties this one didn't break up until dinner was well under way, and in the middle of it our owners streamed into the main dining room, followed by forty delighted and flattered guests. The result was that the remaining five hundred guests were hurt because they were not invited.

After several such incidents, where the owners find themselves proved wrong, the owners may decide that the operator is either a prima donna, or instinctively antagonistic. They become very chummy with the heads of departments, feeling that they can let the high-salaried operator out, take over the smooth-running organization that he, in his knowledge of the business, has assembled, hire a man at much less money, and save the difference. Here is where they really get a "shellacking." Inasmuch as the hotel business is 90 per cent management, one costly decision is all that is needed to show them, too late, the error of their ways.

I can never understand why investors who want to make money on a resort hotel try to make a purchase based on the previous earnings. If the management has been good and showed a good profit, usually the hotel is not for sale except at an exorbitant price; on the other hand, if the management has been poor and the figures are very poor, the hotel can be purchased at a bargain and one has a chance, because of the low overhead, really to make a "killing."

A good resort operator should be able to visit a property, size up the situation in his own mind, visualize its possibilities, and the way it will look given a certain amount of repairs and refurbishing.

When one surveys a resort property with an idea of purchasing it one should catalogue the elements of success and failure with a cold mind, to wit: Is it accessible by automobile, by rail, by air, and by water? Is the climate good during the time the hotel is to be open? Is it in a good resort section relative to the rate structure? Are all outdoor sports facilities available? What is its competition? Are there any serious objections to the property, psychologically or otherwise? Does the type of construction lend itself to your purpose? What is the physical condition of the building? Will upkeep be excessive? What is the situation as to taxes? Are there any natural assets that have not been exploited? Will the local people and local government be receptive or antagonistic to your operation? What are the liquor laws? Is there any opportunity for the staff to find recreation and amusement when off duty? Is it the type of place that your particular clientele will be enthusiastic about?

A seasoned operator can examine all these elements carefully and through experience and instinct make his decision within a few hours.

The wrong architect can ruin a new resort hotel if instead of laying out a hotel from a service standpoint and then, by compromising a little here and there, constructing a pleasing building around the plans, he designs a building which is an architect's dream, in color or a wash drawing, that will sell his services to the owners. Then he will try to house a smooth-running unit in his beautiful picture.

The ideal architects are those who are interested primarily in good planning, utility, costs, income, and low operating expenses and yet who are resourceful and ingenious enough to be keen on appearances; in short, work from the inside out.

I can point out glaring mistakes in many of the finest and largest hotels in the world that a ten-year-old kid should be able to see. On one five-thousand-acre estate a two-million-dollar hotel is so cramped for space that the kitchen is on one side of the patio and a wing containing de luxe suites on the other. If a careless pot washer drops a pot early in the morning, the guests occupying these costly accommodations hear the sound.

If the climate is damp, they locate the linen room in the basement where the linen will mildew. The risers of the stair treads throughout the building are of different heights. Bathrooms and clothes closets are put in the corners of the building.

Bedrooms are laid out so that they are impossible to furnish, and I have come to the conclusion that all architects are bachelors, otherwise they would realize that a clothes closet must serve two.

The kitchens never permit the staff to be efficient, nor is the dining room large enough so that guests can dine comfortably in space at least fifteen square feet per person.

If the hotel has a night club, the entrance is sure to be located where outside guests will chatter under the windows of sleeping patrons.

There are many useful little "gimmicks" of the trade that architects could learn from the operator. For instance, there is a pleasing psychological advantage to having fine-looking tall men and women behind the desk. As the people we want there are not always tall, we plan the floor back of the front desk to be three inches higher than the floor in front.

Then there is the matter of control—the fewer outside doors a hotel has on the ground floor, particularly in the back of the house, the fewer there are to be watched.

In resort hotel operation auditors are wonderful people to have around *if they follow* the operation, but if they are in a position to dictate, they are most harmful. Heaven deliver me from budgets, estimates, and pro forma balance sheets. So many factors are involved which can change the entire picture overnight that a good operator literally has to "think on his feet." He may be shrewd enough to change his entire policy of operation between breakfast and lunch, which may make all the forecasted figures irrelevant. He is primarily interested in a multitude of guests walking in and out of the front door, tariffs that will insure a profit, and the lowest cost possible consistent with good operation, and all this coupled with a gambler's instinct which would turn an auditor's hair white.

There are many factors in the ebb and flow of a resort season, and the operator has to be closely attuned to them, so that if he is subject to criticisms or suggestions they are apt to warp his judgment.

I know of one city hotel being planned where the man who was to operate wanted running ice water in all the rooms. As they were running close to their budget, the architect said there wasn't money available. Looking at the drawing of the building, the manager noticed that there were a number of gargoyles on the building.

He found that the allotment set aside in the budget for the gargoyles was practically the same as that needed to put in the running ice water. But to the architects the gargoyles were more important!

If you can't throw fifty thousand extra dollars on the table and watch it disappear without a quiver, stay out of resort hotel business. It's the foolish money, the last fifty thousand that you can't account for, that gives the finishing touch and makes or breaks a resort hotel.

Kitchens, their operation and layout, have been an obsession with me from the time when as a small boy I stood on a cracker box to serve vegetables in the old Uplands kitchen until I was summoned to New York by the late John R. Todd, of Todd, Robertson, Todd, who built Radio City, to help plan the kitchens for its Rainbow Room. When I started to work in hotels I spent much of my time in the back of the house, for I realized that while the money came in through the front, most of it went out through the back. At the hotel shows and in every large hotel where I had the opportunity I studied kitchen equipment.

The layout of a well-planned resort hotel kitchen is no different from your own home kitchen—there is just more of it! It should operate on the principle of a traffic circle, with one-way traffic flowing from right to left. If it is well planned there is no cross-traffic and no worker has to move against the traffic.

A waitress starting for the kitchen approaches two doors side by side; the door on the right swings out to allow the traffic to enter the kitchen, and the door on the left swings in to allow the traffic from the kitchen to enter the dining room. As the waitress goes through the right-hand door, she enters a sound-lock, or covered hallway, with a door at each end. This hallway is long enough so that the door from the dining room will close behind her before the door entering directly into the kitchen can be opened, thus all noise and odor from the kitchen are locked off from the dining room.

The first thing a waitress does when she enters the kitchen is to remove whatever soiled linen she has on her tray. There is usually a linen chute to the right of the sound lock, or just outside of it in the kitchen.

Next she should dispose of the soiled glasses, as they are fragile. These she deposits on the soiled-glass table, her next point of arrival on her way around the "traffic circle," where they are picked up by operators and put into the glass washer. There are many types and sizes of washers. The ones I have used are about three feet long and wash two thousand glasses per hour. The glasses are scrubbed inside and out with re-volving brush drums, rinsed and polished—the water in these machines is at least 180 degrees—and then enter a steam bath so that they are thoroughly sterilized.

The waitress has moved on to the next table, which is for soiled dishes. This is a very long table made of about fourteen-gauge stainless steel and usually shaped like a huge U, with the automatic dishwasher in the center. There are many different types and sizes of dishwashers, some using wire baskets to hold the dishes and some with conveyors, or endless belts. These machines wash from hundreds to thousands of dishes an hour, depending upon the size and type of machine.

Running along the outer front of this table is a tray rest where the girls can rest their trays while unloading their soiled dishes. The dishwashers stand behind this table, scraping the dishes and dropping the refuse through holes along the back of the table. The dishes are then put through the dish machine and conveyed to the clean dish tables, where they are picked up by boys and carried to the dish heaters, which are spaced throughout the kitchen.

Under the dish table there is usually a chute into which the waitresses put their soiled silver. This silver is picked up, washed, and then put into a silver burnisher, a machine that contains a revolving drum filled with little steel balls and needles, almost like victrola needles. It also contains water and soap powder. When it revolves, the silver is burnished to a fine luster.

At this point the waitress has removed everything on her tray, which she then places on a "setup" table. This may be the top of dish heaters, which are long cabinets with sliding doors, shelved inside, with steampipes underneath to heat the dishes.

The waitress is now ready to pick up her orders and return to the dining room. Across the back end of the kitchen and at right angles to the dish table, et cetera, are the ranges. These may be heated by coal, oil, gas, or electricity. A good-sized resort hotel will probably have an eight-position range, which means eight ranges about thirty-two inches wide and forty-one inches deep, placed side by side with spreaders, or cold tops, in between. These ranges have ovens underneath. At the right end of the ranges are the large roast ovens, fitted with shelves, each compartment thermostatically controlled, each shelf having a door opening horizontally. Here the fowl, turkeys, and meats are roasted. At the other end of the range are the deep-fat fryers—square steel tanks that contain cooking fat. This fat is thermostatic-heat controlled.

Beyond the deep fryers, still in line with the ranges, are the broilers, which may be heated by charcoal, gas, or electricity.

The entire setup of roast ovens, ranges, deep-fat fryers, and broilers extends across the back of the kitchen, a distance of possibly from forty-five to sixty feet, depending upon the size of the kitchen.

Back of the ranges there is a fireproof wall, and extending out from this wall, its entire length, a hood that covers all the apparatus. From the top of this hood extend ducts connected with large ventilating fans that take off much of the heat; but even so the men working on these ranges work in a very high temperature.

Directly in front of the ranges, and running the entire length, is a cook's table about three feet wide made of stainless steel, and in the top of this table are openings to receive two *bain-maries*, great pans about eight or nine feet long, twenty-four inches wide, and nine inches deep. They are filled with water and heated by steam coils. Over the top of these bain-maries are placed stainless-steel meat pans to hold roasts, fowl, et cetera, to keep them warm. These, in turn, are covered with circular stainless-steel covers. Parts of the bain-maries are used to hold pots for sauces, soups, hot cereals, et cetera.

In the center, or at each end, are cooks' sinks.

In front of this cook's table is a high dish warmer with a tray rest on top. The waitress files along, always moving from right to left, picks her dishes out of this dish warmer and picks up her orders from the cooks behind the table. When the waitress has picked up most of her main orders, or entrees and vegetables, she then passes by the cold *garde-manger* and service counters where she picks up her salads, milk, jellied soups, et cetera.

The garde-manger table is a long table much like the cook's table but at right angles to it and nearer the dining room. It is for cold or chilled foods as the bain-marie is for hot foods. Under this table are cabinets for the cold dishes, and back of this table are refrigerators containing butter, cheese, milk, cold salads, and cabinets for pickles, olives, condiments, et cetera, while others contain crackers, dry cereals, et cetera. Also underneath the garde-manger counter at the back are refrigerator compartments, and at the extreme end of the table, nearest the range, is the oyster bar for opening and serving oysters, clams, and other sea foods. On the opposite end of this counter are the waffle irons, the griddles, hot plates, toasters, doughnut fryers, et cetera. The last thing the waitress picks up before she enters the dining room is the tea or coffee, so that it will arrive at the table hot.

There are many items, or gadgets, about the kitchen to make the waitresses' work easier; for instance, the roll warmers which are stainless-steel cabinets usually heated by electricity with thermostatic-heat control containing drawers in which the rolls are placed and kept at an even temperature; the automatic egg boilers—usually placed near the garde-manger counter—small square steel tanks filled with water and heated by electricity. Above these tanks is a row of little egg cups, or baskets, into which a waitress places a raw egg and pulls the basket down into the hot water. There is a clock-timing device on each of these baskets so that the waitress can set it for any specific period and attend to other duties while the eggs are cooking. There are also cream dispensers, electric or gas toasters, and other time-saving gadgets too numerous to mention.

Some hotel men will probably not agree but, space permitting, I like to build a platform about eight feet square and twenty-four inches high in the center of the kitchen, with a railing all around. On this platform is placed a regular executive desk and a chair where the head chef can work and at the same time keep an eye on everything that transpires in the kitchen. As the waitresses pass this desk, on their way into the dining room, he can, from time to time, glance at their trays and see how things are being served before they reach the food checkers.

It has always seemed to me a fine thing to have the chef personally supervise the food before it enters the dining room.

I mentioned that there was a wall back of the ranges from which the hood over the ranges was suspended. Lined up against the reverse side of this wall are four or five large steam-jacketed stainless-steel kettles for making soups and a steamer for cooking vegetables. This steamer is a large steam cabinet with three decks, with complete thermostatic-steam control. Next come the vegetable bins, sinks, automatic potato parer, and a range for the vegetable cook.

It is usual to employ men cooks—some thirty-five or forty of them—but I employ women to cook the vegetables. They seem to have a knack for it that men never acquire.

In walking through a kitchen I take everything for granted, but when I put it on paper it seems endless. The pot washing department; the storeroom with its hundreds of items and cost accounting; the butcher shop and the fish department; the long row of refrigerators; the freezer, meat box, vegetable box, and dairy box, held at different temperatures from below freezing to forty-five degrees, depending upon their contents; the bakery with its great ovens; the pastry department with smaller upright ovens, bakers' stoves, proofing box, and trunion kettles where the icings and confectioneries are made —it is all very interesting.

I believe that if the managing director has knowledge of what goes on in each department it will work to his advantage. This may prove my point. A number of years ago I was operating a resort hotel near another fine resort hotel. A group went to my competitor and requested a banquet for seven hundred people, specifying that the dessert course should include individually Baked Alaskas. Now this is a tricky dish to get in and out of an oven, as the meringue must be cooked quickly before the ice cream melts. The pastry chef in my competitor's hotel threw up his hands at pulling seven hundred Baked Alaskas out of his oven at one time and refused to take the banquet. The banquet committee then came over to see my headwaiter, who brought the problem to me. The headwaiter, pastry chef, and I were in a huddle in the kitchen when a plumber walked through carrying a blowtorch. I instantly saw the solution. The night of the banquet we set seven hundred Baked Alaskas on tables and six cooks working with blowtorches browned them in a jiffy.

There are two other interesting features of a good resort hotel kitchen: the waitresses' waiting room and the room service department. It is a severe hardship on the waitresses to stand at attention during an entire meal. I have been in so-called well-run resort hotels where the waitresses have been allowed to sit down at the table in the dining room when awaiting their parties, but nothing to my mind shows sloppier service.

We always have a room adjoining the kitchen, near the dining-room service doors, where the waitresses can wait until they are called. This room is connected with the headwaiter's desk by an intercommunicating public-address system. A call girl is stationed near the headwaiter's desk whose business it is to know all the guests in the hotel. When she notices guests approaching or entering the dining room, she calls their waitress's number over the intercommunicating system and the girl is at the table by the time the people are seated.

The room service department also adjoins the kitchen and is located near the service elevators. This is a large pantry that has its own linen supply, silver service, and room service tables, and is under the direction of a room service captain who is in charge of the room waiters. This pantry functions from six o'clock in the morning until midnight. It is a busy place during the morning when one hundred and fifty to two hundred breakfasts are to be served abovestairs. Orders are received over the telephone from the rooms by a room service telephone operator and passed on to the waiters, who take the meals to the rooms.

It is not surprising that guests who casually drift in to dinner at eight-thirty or nine o'clock in the evening, in an American-plan resort hotel, little realize that the men who prepared the dinner have been on their feet in the hot kitchen since six or seven o'clock that morning, with very little rest period; or that the waitress was up and had her breakfast at seven-thirty and that it will be ten o'clock in the evening before she gets her tables cleared, set up again, and goes off duty. So, just be a little patient. The help get tired, their feet hurt, and their nerves jangle just as yours do.

I hope the above description has not been boring. Guests naturally take it for granted that well-prepared and well-served meals simply appear on the table with the ease of a magician pulling a rabbit out of a hat. That is as it should be!

Once in a while you find a man who can operate either a city or a resort hotel. To do this successfully almost requires a split personality, as not only his operation but his thinking must fit his environment.

However, the line of demarcation is not so sharp as it used to be, since a number of the resorts have been bought up by chains and are operated practically like city hotels.

The old-time operator who could pioneer a farmhouse to a five-million-dollar plant had imagination and breadth of decision not dreamed of by those who today secure a resort through the purchase of a distress bond issue.

Most resort operators had been country boys. They understood the country and how to make guests enjoy themselves in a resort atmosphere. They were trained along the lines of the American plan, which is only an outgrowth of the gracious gesture of asking your neighbor over to dinner. They realized that season guests need a simple, well-balanced diet of American foods, plenty of fresh vegetables, and plain desserts, and that they quickly tire of highly seasoned foreign dishes that create such a delightful diversion when merely "dining out."

It does not occur to many operators that the most expensive table they can serve is in the end the cheapest.

Guests arriving at an American-plan resort hotel that sets a fine table will usually overorder. Perhaps they have been at other resorts where the food was mediocre. They study the menu and order a number of dishes in the hope that one or two of them will be good; but if they order a number of dishes and every one of them is well prepared, they soon learn to order only the dishes they really want.

While the cost per portion is higher than at the former hotel, still by winning the guest's confidence so that he will order only those dishes he desires, the hotel uses much less food and less food goes into the garbage can. The cost per pound is higher but the number of pounds used is much less.

It is a lark to be handed a wonderful menu and be privileged to order anything without giving a thought to the check. An ingenious little way of helping the guests over their first spree is to put a pair of scales in each bathroom.

A custom which has become universal is having the guests write their orders on a pad. A guest comes to the dining room after a round of golf, a swim, or a horseback ride with a ravenous appetite, grabs a pencil, and starts down through the menu from soup to nuts. By the time he has finished his main course he sees the waitress approaching with the dessert. "I wish I hadn't ordered that!"

In the old days a waitress who couldn't memorize eight orders and serve them correctly, course by course, was not worth her salt, and she didn't have to approach a table with a serving tray and inquire, "Who ordered the peas? Who ordered the beets?" When a guest's appetite was satisfied he didn't order the next course, and thus saved a great deal of waste.

Many times as I pass the dirty dish table in the hotel kitchen and notice the mountain of wasted food I see the hungry faces of Europe's millions. Why do à-la-carte portions have to be so large? Why do room service waiters bring a breakfast big enough for a hod carrier—wasted butter, wasted jam, surplus toast?

When some men become managing directors they believe they can sit behind a desk in a splendidly appointed office and from their exalted positions operate the hotel through channels. They miss the point. Hotel operation is made up of detail —millions and millions of little things that one sees in wandering through his establishment; things that should, of course, be noticed by the heads of departments but are many times overlooked. It is necessary for the manager to develop an observing eye and a pin-point memory.

Things should not be nearly right, but exactly right. He comments, criticizes, and finds fault until sometimes the staff becomes exasperated even though they know him to be right. Someone around the place has to say "No" to the guests and "No" to the help sometimes without the privilege of explaining why. It is a thankless job.

When I operated a number of hotels I had a service inspector who was a corker. When he visited one of my hotels as a guest and sent back a report, which usually ran about fifty closely typewritten pages, I had all the information I needed as to that particular unit.

He would alight from the train, step into a taxi, and give his destination. During the ride to the hotel he would discuss the hotel with the taxi driver, and by putting forth leading questions ascertain its standing. Upon arriving at the hotel he would note the appearance and deportment of the doorman, the time it took for his luggage to arrive at the front desk, whether or not the bellman preceded him through the door or allowed him to enter the lobby first.

He would note the courtesy of the clerks on duty, and whether or not they made the effort to "sell" him one of the better apartments. On arriving at the room, he would notice if the bellman turned on the lights, opened the windows, adjusted the shades, tried the water faucets, flushed the toilet, and checked the bathroom for towels, soap, et cetera, placed the key of the room on the dresser, and politely inquired if any further services were needed, such as a radio and room service.

My inspector had his own small radio which was always out of order in some minor detail. Usually by a call he could get a mechanic up to fix it. Were the man's overalls clean? Was he polite? During the time it took to make the repair the conversation would drift as to how the mechanic liked his job and to the popularity of the resident manager.

My inspector had a coat with a button off. How long did it

take to have it sewed on? Before leaving the room he placed cigarette ashes under the bed. How long did they stay there? He would call the chief telephone operator and say that he was leaving the hotel and expected some telephone messages, would she take them? He then went out of the building and called himself back. How long did it take to get the hotel? Was his call handled promptly and efficiently? When he arrived back at the hotel was the call slip in his mailbox?

He was particularly finicky about his food and would make unwarranted complaints in the dining room. How did the captain handle it? What was the waiter's attitude?

As he usually stayed four or five days in each hotel, sooner or later, by hook or by crook, he got the lowdown on all the different departments.

Once an organization who owned a hotel wanted me to take an operating contract. The board of directors was a large one, thirteen people, many of them women. They were an ultra-conservative group and went to great pains to impress upon me the high moral plane upon which the hotel was operating. "We are more careful," they said, "particularly in regard to moral standards, than any other hotel."

I had a surprise for them! As soon as I heard that they were contemplating my management I had sent my service inspector to spend a week at the hotel as a guest.

The last night of his stay he had asked the elevator operator, "How can I get a girl up to my room?"

Eventually a girl came to his room, and he had both the girl and the elevator man arrested. When I read them his report it was a bombshell. They had been so smug!

One person who never worries me is the *always* dissatisfied guest—the chronic complainer—he is one person who will never leave.

No man with the responsibilities a managing director has can go very far toward greeting the public. He has affable floor men of good appearance and pleasing personality who can do it much better. Those who greet the public all day should not have a care in the world. The fact that the ice-plant compressor has gone bad, or there has been an accident in the engine room, are no affairs of his.

He is aces with the guests, as he should be, and gets credit for things with which he has not the remotest connection. The guy in the back office in his shirt sleeves had the headaches.

This has fooled many new owners. They see a smooth-looking gent with a gardenia in his buttonhole standing in the lobby of some hotel exuding personality. Of course he hasn't anything on his mind. So they think it will be smart to hire him to operate their new hotel in Florida or California.

Having had no experience whatever with the operating problems of a hotel other than to greet new guests and wish the departing guests Godspeed, the first time he is confronted with an operating problem that calls for experience, cold business judgment, and acumen, he is up that well-worn stump and the owners pay.

All hotel operators continually receive letters from people outside of the profession who wish employment. They have been bond salesmen, insurance men, et cetera, and are used to meeting the public. What they do not understand is that each and every employee of a good hotel is a specialist. When one applies for a position in a hotel the first questions are: What can he do? Is he a fry cook, a cashier, a night auditor, or a room service captain? Does he know his stuff? Or will he have to learn it at the expense of the hotel?

The amateur does not realize that an operator hires his maître d'hôtel, who, in turn, hires everyone in his department; and if things do not go well in his department the operator simply gets another maître d'hôtel.

To a certain extent the hotel operator is absolutely defense-less and at the mercy of his employees. In any other business a presentable, well-educated, and highly trained person repre-sents the firm, and presumably exercises the tact and good judgment necessary to the position; but in the hotel business every employee who comes in contact with the guests, from the bootblack to the resident manager, is a representative of the firm. The staff of a hotel reflects the policy and mental attitude of its operator. If the boss has complete command of the situation and is confident, his crew is confident and will render good service.

From the foregoing one might think a managing director's life is nothing but headaches. Happily this is not the case. There is a terrific fascination about the life that gets into one's blood, and the tempo of the environment keeps one young and mentally alert.

There is nothing so interesting as human nature! I like to observe it from an inconspicuous corner table in the "Champagne Room," or whatever the name of the hotel's supper room.

One can detect a network of crosscurrents—humor, pathos, and sophistication—not easily discernible to the casual eye! The lovely old star of silent pictures, holding her head painfully high so as not to show the wrinkles in her neck; the kid with the little brunette angrily insisting that he is *so* old enough to order liquor; a matron, her face pinched with anxiety, watching her marriageable daughter dancing with a wealthy bachelor; the beautiful blonde on the far banquette having "fumbling trouble" with a gray-haired playboy.

A married woman is staring starry-eyed at the bandstand. Why kid herself? The leader is nuts about the pert little cigarette girl with promise in her eyes who's crazy about the sax player!

Everyone who is the guest of a hotel, particularly a resort hotel, is "living in a goldfish bowl."

The very nature of the service required gives the staff an insight into the lives of the guests to a degree that would surprise them. The old "grapevine" starts to work the moment a guest registers. And while the managing director is not interested in the daily lives of his guests except to see that their wants are adequately cared for, he cannot avoid knowing a great deal about the people domiciled under his roof.

Bits of information constantly cross his desk—the cashier reports that a wife signs all the checks. The night watchman reports a nightly battle in 817. The room waiter overhears scraps of conversation that portend trouble. The chambermaid notices that 706 has costly baggage and very little else.

The telephone operator calls the night manager: "The man in 902 has been talking with Los Angeles for hours. His bill is now one hundred and twenty-three dollars. What shall I do?" As the report comes back the calls get crossed and they hear him say, "So you're going out with other men! Well, good night and good-by!"

The hostess is worried about the morose young lady in 512.

A bellman summons a guest from the dance patio and avoids an embarassing situation. An alert maître d'hôtel stops a captain from seating a newly married couple at the next table to the husband's "ex."

A very contrite debutante comes to me and says, "I'm in a terrible jam." I am not surprised. I had a tip from the doorman. I have known her since she was running around in three-cornered pants and feel like giving her a good spanking.

The house physician reports that Mrs. Adams in 1114 has had a stroke and that poor old man Adams is beside himself with bewilderment and grief. People in an emergency are so helpless away from home; there is much you can do for them.

So it goes, twenty-four hours a day, seven days a week.

A queer phenomenon of hotel life is that anyone who loses anything always knows exactly where he—or she—lost it. Usually she is positive it was taken by an employee. This is rarely the case, as hotels, for their own protection, are extremely careful whom they hire.

The loser cannot understand why the manager is not

alarmed. Instead, he calms the guest and has the housekeeper accompany her to the room, where, nine times out of ten, the missing article is found.

This summer at Montauk Manor one of our maids found a hundred-dollar bill on the floor of a room she was cleaning, and I'm glad to say she received a liberal tip.

Unfortunately it is not always so simple. In one hotel a woman guest reported the loss of a diamond brooch that was heavily insured. Her jewel case had been pried open but the rest of her valuable jewelry was intact. This made the insurance detective sure it was an inside job. But her husband was prominent, and the matter had to be carefully handled.

The report the detective eventually sent his firm saved us a lawsuit. He had traced the woman's life and found she had been in show business as a girl. A former friend of those days needed money, and she had stolen and pawned her own brooch.

Occasionally we have a professional thief who is extremely clever. A famous theatrical star brought a group back from a night club to her suite one night. Among them was a young woman no one seemed to know, who, when leaving, donned her hostess's expensive mink coat and left in its place her own cheap mink-dyed fur.

Sometimes guests stage fake accidents, hoping to sue. Only last year a woman placed a suitcase outside her door and purposely fell over it, claiming internal injuries and shock. She might have made it work but for a keen-eyed chambermaid who had seen the whole thing.

I have quoted Father: "There are only two kinds of people around a hotel—guests and help." Father might well have added that in many ways they both have to be handled in the same way. For instance, when a clique forms among the employees, usually with a ringleader, and this clique is detrimental to the hotel, the most effective cure is to eliminate the whole group. By the same token, if a clique forms among the guests, and it usually forms among the oldest and most valued guests, they should be eliminated just as promptly.

When such a group, taking possession of the lounge or the cabanas, begin to look down their noses at new arrivals and remark, "Well, I wonder how they got in here?" it is time to take action, and there are many graceful ways of doing so. These guests never seem to realize that it takes a large amount of money to operate a resort hotel and that while each is paying a substantial rate the aggregate amount this entire group pays is a very small portion of the daily receipts.

Then they begin to tell you how to run your hotel. I grant there are many ways of operating a hotel, but it is impossible to operate it under a number of different policies at one and the same time. It is usually best to stick to a policy that has been successful over the years.

Another of Father's axioms: "If you operate a hotel well enough long enough you usually win out."

By and large the ideal clientele for a resort hotel and the most enduring is a carefully selected homogeneous, cosmopolitan group, so that if, for any reason, one segment is affected adversely it will not be serious.

Guest relations—handling of the everchanging human element—is more a matter of instinct: knowing how people are apt to react under certain circumstances; the ability to spot a "phony" instantly and to shrug off the "hail fellows well met" and those with an exaggerated sense of importance which clutter up all hotels. The infinite patience necessary to listen to woes—real or imaginary; to be kind, considerate, and tolerant, for after all morals are a matter of geography.

I am not naturally a patient man. I wish I were. Sometimes patience pays off more than anything else.

When I was operating the Vendome Hotel in Boston, a very lovely old aristocrat occupied one of our apartments for years.

One day she called me to her apartment and said, "Young man, is there anything wrong with your nose? Nobody else in this place has a nose they can smell with. Do you detect a horrible odor in this suite?"

I replied that I certainly did! I had the carpenter take up a little of the oak flooring and had the plumber come up to pound and pound! The little old lady was delighted. An imaginary worry had bothered her for days, and it was so easy to put her mind at rest.

That old lady thought I was the finest hotel manager in the world, and she was my best publicity agent.

I tell my assistants, "Watch people's habits—they are more telling than their fingerprints." Mostly they are not conscious of them, but they are indicative of their likes and dislikes. Finding out where they came from helps indicate their wants. Men are apt to be especially fond of certain dishes they ate when they were children. Little details mark the difference between fine hotel keeping and simply running a hotel.

The fewer rules you have for guests and help the fewer you will have to break.

Guests can be peculiar! I was in Miami Beach the other day stopping with my good friend, Neil Lang, the general manager of the Roney Plaza, and in the course of conversation he remarked:

"I think the impact of bad weather on the disposition of resort guests is an amazing if understandable phenomenon. People who come South, for the most part seem to be sun worshipers. Nothing seems to be quite so important to a Miami Beach vacationist as the ability to alight from a train or plane in a northern city sporting a coat of tan.

"Let it rain for a few days and the southern resort operator finds his problems multiplying by the hour. Rooms shrink, closets get smaller, the food gets terrible, the liquor even worse, and mattresses develop lumps that were never apparent when the sun shone.

"Driven indoors by bad weather, the guests find it difficult to amuse themselves. The weather is the subject of the moment and watched carefully. At the first sign of sun everyone heads for the beach, the hotel again becomes a nice place to behold, and everyone is smiling and happy."

While I am rambling about in this chapter I might as well mention the controversial subject of "tipping." There seems to be an *idée fixe* that tipping is a pernicious practice! It is my considered opinion that, within limits, it is the most practical and satisfactory system that could be evolved.

It started in England several centuries ago, when there were signs in taverns reading "To Insure Promptness," later condensed to "T.I.P."

The rates of a hotel must, of necessity, be based on the cost of accommodations or of a meal plus a reasonable profit. If the employee is hired with the understanding that tips are available, his wages are lower and therefore the cost of the accommodations, or meal, is lower than it would be if he were hired on a no-tip basis. So, in the end, it adds up to the same for the public.

It is a fact that the majority of people experience a certain amount of pleasure in rewarding an employee for good service and little extra attentions, and the gamble of the tipping practice makes the servants' work fascinating.

As to amounts—15 per cent roughly holds good in a restaurant; in a bar or night club, more. A few years ago a man stopped me as I was coming into the dining room and said with all sincerity that he was giving his waitress two dollars and fifty cents per week, but she had conveyed the idea, in a courteous manner, that she did not feel that this was enough.

I asked him, "How many persons are there in your party?" He replied, "Four." I said, "If you have a meal and give the waitress a 15-cent tip, would you think that was excessive?" He replied, "Certainly not!"

I said, "Fifteen cents per person, and four in the party, would make sixty cents per meal, and three meals per day would be one dollar and eighty cents per day; thus one week would equal twelve dollars and sixty cents."

That had not occurred to him.

The hotel operators of America are long-suffering. I do not believe the general public has the slightest conception of the difficulties they have surmounted in these last few years of labor troubles, shortages of food and materials, and government regulations. It has been by a miracle that they have provided bed and board for millions.

Did you ever stop to think what would happen if every hotel and restaurant in America closed their doors some morning?

A flaw in the present situation is that during the past few years hotel accommodations throughout the country have been at a premium. The slipshod operator who was either too tired or too indifferent to care has been able to operate successfully in spite of his incompetency. This is discouraging to the well-grounded operators who are really trying.

The saddest thing in the whole hotel industry is to see a very fine resort hotel being run as it should be and entertaining a very fine clientele, and then, because of the very successful operation, see it sold. The new owners, believing that they can do much better, hire a manager who is not well grounded in his work and then hem him in with an entirely different operating policy than the one that made the hotel a success. A few years and you drive past to see a once enchanting place despoiled by shiftless management, with indifferent food and slipshod housekeeping.

Right management, an efficient crew, and a fine clientele keep a hotel a success. Father used to say that the clientele furnishes a hotel, and all one has to do is walk in a lobby and look around at the guests to know what kind of hotel it is. So often you hear people say: "Do you remember the beautiful such-and-such hotel? Have you seen it lately?"

The rundown hotel is one of the first to suffer in a depression. The hotel with the steady year-in-and-year-out clientele weathers the storm.

No one knows what causes good seasons or poor seasons in resort hotels. I have seen terrible weather up North all winter and people there, flush with money, while sunny Florida had a bad season. I have seen winters when the weather in the North was like spring and business conditions bad, and Florida had a wonderful season. There doesn't seem to be any rhyme or reason. One thing I know, from the day a resort hotel opens until it closes, the resort hotel operator is under terrific strain. So many things can happen to ruin a season—transportation strikes, weather conditions, national emergencies, stock market slumps, epidemics, trends toward cruises, and a million-and-one other things.

The hotel industry has done well during the war and the years since, so at first blush one would think it a good business in which to invest. One should bear in mind, however, that things looked as promising after World War I, yet within a decade or so there were only about 20 per cent of the hotels in America that were not in the hands of receivers.

Whether this condition will prevail again depends somewhat on whether there is enough overoptimism to start a boom in new hotel construction.

Some say that it is a good time to build hotels because mortgage money is cheap, but by the same token cheap money is available to the refunding of mortgages on old hotels.

Top management, guided by long experience, seldom, if ever, makes a mistake, but "fools rush in where angels fear to tread."

Most industries can radically curtail their operations when business falls off, but the hotel business is a twenty-four-hour service operation which must be maintained at all times regardless of whether business is good or bad. Hotel operation is not so flexible as other large industries although its volume of business is more so.

The break-even point of hotels is often stated in relation to the percentage of room occupancy. But there is another factor, the price per room. Occupancy may be fairly high, but in times of recession the higher-priced rooms are not "sold" and the "average rack" (average number of persons per room) may be low, so that the dollar volume is low.

Low room occupancy not only affects the general spending around the hotel, in the bar, restaurant, et cetera, but psychologically people spend less. The hotels that are hardest hit have a tendency, through desperation, to "sell" their rooms below cost, which in turn affects the price structure of other hotels.

In building a new hotel there is a danger of overoptimism in the estimating of percentage of occupancy and in revenue to be received from restaurant, bar, concessions, et cetera.

With hotel occupancy the last few years running 90 per cent or better, hotels have made money even with the high costs of operation, but I am wondering what will happen if the average occupancy drops to around 75 per cent.

It does not seem that new hotels built at this time will do so well financially as the better hotels already built. The cost per room of new construction is very high. Companies building new hotels disregard the drain of mortgage interest and depreciation, renewals, repair, et cetera. The seasoned hotel operators "in the know" are not at fault. It is the overenthusiastic investing public that get themselves into trouble.

A new hotel is like a new automobile. It is a shiny thing of joy to start with, but it soon gets into the used-car class and before long it is just another hotel whose overhead is higher than its competitors'.

I remember when I was a young man, an older hotel man, who ran a very successful New York hotel, said, "Karl, they are building a lot of new hotels in New York. This doesn't disturb me, but I hope no one ever builds an old one."

WHEN I was in the Navy many warrant officers who had made a lifetime career of the service and were facing retirement were always talking about chicken farms. Some even subscribed to poultry magazines. My newspaper friends liked to dream of owning a weekly paper in some small town. By the same token, many big hotel operators look forward to the time when they can buy a small hotel and settle down to a life of ease.

When Father was a young man he and a couple of friends took a sailboat trip one winter and spent some time at Melbourne, Florida.

He never got over talking about it. "When you get old and want to retire," he told me many times when I was a boy, "go down and get yourself a little place on the Indian River at Melbourne." That seemed most unlikely during the exciting years. But when I did make up my mind to buy a small hotel in Florida and retire, and was driving around the state looking the situation over, the one hotel that appealed to me was the Trade Winds Club in Melbourne, and I bought it, along with a home on the Indian River. I bought the house without even seeing it. A friend of mine telephoned me at the Sagamore that it was for sale, and I bought it as mere speculation.

When my wife and I went South that fall and looked at the house for the first time, I told her: "This is it! This is the end of the trail."

My wife agreed with me.

The beautiful little Trade Winds Club and the Bahama

Beach Club and pool adjacent, which I also purchased, were an answer to a resort hotel man's dream—a miniature Boca Raton.

I had a grand time landscaping the grounds, setting out an orange grove, building an outdoor dance floor and fishing pond. There is burning pride in the ownership of a little hotel —everything is so personal. The year 1945 found me with a fine business, a splendid clientele, and the home we had always talked about. So I retired on the Indian River—for a couple of months!

One morning I was fishing on the dock in front of my house, sitting out there in the sun, just me and the pelicans. There is one old pelican that doesn't do anything all day except sit on a post. We call him "the Caretaker."

Our communion was interrupted by a phone call summoning me to Miami, to see Mr. Oscar Miller (president of the Security Trust Co.) and Mr. Lindsey Hopkins, Jr., of Miami Beach and Atlanta. I had never met Lindsey but I knew that his father had reorganized the Carl G. Fisher Corporation of Miami Beach, and that Lindsey had reorganized the Montauk Beach Company, Montauk, Long Island, which had been another Carl G. Fisher project.

I also knew that the Carl G. Fisher Corporation owned the beautiful Flamingo Hotel on Miami Beach, and that the Montauk Beach Company owned the Montauk Beach properties on Long Island, New York, some thirty-five hundred acres of rolling countryside, unique in its wild beauty and strikingly reminiscent of the Scottish moors.

Alan Howard, of the *Social Spectator*, had once sent me a beautiful brochure of this property showing the Surf Club with its cabanas, yacht club, golf club, riding stables, and Montauk Manor, where this last chapter is being written.

Both properties had been in the hands of the United States Navy during the war and were about to be turned back to their owners.

After a morning-long conference the gentlemen offered me the management of the two hotels.

At first blush the proposition did not appeal, inasmuch as the Navy had used the hotels to house its personnel and the situation presented obstacles and headaches too numerous to mention. The more I talked it over, however, the more I became intrigued with the situation. To tell the truth, I was more intrigued with Hopkins and Miller than with the hotels. I found myself talking to a couple of young men with signal ability, foresight, and a keen appreciation of "what it takes" to put properties over, and they engendered in me a mounting enthusiasm, so I accepted the job.

It is difficult for the layman to contemplate the task of taking two large resort hotels, the entire clientele of which had been lost, the furniture and equipment completely obliterated, and the interior of the buildings badly damaged, and in a matter of weeks to open two fine resorts, completely rehabilitated, refurnished, redecorated, staffed, and ready to welcome guests. And at a time when supplies, labor, equipment, and furniture were virtually impossible to get! It never could have been done if the owners had not had the nerve and resourcefulness to co-operate with the contractors and myself and see it through.

During 1945 the Flamingo housed some eight hundred navy personnel. The Navy had agreed to have these people out of the hotel by November 1, but through one cause or another they were reluctant to leave, and I could see that they were going to delay us unduly.

On November 1, at seven in the morning, C. F. (Red) Wheeler, the general contractor, hit the building with four air hammers to demolish a long flight of cement steps that ran from the ground up to the first story. The noise was terrific, the dust rose to the ninth floor, and the Navy left forthwith.

I had to smile. They had really got themselves a contractor

who was hard to stop. It was a pleasure to see him fly at the building with no lost motion.

From then on it was a running battle to meet the opening deadline of January 10—seventy days including Sundays!

We decided upon some major changes. In previous years the lobby had been on the second floor. It has always been a source of irritation to me to see guests arrive from the train or by motor, tired and wilted, and be paraded across a lobby floor to register and back to the elevator, when the lobby was filled with guests dressed for dinner, so it was decided to tear out the lower floor of the main building and put the registration desk opposite the entrance and the elevators, where it belonged.

For the first two weeks all we did was tear things apart. It was frightening. Wheeler and I had conferences with the owners at odd times during the day, and almost any time during the night, deciding this and that, sitting on boxes, bales, and piles of lumber, and the air was blue with conversation. There wasn't a "yes" man in the crowd and this built for mutual respect and got things done.

I recall Oscar Miller sticking his head out of a third-floor window one day and calling down to me with a grin, "Abbott, are you going to have this hotel open by January 10?" I laughed and told him, "I will if you'll go back to Georgia and run your farm!" He got a kick out of it. Oscar was doling out the money and trying to keep a halter on me to keep me from kicking over the traces. But it is the foolish money spent that makes a resort a success, and I think I had Oscar convinced before the job was over.

Plumbers and steam fitters crawled through the building like ants; sub-contractors swarmed in with tile, electrical fixtures, ventilating ducts, intercommunication systems, and hundreds of other items. Sixty or seventy painters arrived on the property in white overalls, like a flock of seagulls.

There are fourteen cottages on the Flamingo grounds, and

one morning before the men came to work there was an argument as to whether or not these cottages should be painted, and the conference was adjourned until late that afternoon. When we got together again, along about quitting time, all the cottages had been painted. And that was that!

There was a help's dormitory of one hundred and seventy-five rooms, and while we were discussing the matter this building got painted too—inside and out. That gang of painters painted everything that stood perpendicular and varnished everything horizontal—they painted the entire exterior of the building in nine days and the whole interior in two weeks more.

Someone sent a load of lumber to resurface the dock and non-union carpenters to do the job, so all the union men went out on strike. In the middle of this pandemonium about $80,000 worth of stainless-steel equipment arrived for the kitchen and had to be set in place.

A large dance terrace was built, overlooking Biscayne Bay, and new furniture, bales of carpet, china, glassware, silver, draperies, and other things cluttered up every available inch of public rooms and hallways.

In the middle of this I had other problems—the incessant bickering about city ordinances, restrictions, and licenses; the O.P.A. and the liquor board; the securing of an efficient staff, including a band, beauty salon operators, barber, swimming instructors, tennis pro, dockmaster, masseuse, dance team, and all the necessary people to cater to an exacting clientele; advertising program; purchasing uniforms for the staff; the renting of concessions. Detail upon detail, and all important. Miss one and it threw the machinery out of gear.

We set up an office in the largest cottage, where the reservation manager, Dick Barney, and his three stenographers held forth in the large living room and my secretary and I had desks in the opposite ends of the room. Everyone roomed on the second floor. It was cool that fall, and the only heat we had was from a fireplace. We made one bedroom into a kitchen and another into a dining room. It was really "camping out."

We had a woman to keep the place clean and wait on the table, and a fry cook from our regular crew came down early to cook for us. He was a jovial Italian and the only dessert he could make was bread pudding. We had bread pudding every night for two months. Bread pudding with peaches, bread pudding with raisins, bread pudding with grapenuts, and just plain bread pudding. I used to love bread pudding, but I haven't eaten any since.

We also had with us decorators, a bookkeeper, the housekeeper, and a couple of men who were checking in supplies, so we had quite a family. "Red" Frank Wheeler came into our "office" one day and said it reminded him of a scene from *You Can't Take It with You!*

When he walked in Dick Barney and his secretaries were working like crazy taking reservations over the telephone and trying to get out some of the thousands of letters that were the product of the files I had built up over the years. I was attempting to dictate to my secretary on the other side of the room, and she was also wiring for supplies, checking bills of lading, sending tracers on missing merchandise, and answering two telephones at the same time. A plumber and his helper were at work in a closet fixing the hot-water heater, creating a virtual anvil chorus. Two drapery salesmen were having a screaming argument, "I want it cerise!" "No, I want it purple!" A darky was bringing in wood and slamming it down by the fireplace in case the evening turned cold. The boss painter was complaining to me that some of my staff who were installing furniture and whom we called "the chain gang" had walked all over the new varnish on the ballroom floor. And to make it just dandy, a beautiful dance instructress was trying to demonstrate a new dance called the "Flamingo" that she had evolved for opening night.

To the uninitiated this madness would have seemed utter confusion, but we were getting things done, and fast.

We worked from morning till midnight, through Sundays, Christmas, and New Year's. On New Year's Eve we stopped for a couple of hours and had a party. Everyone brought something—a box of candy, some pastry from a bakery, cheese and cold cuts from a delicatessen, a carton of cigarettes, a bottle of scotch. It was fun! We had been opening the hotel on cigarettes and black coffee and it was nice to relax if only for an hour or two. Everyone did a specialty—a song, a recitation, droll stories, and a swan dance by the installation men with some draperies for costumes.

On the second day of January the staff arrived—some two hundred and twenty-five of them—and began the routine of setting up the guest rooms, the dining room, public rooms, and kitchen, and on the afternoon of January 10, when the band started playing at cocktail time on the dance terrace, everyone was standing at his station as if he had been there for months.

The opening was splendid and on schedule.

The Flamingo filled rapidly with guests, who lounged in the cabanas without the slightest realization of the tremendous effort that had been expended. It was a gay and prosperous winter and the hotel and cottages were filled to capacity for the entire season. It was an era of free spending that surpassed anything I had ever seen.

I remember sending an armored car to the bank one morning for $30,000 in cash. This was all gone by nightfall, having been advanced to guests who were going to the race tracks and "The Brook" and other swanky night clubs for the evening. One bellboy told me that he had made fifty dollars in tips one evening in the lounge pulling up chairs for the guests and lighting cigarettes.

While my ears were keenly attuned to the hum of the wheels within wheels that make up the operation of the hotel, my mind was not on it—my attention was already focused on the situation that confronted us at Montauk in the spring.

We closed the Flamingo on April 10 and the owners sold the hotel on the handsome showing we had made. The last guest had not left the Flamingo before Dick Barney was booking Montauk Manor from the New York office. About May we arrived at Montauk Manor to do the same thing all over again. Thirty-one days in May, thirty days in June, sixty-one days until July 1—nights and Sundays.

A dance terrace to build in the patio and a night club below stairs; more cabanas at the beach; a new kitchen; a complete renovation.

Again there was the cajoling of supply people, pleading with freight traffic managers, browbeating installation men, six hundred cases of scotch (when there was no scotch) and getting it on the strength of friendship and past favors rendered; two hundred loins of pork and a hundred prime ribs of beef literally pulled out of thin air when there was no meat.

Again I ask—no sentiment in business? Give a man friends and he is hard to lick.

All spring I had been going almost nuts about the Montauk refrigeration. The Navy had changed it over to suit their needs and we had to change it back. It was just one delay after another until two days before we opened we started to chill down the boxes. For this reason we'd had to store our meat with our purveyor, Wyman Smart of Bolton and Smart in Boston. The day he was to ship it there was an express strike over the country, and a trucking strike on Long Island. Here was one for the book! How to get meat from Boston?

Wyman had it shipped by truck as far as New London, Connecticut, and someone in this wonderful crew of mine (I never dared to find out just who) got the meat on an army boat that was supplying the forts in the Sound that landed at the naval pier in Montauk. They hadn't got the last barrel into the hotel before I had the whole Army and Navy down around my ears. But by that time we had the meat.

Among the first to apply for reservations were Ambassador James J. Gerard and Mrs. Gerard. He had been Ambassador to Germany during World War I. After they had been our guests for four seasons at Montauk he and I were talking one evening, and he happened to tell me they had been guests of Father and Mother at the Royal Palm in Fort Myers back in 1904. "Your mother had the cook prepare a special guava shortcake for Mrs. Gerard and me," he said. "It was so delicious; I remember it to this day."

This was on Labor Day 1949. He had remembered that shortcake forty-five years.

Here and now I want to speak of the crew.

I have said before that a hotel man is no bigger than his staff. A hotel is run on loyalty, and that loyalty must be earned. It can't be bought for a few extra dollars a month. It must be proven by reciprocated loyalty over a period of years.

My assistant, Leo Nolan, maître d'hôtel Maurice St. Clair, Engineer Harold Harvey and his wife, the housekeeper, and the colored superintendent of service, William Gamble, have all been with me for more than twenty-five years. Rena, our personal cook, has been with us for twenty-seven years. Many of the employees in lesser stations have been with me as long. They are the salt of the earth.

These people are specialists. They know their jobs and handle their departments with an automatic precision that leaves little ground for criticism. They have been no small factor in building toward my reputation and the reputation of the hotels I have operated.

The Manor, rehabilitated, refitted, painted inside and out, refurnished and redecorated, opened on schedule, July 1, and in two days the S.R.O. sign was up.

On opening day a beautiful car stopped at the entrance and a very dignified-looking gentleman and his wife got out and came to the desk. The hotel was crowded at this time and available accommodations very limited. The man glanced around the lobby, turned to the clerk, and said, "My wife and I would like to have one of your better suites for the week end." The clerk said, "I am sorry, but we have no suites available. I can give you a nice double room with bath." Whereupon the man turned to his wife and said, "Is that all right, dear?" To which she replied. "Yes, sir."

How stupid can a girl be?

Another wonderful season. Labor Day with its capacity crowds came and went. The staff was beginning to look haggard; they had literally been on their feet since the preceding January, and I was beginning to wonder how much work this wonderful crew could take.

About this time a friend of mine, Ed Wright, came up from Saint Petersburg, Florida. He was the owner of the Belleview Biltmore Hotel at Belleair, near Clearwater, Florida. The Belleview Biltmore is one of the largest hotels in the state. This had been in the hands of the Army during the war. It sat in its own private domain of some six hundred acres and was surrounded by golf courses, cottages, and service buildings.

Ed had an idea that the hotel should be renovated, refurnished, and opened for the coming winter, but he had been told by two or three top-flight hotel men in New York that it was an absolute impossibility in the time allotted. They thought that possibly someone might be able to open *one wing!*

Another challenge. More green pastures. After staying with me at Montauk a couple of days, Ed decided that it might be better to sell the hotel to a syndicate rather than undertake the task himself.

The wheels started revolving again—contacting brokers, letters, telegrams, phone calls; flying trips to Florida; conferences in New York; and we finally sold the hotel to a representative group from Detroit.

The days went by. Decisions had to be made; delay piled upon delay; financing had to be arranged; papers drawn; contractors hired. And almost overnight we were again at the fatal date of November 1. This job was twice as big as either of the other two.

When I arrived at the Belleview Biltmore there was not one movable thing left in the hotel. The building was tremendous. The corridors seemed miles long, the public rooms enormous. It was a real resort hotel in the fine old tradition. Its reputation these many years had been pre-eminent, but again the clientele had been lost.

The new owners wanted to do the job right and they did. Bills were thrown across my desk at the rate of $80,000 a week—replumbing, refurbishing, golf courses to be put in shape, refurnishing, and redecorating. A carload of paint arrived. One thousand box springs and one thousand mattresses (five carloads) arrived in a single day. John L. Lewis took this exact time to call a coal strike which threatened a freight embargo and I had to sweat this one out—sending men to junction points to get things rolling and get them under the wire; four round trips from Florida to New York in one month, selecting materials, setting up a New York office, and attending to the multiple details of getting things under way.

At the Belleview Biltmore I set up my private office in one of the big suites with living quarters near by. One morning when I got out of bed I couldn't walk. Something had happened to my right leg. I had a man drive me to Melbourne and went to see my old friend Dr. Ike Hay. I felt if I could get to him I would be all right. He bawled me out, took me down to the hospital, and operated under a local anesthetic. He told me to go home and stay in bed for a week. A week! Great day in the morning! We were counting hours, not weeks! That afternoon I was driven back to the Belleview Biltmore.

I tried hobbling around with a cane, but it was no good.

So I was confined to my office and living quarters and hired a Negro boy to help me hobble back and forth and be my valet.

I was sitting in my office, stewing and fretting, wondering what was going on all over the plant. Miss Lillian Riley, my secretary, unknown to me, borrowed a wheel chair. The damn thing was outside my door the next morning. I swore I would never ride in it. But it sat there, gaunt and stark, all day. The more I looked at it the madder I got. But I couldn't stand it— I had to know what was going on. So I finally acquiesced and my colored boy pushed me around the building. After a while it got to be a lark. I had a cane with a big handle and soon had the colored boy racing me down the long corridors while I played polo with empty paint cans. Thank goodness I was out of that chair before the hotel opened.

The beautiful old Belleview Biltmore blossomed like a rose. The new furniture in the stately public rooms gave an air of grandeur not found in many of the recently built, modernly engineered hotels. Again luck was with us. We filled the house to capacity.

What a thrill I had of an evening seeing the tremendous lobby crowded with men in evening clothes and beautifully gowned women enjoying themselves in a hotel that had stood so long like a great white ghost, its long, empty hallways echoing to yesterday's footsteps.

One evening we had almost five hundred people playing bingo. Every available chair and couch in the lobby was filled and people were sitting on the grand staircase. Two loud-speakers carried the numbers to the crowd. The grand pot was something around four hundred dollars. When the last number was called the lady who was the winner was so excited that she called "Pluto" instead of "Bingo," and fainted dead away.

As there was no night life around Clearwater to speak of, the thought occurred to me that we should do something spectacular to entertain the guests in the evening after dinner. The hotel had a large ballroom with a high vaulted ceiling and I saw an opportunity to do something with it.

We built it into a beautiful night club called "The Starlight Room," comparable to anything in the state of Florida. This room accommodated about three hundred people and we had a good band which broadcast twice a week.

One evening Bill Cunningham, the columnist and radio commentator from Boston, came over to my table and we got to discussing New England and the fact that so many resort hotel men came from there originally. The next morning Bill came up to my office and chatted with me for an hour. He was interviewing me, but I didn't know it.

The following Sunday the Boston *Herald* carried a front-page story, "Best Resort Hotels Run by Yankees!" by Bill Cunningham. It also ran half of page three quoting me almost verbatim, paragraph after paragraph, naming names and giving dates. It was the finest piece of reporting I ever read.

When he left Bill said, "You should write a book." I said, "Maybe I will." I'd been hearing that from family, help, guests, and folks in the hotel business for years. Whenever I started yarning, someone would be sure to pipe up, "You should write a book."

The hotel closed April 5—just eighteen months from November 1, 1945, when we started work on the Flamingo. Starting from scratch three fine resort hotels had been renovated and put back in service and three fine seasons were behind me. They tell me this is some sort of fool record in the resort hotel business.

I went over to my home in Melbourne to recuperate.

After I'd relaxed a couple of weeks my secretary, Miss Riley, reminded me that I had said I would write a book.

I said, "What do I know about writing? I wish I'd kept my big mouth shut. As an author I'd be a barefoot boy walking through the tulips."

I went out on the dock and began to fish. "The Caretaker" was still there, sitting on his post. I was as happy and relaxed as that pelican, looking out over the beautiful Indian River into the past. It was the first time I had ever looked back. There had never been time before.

The latest years had been the biggest. The hardest job I had ever done was the one just finished. But beyond were all the others, the beautiful hotels over the past thirty years. How much ground they would cover if placed side by side—11,000 acres around the Profile alone.

There had been the wonderful guests, the great and near-great, the battalions of personnel.

Beautiful caravansaries! Wonderful people!

I looked back, all the way to Father and Mother and our first little inn clinging to the hillside in Bethlehem.

It was a long look back to those days. They seemed clearer and brighter for some reason.

All of a sudden I yelled for Miss Riley. Right there on the dock, with the old pelican looking on, I started to dictate:

"Father ran a small hotel. He used to lean against the desk and say, 'What we need is folks.' He kept a pen in an Irish potato . . ."

CLOSED
–FOR THE SEASON–